God Says, We Say
The Interpersonal Act of Redemption

God Says, We Say
The Interpersonal Act of Redemption

Robert E. Joyce

LifeCom

Published by
LifeCom
St. Cloud, Minnesota, USA

© 2010   Robert E. Joyce
All rights reserved

ISBN 978-0-578-06653-0

No part of this book may be used or reproduced in any manner whatsoever without written permission. No part of this book may be stored in a retrieval system or transmitted in any form or by any means including electronic, electrostatic, magnetic tape, mechanical, photocopying, recording or otherwise without the prior permission of the publisher.

For information, address *LifeCom*, Box 1832, St. Cloud, MN 56302

Contents

Preface	vii
Introduction	1

Part I Searching for the Inside Story

Chapter 1	The Suffering of the Innocents	11
Chapter 2	Strangers in Being	19
Chapter 3	Crying for Salvation	29
Chapter 4	Beneath the Book of *Genesis*	43
Chapter 5	What about Adam and Eve?	49
Chapter 6	A Defect in Traditional Theology and Philosophy	65

Part II Where Did We Come From?

Chapter 7	The Roots of Being	73
Chapter 8	The Unlimited Being and Freedom of God	85
Chapter 9	Intimacy Offered and *Unreceived*	91
Chapter 10	The Roots of Becoming	99
Chapter 11	Where Is My Oneness?	109
Chapter 12	Being Conceived and Being Deceived	117

Part III Contemplating Our Condition

Chapter 13 What Happened to Friendship? 131

Chapter 14 What Happened to Freedom? 149

Part IV Hope for Final Intimacy

Chapter 15 Recovering 165

Chapter 16 A Call to the Three Traditions 181

Chapter 17 Critical Questions: Challenging the View 195

Works Cited 271

Glossary 273

Preface

Sincere believers know and love the truth. But they make claims and draw conclusions that beg for better explanations. This book is the second in a series of three that are written to offer deeper meaning to believers, and also to those who are earnestly seeking God, who is worshipped and celebrated by Jews, Christians, and Muslims.

People who acknowledge that there is one personal God are called theists. They are spiritual children of Abraham, brothers and sisters in a common divine communication intended for all people. As a theist, I praise and thank God for the divine Revelation. I hope to advance our ability to *receive* this Revelation. My basic purpose is to provide deeper premises and perspectives so that we will be better able to receive.

I have tried to avoid concepts and terms that are technical, so that the book is accessible to most people who are keenly attracted to the mystery of creation and the origin of evil. But if the reader thinks that some passages of the book are difficult to understand, such can be skipped without missing the fundamental message of the new theistic perspective. One can also refer to the first book in the series, *God Said, We Said: The Interpersonal Act of Creation.* That book deals largely with the theme of Adam and Eve as archetypes of our creation out of nothing (*ex nihilo*) and confronts the origin of evil.

Also, the third book of this trilogy is an even more concentrated development of the new view. The book, *God Will Say, We Will Say: The Interpersonal Act of Salvation,* highlights the culmination of our interfacing with God, at our death, when we encounter the critical moment of being and existence: salvation or condemnation forever.

In any event, I am profoundly indebted to the basic teachings of the Catholic Church, to which I am committed for life. My hope is that these new viewpoints for receiving Revelation might serve to amplify and enrich the meaning of those teachings. Some Catholic doctrines are common, and some are unique, within the three main traditions of theism. Despite any first impressions to the contrary, I think that nothing said in this book of exploration is opposed to the Church's teaching authority.

Discordant notes are sounded, however, concerning the present state of *theological* development. Theology includes the endeavor of explaining the truths received in Scripture, Tradition, and Nature—and harmonizing them.

The book's anecdotes and examples have varying characteristics. All are based on real happenings. Some are fictionalized, at least partly, either to protect the parties involved or to bring some points to a finer pitch. Some serve more as parables than as reports.

For review and helpful comments on certain aspects of Jewish and Islamic teaching, I am grateful to Professor Seth Ward, currently teaching at the University of Wyoming. At the time, he was Director of the Institute for Islamic-Judaic Studies, located at the University of Denver. His review occurred in the early stages of writing and he cannot be faulted for any inadequacies in the final rendition.

Thanks to all those who read the manuscript in various stages of development. Readers of the whole book include three people who deserve particular mention.

James T. Joyce, my brother, is a writer who afforded immediate encouragement and suggested developments for the overall work.

The late Dorothy T. Samuel, friend and author with penetrating faith, gave valuable help both on the content and the presentation.

Mary Rosera Joyce, my best friend, beloved spouse, and fellow philosopher, has been involved with every phase of this work. She and I have discussed all of the major points and so many secondary ones that she could have written the book herself. In such case, she would have provided her own distinctive angles with a very similar message.

Thanks are due to Mary particularly for ideas and phrases such as passive-reactive energy, the need to anchor the beginning of the book in *Genesis,* the idea of renewal in the roots, and the concept of humans being rational persons—and not animals in anything but a figurative sense.

Mary and I have been married in life and in thought since 1961. I deeply cherish her loving work with this book and the others I have published.

The ideas for the present endeavor have been gestating since 1964. The key insight came to me suddenly in the midst of an informal discussion with a small group of University faculty members who were concerned with creation and evolution.

Along with the other two in the series, this book initiates a basic development and a deepening of the meaning of creation, sin, and redemption. I welcome readers' questions, suggestions, comments, and critique.

Robert E. Joyce, Ph.D.
Professor Emeritus
St. John's University
Collegeville, Minnesota
July, 2010

LifeCom
Box 1832
St. Cloud, MN 56302

Email: robertjoyce@charter.net
Website: www.lifemeaning.com

Introduction

> The [*understanding of faith*]...demands the contribution of a philosophy of being which...would enable dogmatic theology to perform its functions appropriately.... It must turn to the philosophy of being, which should be able anew to propose the problem of being...without lapsing into sterile repetition of antiquated formulas.
>
> Set within the Christian...tradition, the philosophy of being is a dynamic philosophy which views reality in its ontological, causal and communicative structures. It is strong, and enduring because it is based upon the very act of being itself...in order to reach the One who brings all things to fulfillment.
>
> (Fides et Ratio, n. 97)

In these words, John Paul II urges a viewing of God and of creation that is definitely more light-gifting than what has been developed so far in the history of thought by the mainline of Christian, Jewish, and Islamic thinkers. He wants the meaning of creation, redemption, and salvation to grow deeper *roots*.

God Says, We Say attempts to forward such growth. Along with its companion books in a trilogy, *God Said, We Said* and *God Will Say, We Will Say*, this book presents a worldview for theism that gives hope for reconciliation between conflicting forms of belief, granted that the participants are open to the real *infinity* of God's goodness, power, and freedom.

Sources for the New Millennium

The prospect for constituting an elemental deepening and renewal of theistic thought comes from several main sources. The critical call is for a deeper coalescence of the spiritual and the intellectual sources for development.

Individuals and communities must turn to fuller, more heartfelt ways of prayer and repentance. Only with a conversion of *will* is it possible to achieve *intellectual* attainments that articulate adequately the meaning of belief. The history of theism includes the eventual confluence of the mystical and the metaphysical, of holiness and wholeness.

The present book and its two companions draw upon 20th century advances in psychology and in philosophy. Two perspectives merit particular mention.

The first comes through analogy with the psychoanalytic. The psychological attention to the human mind's unconscious life has gained a significant measure of respectability and systematic regard. In *The Forgotten Language*, Eric Fromm has written tellingly about the moving power of dreams and myths, recognized by many people throughout history. Much earlier, attention to the unconscious was provided by Schopenhauer, von Harmann, Janet, Binet, and others. Emerging from some of his study with William James, Boris Sidis wrote on many topics parallel to Sigmund Freud, who nonetheless can be credited with pioneering work in the systematic study and practical use of the unconscious.

This awakening to *psychic* depths can make way for an awareness of the *spiritual* unconscious. We can become not only attentive to the profound emotional unconscious, but to an unconsciousness with respect to the deepest meanings of being, origin, and destiny—far more influential than the depths of human emotional life probed by psychology.

Jacques Maritain, for instance, in his *Creative Intuition in Art and Poetry*, has identified the powerful similarity between the human psyche and its analogous counterpart, found in the human spirit, the unconscious "life of the soul" that he aptly termed the *preconscious*. In my view, the spiritually unconscious dimension differs much from the psychic unconscious, as it does for Maritain. But I am convinced that this preconscious dimension also emanates directly from what I wish to identify as the *protoconscious*. Such originative consciousness is gifted with our creation *ex nihilo* (*out of nothing*).

Introduction

The second perspective for a conversion in consciousness comes from the meaning of *being*. Religious thinkers have made progress in this area of understanding and in some of its implications. They have benefited from a philosophical awakening to *being*, especially within the tradition of Thomas Aquinas. Contemporary theologians and philosophers like von Balthasar, Wojtyla, Ratzinger, Maritain, Gilson, and others have been moving gradually in the direction of a perspective that is more ontological and less cosmological.

These key insights into both the *spiritually* unconscious and the primacy of *being*—especially with prospects for integrating them—constitute a relatively new environment for *receiving* traditional Revelation. Earlier generations of believers had ample access to the sources of basic Revelation. But they did not have the perspectives afforded by these relatively recent developments and their potential for a special deepening of theistic meaning.

The new sources, concerning the unconscious and the meaning of being, provide an opportunity to understand rather decisively the essential freedom of every human person. These fonts of meaning might be taken, as well, to forward awareness of a kind of *spiritual repression*: how we might be suffering from repression with respect to both God's pristine creation activity and the origin of evil.

The theories proposed in *God Says, We Say* and in the rest of the trilogy are working from, but go beyond, the resources afforded by the relatively recent discoveries from the depth psychology of the unconscious and from the philosophy of being. The perspective of the trilogy constitutes an effort to reveal a truer ontology of creation and sin. While not necessary, awareness of these particular recent developments might help readers more readily to get in touch with the new perspective. The Glossary found in each book offers another way to see how the traditional is being cast in a new light.

Some might claim that these books propose a theory of beginnings like that of Origen. A streak of similarity does exist between my orientation and that of the devout, massively erudite, problematic theologian of the third century. But present theory was envisioned more than forty years ago, without awareness of Origen's theories, *and on different grounds*. Some of the more obvious differences are indicated in the last Chapter of this book (Chapter 17) that deals with questions and responses.

4   God Says, We Say

Only during recent history can one find the practical possibility of developing the meaning of Revelation as suggested in the present trilogy. Julius Muller, a German Lutheran theologian of the mid-19th century, did indeed articulate a profound sense of personal responsibility for the origin of evil in our lives. But he was not able to explore the prospects for meaning in the unconscious life of the soul. Earlier, in explicating the source of religious commitment, the philosopher Immanuel Kant also touched upon a kind of *agent will*. But he was self-blocked from any viable metaphysics, and the basic framework had not yet surfaced for appreciating repression in the unconscious life of the soul. Only within the 20th century did there emerge prospects for taking seriously and systematically the depths of the unconscious.

God Says, We Say: The Interpersonal Act of Redemption proposes no new doctrines. Yet it might be considered to hold a fundamental development of the traditional doctrines on creation and the origin of evil. It would seem to offer potentially deeper implications for perennial teachings. The reader, of course, can consider these new themes and proposals as serious concerns without having to regard them as definitive articulations.

In recent times, many Christians have been captivated by the "theology of the body," developed and articulated by John Paul II. This philosophically-attuned attention to the human body as nuptial, and as truly an image of the living God, can lead people gradually into a heightened consciousness of the meaning of particular theistic revelations. Similarly, we unconsciously hunger for a "theology of *being*" that will lead us to see hitherto unsuspected relationships of God with created persons and of these persons with one another.

My hope is that the reader will consider attentively and prayerfully what is said and will attempt to apprehend how the ideas might be in accord with past and present inspiration from the Spirit of the living God. Genuine discernment can be accomplished only by prayerful, open-minded, faithful attunement to the sources of Revelation and to the best and lasting interpretations of the theological community.

Within the Authority of Faith: A New Vision

Each of us requires an authority that is *other* than self. When we claim to propose or to assimilate some new vision for the theistic worldview, we naturally look for a guiding light and a steady mind.

Introduction

We have need of an authority to guide us not only in morality, but particularly in matters of Faith and Sacred Revelation.

The authority within your faith might differ from mine. But the authority of your reason should include a major recognition common to mine: *our reason is not its own authority.*

The "authority" of *my reason* itself tells me that it is not its own authority and that it exists for the sake of truth—which is neither mine nor yours, but God's. We do not create truth. We discover it. Often the attainment comes through difficult dialectical reasoning done in the spirit of true dialogue. But in the midst of matters of faith—requiring more than mere reason—there stands always an underlying authority.

The authority of *my faith* comes through the essential teachings of the Catholic Church. *Yours* might come through a different domain of faith. Nonetheless, we can respect each other's efforts of reason and acts of faith. We can work together to explore and to amplify the meaning of some of our common, seriously held beliefs.

Instead of separating faith and reason, we can come to see their unity within difference. Efforts are constantly being made in this regard. They were given a special momentum by John Paul II in his Encyclical, *Fides et Ratio* (1998). The needed gift of integrative insight was heralded there. "…Even in the philosophical thinking of those who helped drive faith and reason further apart there are found at times precious insights which, if pursued and developed with mind and heart rightly tuned, can lead to the discovery of truth's way. Such insights are found, for instance, in penetrating analyses of perception and experience, of the imaginary and the unconscious, of personhood and intersubjectivity, of freedom and values, of time and history" (48).

The Encyclical itself depicts philosophy and theology as forming a circularity of concerns. Joseph Cardinal Ratzinger, who became Pope Benedict XVI, has furthered the idea of complementarity by challenging philosophies to keep open to the guidance of religious revelation. He underscored the obvious need for philosophy to take notice of empirical perceptions that regularly emerge within the various scientific disciplines. Similarly, he said, "(Philosophy) ought to regard the holy traditions of religions and especially the message of the Bible as a source of perception and let itself be made more fertile by this" (Ratzinger, 208). This means that any really holistic philosophy will be open to the data of Revelation as well as to the data of sensation—without becoming a theology or a biology.

My intention is to work within the spirit of these contemporary Christian leaders. Pope John Paul II constantly tried "to promote, in charity and service, the solidarity of the entire human family." In the midst of the United Nations assembly in 1995, he said,

> As a Christian, my hope and trust are centered on Jesus Christ, the two thousandth anniversary of whose birth will be celebrated at the coming of the new millennium.... Jesus Christ is for us God made man, and made part of the history of humanity. Precisely for this reason, Christian hope for the world and for its future extends to every human person. Because of the radiant humanity of Christ, nothing genuinely human fails to touch the hearts of Christians. Faith in Christ does not impel us to intolerance. On the contrary, it obliges us to engage in a respectful dialogue. Love of Christ does not distract us from interest in others, but rather invites us to responsibility for them, to the exclusion of no one....
>
> (Vatican News Service)

God Says, We Say: The Interpersonal Act of Redemption tries to make the relation between sin and pain much more understandable, thereby providing an holistic shareable interpretation. The mysteries of creation and of evil are treated as super-intelligible—more and more knowable. They are not obscure, but quite intellectable, just as other mysteries, such as the natural mystery of the ecology of plants and animals or the supernatural mystery of heaven as the friendship of God. This present book envisions a new level in the culture of belief, along with a new dimension to the culture of love—a fresh kind of joy and sorrow in life's meaning.

The new joy comes through being able to love God as Creator and Savior in a way that is profoundly more *personal* than ever before. The new sorrow comes from stronger awareness of how we must have originated in the *heart* of God, but haltingly so. Practically speaking, we can begin to discover deeper meaning for the perennial question, "*Why* do bad things happen to good people?"

Instead of sliding away as usual into advice on how to suffer well, we can confront that question head on. We can retain the advice and

Introduction

still know more fully *why* there is any suffering at all. This truth can put us on better speaking terms with Adam, Eve, and God.

*****

A Word about Thinking

We will be thinking about the most profound depths of reality. This endeavor requires the exercise of a mind that is active in a wise manner, respectful of common sense and scientific reasoning, yet actively engaged within and beyond them. In order that we attain the *uncommon* sense known as wisdom, we must get in touch with our ability to see things whole and against the wide sky of *being*.

Because the key ideas of this book are relatively new, they are presented repeatedly from various angles. The approach required is more-than-linear. It is global. The reader who is conscientious might thereby benefit from meditating on the new perspective in ways that could engender a deepening of personal worldview.

The self-centered, earth-bound views of pragmatic consciousness must be put on hold. We are looking fully into meanings that are paradoxical, involving the union of opposites.

The common logic of identity and separation, so necessary in both speculative and practical matters, will be needed, but can hardly be sufficient. Much of the truth in faith and philosophy is not like the *either-or truth* found in mathematics (e.g., "6 x 7 = 42, not 41.8," and so forth) and in practical matters (e.g., "this candidate will either win or lose the election").

By contrast, the truth of *being* permeates everything and is super-relational. Relating to everything, *being* is analogical, not univocal or *merely* logical. More than anything, the truth of *being* is a *both-and* kind of truth. It is inclusive of all lesser kinds of truth.

So, when we are thinking about *God, life*, our *origins*, and our *destiny*, one single meaning does not "fit all." The same word can have significantly different meanings. Depending on the context, as well as the worldview, the terms we use shift in meaning.

8 God Says, We Say

In ordinary conversation and writing, we are strongly inclined to think about matters of simple practicality—where words can have meanings of only one or two dimensions. Such words necessarily have *univocal* and *separable* meanings. These everyday words have the *same* basic meaning each time they are used. One and the same word is said of diverse things with essentially the same meaning. Words like "dog" and "house" most often mean the same each time they are used.

So, when we enter philosophical and theological matters, we are not as inclined to think in terms of *both-and* meanings, wherein the same word can have quite different, yet related, meanings on various occasions. The mysteries of reality and of our limited minds require agile adjustments.

Theists, therefore, are called to do paradoxical (both-and) thinking when relating to the greatest revelations about God. For instance, believers acknowledge *both* the withinness *and* the otherness of God. The divine Being is known to be fully *within* creatures, as well as completely *other than* creatures. These features of the immanence and transcendence of God are then basic truths that incomparably integrate opposites: God's *withinness* (not insideness) is seen as one with God's *otherness* (*not* outsideness or "beyondness"). They are united, but not identical at all.

Theists profess that God is *both* infinitely "close to" *and also* infinitely other than created beings. Theists are neither pantheists, who think that creatures are ultimately identical to God—or form a part of God—nor deists, who think of creatures as separate from God. Theists *distinguish* clearly—*without separating*—uncreated Being from created being.

Failures of human understanding are legion and curiously often quite "complementary." For everyone who claims that "the sun is God" or that God is "in the starry heavens" there are many who think that God is the same as themselves or that they are part of God.

But theists hold that God is not separate from us, like a physical and spatial entity, nor identical to us, even in part, however much we "look inside." Fixated areas of the human mind that impede a true awareness of God have to be relaxed and awakened by paradoxical

Introduction

thinking. Truth is *both* either-or *and* both-and; not *either* either-or *or* both-and.

There are truths that are either-or (such as, "you will be either saved or lost forever"); and there are truths that are both-and (such as, "God both can and cannot save you," depending on how well you exercise your personal freedom). While retaining respect for *either-or* truths, we must tap into the *both-and roots* of truth in order to grow in vigorous understanding.

God Says, We Say requires the kind of paradoxical thinking that sees truth in the mutual unity of opposites. The transcendence and immanence of God is but one prime example of many such truths.

This book includes other paradoxical truths. Particularly relevant in light of the new theistic perspective is the meaning of being and of becoming. Creation *ex nihilo* (out of nothing), the creation of our *being*, has been constantly confused with creation *ex aliquo* (out of something; dust, a rib), the creation of our *becoming*. The book calls attention to our "cosmolock," our minds' lockage onto the world of matter and motion (cosmos). It points out how we tend, in one way or another, to reduce *being* to *becoming* instead of giving respect to the two different terms. *Becoming* is a kind of *being*. But not every *being* is a *becoming*. God, for instance, does not become anything by growth or transition of any kind.

Important words within our everyday life—terms such as self, gift, causality, soul, and so many others—can have either being-based meaning or becoming-based meaning. It is helpful to see how these diverse meanings interface.

So, we need to refrain from a simple *either-or* mentality about our deepest kind of identity. Perennially, we have been short-circuiting God's love for us by leaving out the *true* infinity of God and the *perfection* of originative creation (*ex nihilo*). We take finite persons as found in the cosmic, imperfect world and "forget" they were, and still are, *perfect* as effects of creation *ex nihilo*. Created human persons are *both* perfect *and* imperfect, not simplistically imperfect. That is a paradox second to none.

In any event, when we are trying to understand the new view, with its different angles and levels of meaning for common terms, it would be wise to hold back our tendencies to make univocal and simplistic judgments. By such restraint, unnecessary disagreements can be minimized, while genuine disagreements can become better focused.

All the while, we can hope for agreements—*both* old *and* new.

******

A Word about Reading

Of the worldview offered in these pages, not all "parts" can be seen at once. The reader needs to consider patiently the elements, one by one, with an eye to the eventual formation of a whole view.

The chapters are designed for a cumulative effect. Later chapters reinforce earlier ones. They provide various angles in an attempt to spur the reader's consciousness into another level or dimension: a fresh verticality of sight that cuts through the ordinary, "horizontal" levels and kinds of being.

Thank you for your participation in the exploration of this new theistic view.

******

Part I Searching for the Inside Story

Chapter 1

The Suffering of the Innocents

Why does God not stop the killing of innocent babies? Atheists have had a field day with that question. Even good Jewish, Christian, and Islamic people have come to wonder why, each year, millions of innocent children, inside and outside of the womb, are deliberately slaughtered, by their parents? Why does God not prevent a calamity like this from happening?

We can understand why bad things happen to guilty people. But why do bad things happen to those who are perfectly innocent? Is God a 'monster in the sky,' or only existent in some other locale? Is God not powerful enough to prevent injustice? Or not good enough? If not powerful enough or not good enough, is God really God? Or perhaps we are confused about the meaning of justice, peace, and love?

Blaming and Naming

Are we not *unconsciously*, if not consciously, blaming God for the suffering of innocent people? In the three traditions of theism, we do not seem to understand—consciously—how God can tolerate bad things happening to good people. So, we claim that it is a mystery and often piously refrain from posting our thoughts and sentiments. We can unconsciously and implicitly, however, be blaming God, while professing our belief that God is infinitely good and infinitely powerful. Our blaming is repressed. We deny that we really know it.

Most of us realize that God could not possibly *will* any evil to anyone who did not deserve it. For Christians, only the Redeemer himself and his mother suffered unjustly, on behalf of redeeming and saving us. Even with respect to the angels in hell, we can affirm that God allows their self-torture, since it is caused, at the moment of creation, by their complete unwillingness to love. God infinitely

12 God Says, We Say

respects our exercise of *God-gifted* freedom. This freedom, a gift to each person, is absolutely ours, and not a loan or a lien.

We are inclined, however, simply to dismiss the question of how there can be real evil if God is both *infinitely* good and *infinitely* powerful. We might be trying to keep at bay the wondering within our hearts and minds, so that we can go on believing in the infinity of God's goodness and power.

Doubters about Infinity

Many, however, doubt the infinity of God's power. In his famous book, *When Bad Things Happen to Good People* (1981), Rabbi Harold Kushner clearly and vividly articulated the doubt and even the denial of God's infinity of power. He held for the absoluteness of God's goodness, but he doubted and even denied God's 'almighty power.'

Many people have agreed with this notion. Countless theists have abandoned faith in God's *infinite* power—especially in the light of the Holocaust and of various other kinds of tragedy for individuals and populations.

Facing the Abusing God was published in 1993 by the theologian David Blumenthal. He has established a following in the movement called "protest theology." It is inspired by Blumenthal, Eli Wiesel, and others. These ardent adherers to the ancient tradition, as they see it, believe that God really did overstep his boundaries and did abuse his people in and through the Holocaust. They actually ask God to repent to us, in addition to our ordinary repentance to God. In doing so, they give unintentional comfort to atheists. Many people have always laughed at theists, who believe that God is both infinitely good and infinitely powerful, and yet can *allow innocent people* to suffer the extremities of pain and protracted torture.

The 'theology of protest' seems to be a reaction to the classical meaning for God. Practitioners who claim to be facing the 'abusing God' are responding by denying that God is somehow perfect, much less infinitely perfect. It appears that these protestors have become so "cozy" with God that they can 'tell God off,' so to speak. They leave us inferring that God is not infinitely *good*—whether or not God is infinitely powerful. They have "creaturised" God by insisting upon human standards for God's 'behavior.'

Chapter 1   The Suffering of the Innocents

Rabbi Kushner, however, opts for there being no such thing as infinite *power*, since God cannot prevent tsunamis, tornadoes, and other acts of nature that ravage human beings at times. According to his scenario, God is seen as completely compassionate with those who suffer unjustly and will provide immense comfort to them when they sincerely ask. But God is thought necessarily to be unable to remove the *causes* of pain and anguish from them. He has not the power.

In effect, Nature trumps God.

An Improved Response for Believers

Instead of demurring on the question, Christians and Jews should take back their heritage. God is infinitely actual, unlimitedly good, and able to do anything real, other than sin. Many Christian texts over the centuries have provided genuine comfort by telling us how to suffer with our Savior. But hardly any yield basic reasons *why* we suffer—especially why little, innocent children suffer torments and are so often destroyed, even being torn alive, limb from limb, within their own mothers.

The God of the Bible, of course, cannot do just anything. God simply cannot 'make a square circle' or 'do a sinful act.' Such is contradictory and absurd. But God *can* stop volcanoes, hurricanes, and wars from erupting and killing helpless populations. As divine goodness and power miraculously preserved from harm Daniel and his companions in the fiery furnace, so this goodness and power can preserve the life of any soldier landing on the beaches of Normandy under 'impossible fire.'

For doing such deeds of greatness, we can trust in God's power and effectively draw it into our sphere by prayer, penance, fasting, and humility. These are decisive factors, if done sufficiently, for God's infinitely abiding mercy to become effective in our lives.

We ought not to *blame* God—consciously or unconsciously—for anything. But God often requires our faith-filled help in the doing of miracles. Even the slight mistrust at striking the rock was enough to prohibit Moses from entering into the Promised Land with people he had led for forty years in the wilderness.

If we are to be faithful to our calling as the people of God, we must *stop* faulting God—*even unconsciously*. We need to place the responsibility squarely on ourselves. How dare we think that God might not be unlimitedly good and unlimitedly powerful? To think so is to *deny that God is God.*

We are deeply inclined, however, to deny our own responsibility for whatever good or evil happens *to* us. So, we are being called to recognize that *we might not be nearly as good as we think we are.* Kushner's 'good people' are not as good as he thinks they are. Even as the Rabbi extols his own virtues of a lifetime of service to God and his people, he seems to be unaware that he is *conceived* in sin, and that there is genuine reason for it. The prophet David cries out to God for all of us, "For behold, I was conceived in iniquities; and in sins did my mother conceive me" (*Psalms* 50:7).

Christians believe in original sin. But they do not believe that we committed *that* sin by stealing cookies from the cookie jar at age four or five. Nor do they think we sinned with Adam and Eve under a tree. So, whence comes the *origin* of evil in *our* lives?

Our sin *and the sin of Adam and Eve* comes from the depths. It comes from our deepest hearts. Its beginning must have come from the moment of the creation *out of nothing* (*ex nihilo*). Since we are created *persons*—not plants or animals—we must have responded with Adam and Eve and the angels to the immediately interpersonal love of God *loving* us into *being*.

We were gifted with our own being, from within *the infinite heart of God*, and we hesitated to receive ourselves as perfect finite beings in God's image and likeness. By receiving our perfect being freely and immediately, but imperfectly, we *made* ourselves imperfect.

We must ask ourselves seriously some poignant questions. Could God love us into reality by gifting us with an even slightly flawed being and with an imperfect freedom? Could Adam and Eve and we ourselves have had our *absolute beginning to be* from the dust of the earth? Could God create anything *ex nihilo* ('fresh from nothing') that was directly and immediately imperfect, such as dust, a rib, or anything of passive potency—the passive base of material creation?

If so, God is *not God*. God is not infinitely actual, with infinite goodness, infinite power, infinite freedom and infinite wisdom. God is basically a mega-creature and is like *us* in 'doing what pleases' rather than doing what is infinitely and necessarily true, good, and beautiful.

Chapter 1 The Suffering of the Innocents

Why We Are Conceived in Sin

Our whole theological tradition—not the Revelation itself—has burdened us with the notion that God created *directly out of nothing* the birds and the bees, the wind and the trees, and all manner of passive potencies. Yet these particular kinds of creatures, the *sub-personal* ones, are intrinsically imperfect, having space and time and physical composition that, in principle, lack completeness of being. They are *derivative kinds* of being whose existence serves *fallen* human persons. No sub-personal being has intellect and will; and so it cannot receive its very own being as a gift from God. Each one is intrinsically incomplete and imperfect, from molecules to monkeys.

As St. Thomas Aquinas noted, only persons are complete being. Only persons are perfect in principle. What is finitely perfect can come to *be* only by the causal act of the *infinitely* perfect.

Nothing imperfect comes directly by an infinite act of love. God is the *only* agent of the *ex nihilo* act of creation. All is perfect at this non-durational moment *within* eternity, in which God gifts other beings to *be*—that is, finite beings (persons) are infinitely loved into being. Absolute creation involves *only* persons—complete beings, with intellect and will to know and love, to receive and give self. Out of nothing, God gifts all persons—angelic and human—with full and perfect finite being.

There is no other agent in the activity of creating out of nothing by whom even the least imperfection or flaw *could* result. The act of creation could not have transpired as an act of time or space. Those dramatic parameters of cosmic being are intrinsically *imperfect*. They are the bounds of passive potency, the kind of being that can be "done to," or determined by, another or many others.

At that same moment of creation (*ex nihilo*), "simultaneously" so to speak, we gifted ones were fully free to receive the gift of being and of being ourselves. We were able thereby *fully to unite* with God and with all creation forever. Our freedom of will was immediate and perfect. Within the infinite heart of divine Being, we must have responded necessarily and freely from the heart of *our* fully-gifted being.

In the same non-temporal moment that we were gifted with our beings, we necessarily and freely acted as we willed. The giving and receiving of *being* were an ontological exchange between God's necessarily interpersonal act of gifting us to be and our necessarily interpersonal act of receiving—well or not so well or not at all—the gift of who and what we are.

Multitudes of angels and perhaps many or a few human persons must have said, immediately and fully, *yes*, thereby uniting firmly and forever with God's infinite love. Other angels and perhaps many or a few human persons said, immediately and fully, *no*, thereby locking themselves into self-torture forever, *completely perverting* their functional freedom so as to make repentance impossible.

And then there were we. We said less than fully *yes*. Effectively, we said *yes-no*, that is, *maybe*.

Yet, not all *human* persons necessarily said *maybe* at the moment of being created out of nothing. Not all were destined to be members of "Adam's fallen race." Many or a few could have said *fully yes* and entered heaven with the *yes*-saying angels. They would have been freely and immediately lovers of God.

Moreover, many or a few human persons could have said fully *no* and confined themselves in hell with the *no*-saying angels. These might have been freely, immediately, and spontaneously "insanely jealous" of God and of God's *infinite* kind of being.

We fallen-but-not-dead human persons, however, must have said to God and to our own gifted being, immediately and fully, *maybe* (*yes* and *no*, as it were), thereby crashing our beings. We thereby imploded and exploded. We imploded our beings upon themselves and, as well, exploded our pristine freedom into a kind of dull and uncontrolled 'fragmental freedom' that was destined to be known as cosmic elements and particles.

Our bad exercise of first freedom caused a collapse from within. From that devastated condition, we are now being rescued (out of 'the dust')—perhaps, in part, through a kind of partial evolution. We will even come to salvation, should we be eventually *fully willing* to repent and to be saved. In any event, we are becoming "cosmically poised" for our final decision at death.

Because of the *yes* in our *maybe*, we are candidates for redemption and salvation. Because of the *no* we are in jeopardy of everlasting ruin. But we can hope to muster enough good will from out of the ravages of our first act of botched freedom-in-being. By the power

Chapter 1 The Suffering of the Innocents

of God's Scriptural word; by the supernatural agency of sacraments and sacramentals; and by many interpersonal ministries *cooperating* with God's *infinite* power and love; we who are really repentant persons can return to, and enter, the heart of God's infinite invitation to *be* and to be who we really *are*.

The Answer to "Why Me?"

If we were to realize as true what has been sketched here about our perfect creation and originative sin—sinning with Adam and Eve and multitudes of other human persons *"right from nothing"*—we could *stop blaming God unconsciously* for the cry in our hearts, "Why me?" We could finally have a sound answer to atheists about *why* innocents suffer: they are not nearly as innocent as they look.

We could begin to believe with wholeness in the God of Jews, Muslims, and Christians who is *both* infinitely good *and* infinitely powerful. We could believe that God's little ones on earth need enlightenment and healing from their personally originative sin that blocked out the vision of the perfect being they were being gifted to be. No more "Why me's?" There might then blossom in our souls, "Why *not* me?"

We would know more than we might, at first, want to know about the answer to the 'problem of evil.' But we would stop overlooking the prime aspects of God's loving creation *out of nothing*. And we would then be freer to acknowledge our *originative* sin, namely, our meagerly grateful response to *being*, from which we suffer together, largely unconsciously. Free and immediate *hesitation to be who and what God gifted us to be* has multitudinous consequences. We are now living by them and within them.

Chapter 2

Strangers in Being

A woman was viewing the dead body of an elderly man in the funeral parlor. Her friend, the widow, said softly, "I never really knew John." After many years of marriage so little of this *person* had emerged through his personality. And his wife's sensitivity had grown enough that she had come to recognize the loss to his family and friends even while he lived.

This might seem to be an extreme case. But it must be said that we live and die in a world full of strangers.

Why are we even *like* this? What must have *happened* to us? An infinitely good and infinitely powerful Being created us. So, there could not have been any flaws in the Divine act of creation. Yet we are living in the backwater of creation, called the cosmos. We are largely estranged from ourselves and from one another. All of us are riven with physical, emotional, mental, and spiritual hazards, with potentially torturous maladies, and with inevitable death.

Floundering Vision

Why are we subject to this alienation? What does it mean? Is it coming from the infinitely loving God and from our perfectly gifted self?

If we say it all started with Adam and Eve, we would seem to be blaming God for letting them hit us with *their* original sin. Can God really "stand by" while any innocent creature is *unjustly* harmed? Could not God have gifted us into being as innocents, with different first parents, ones who would not have sinned? Or could not God have created us as fully mature and free, and even without any parents at all?

Let's face it. Tiny infants inside and outside the womb, as well as the holiest of saints, are vulnerable to the most horrendous evils.

20 God Says, We Say

Does God then overlook their being tortured? Is God really able to prevent it? Holocausts and purges aside, even in ordinary civilized life, the world has plenty of perils and pitfalls.

And why do we seem rather opaque about the perennial question on "the suffering of the innocent"? Are we not sensitive enough to see *why* we suffer?

Obviously, we are not. Our vision is weak when it comes to *why*. We wobble around trying to find a stable vantage point from which to observe the creation scene. But our efforts inevitably prove futile whenever we think in terms other than sheer *being* itself.

At every opportunity, human history wanders away from *being*. A primordial weakness makes us unable to ground ourselves and our conscious lives in *unqualified being*.

People rarely stake their conscious lives on being itself. They inevitably pledge allegiance to different *kinds* of being. The state, pleasure, power, money, humanity, one's society, one's children, one's self, and even one's *conception* of God are some of the usual fixations of human consciousness. And they are all *kinds* of being. Even God is a kind of being. Although God is the infinite kind, God is not outside *the community of all that is*.

It seems that human beings, East and West, try to make their lives meaningful by passively allowing themselves to become primarily a function of *one* kind of being, and by regarding all other kinds as subordinate to the Big One. The history of *our humankind* amounts largely to the history of prejudice in being.

After All, It's Only a Being

We take being for granted in our conscious thought, as well as in our subconscious. If someone comes into the room and asks, "Who are you?" we are likely to respond by giving our name. But we would not think of indicating something by way of grounding, such as, "I am a unique gift of God," or "I am a unique being who is able to determine who I am." And if someone were to ask about our companion, "Who is this person?" immediately we might respond, "This is Jane Smith," rather than mindfully pause, perhaps more honestly, before the profound meaning of the pronoun *who* and the unique being of the person herself, and say, "I hardly know!"

Chapter 2   Strangers in Being

We are not able to wonder well—in an unqualified way. Rather than bringing ourselves to face the more fundamental question *"Why is being,"* we concentrate almost exclusively on questions such as "What is this?" or "What is that?" But, in addition to asking about the essences and definitions of things, we are called to ask *"Why* is this being?" We could even push forward with this question to the extent of wondering *"Why* is God?"

In the course of human history many have seen that we cannot take the existence of ourselves and the beings around us for granted. We must affirm the *being* of God as the ultimate cause. Religious faith encourages us to be grateful to God for all the gifts of being. But another truth is hidden in our hearts. How wondrous it is that *God is at all.*

Most of the time, theists take God for granted. God is conceived as being the divine Kind of being: infinitely good, powerful, loving, merciful, creative, and salvific. These and many others are attributes of God, indicating the *kind* of Being God is. But what if there were really nothing-at-all, not even God? Granted, such is an hypothesis contrary to possibility. But the kind of Being with all the attributes of the divine Being (even as the three Divine Persons) calls for our gratitude and praise. How great it is for God just to *be and to be eternal.*

If we would ask ourselves *why* is being—why is there something rather than pure nothingness, why is there any being at all, including the infinite being—we would change our attitude toward everything. We would discover that things *do* their being in a way different from the way we think as we go about taking being for granted.

Changing Attitudes

Our attitudes of quietly objectifying one another and of mindless subservience can begin to change and be transformed. We can start to see everything as a co-end in itself. Every unique, individual being is a good-in-itself-with-others, as well as perhaps a means to something else. Every hair of one's head, every feather of a bird, the call of a loon, the scent of a rose—everything accidental as well as substantial—has an absolute, but highly relational, finality. Not even the slightest thing need be treated simply and exclusively as a means to an end.

22 God Says, We Say

The transforming goodness of every being in our workaday lives is still rather minimal. But that is because of our response, or lack thereof, and is not due mainly to the condition of the being itself. If we want the meaning and worth of each little being to increase, we are going to have to start *willing our own act of be-ing* and stop "letting God do it"—stop assuming that God is doing our *be-ing* for us.

We are still latent pantheists to some extent. We assume that God is responsible for every act of be-ing and that our individual act of be-ing is not something we *are*. We think that God "makes us be" and thus is doing our act of being for us while we respond with individual acts and attitudes that modify by affirming or denying this created act of be-ing. We fail to realize that while God gifts us with an act of be-ing, this act is an act that we both are and *do*. We *do* the *gift* that we *are*.

But somehow we are going to have to recognize that *be*-ing is, in a critical sense, an *act*, even as walk-ing, talk-ing, and breath-ing are acts that we are *doing*. At any given moment, I am breath-ing, I am think-ing, I am be-ing.

I have been taught from earliest age to think, at least implicitly, that be-ing—unlike breath-ing, think-ing, and the rest—is something God does for me. Because God gave me my being out of nothing, I get the idea that God made me dependent on God for that gift and that the be-ing itself is dependent on God.

It takes considerable reflection and discussion to realize that God does God's own be-ing and that God could not do my be-ing for me unless the divine were to become me literally. But since God could not become me without truly ceasing to be Self, there seems to be only one being left with the primary responsibility for my be-ing—and that is I.

I *Am* My Being

I cannot delegate my act of be-ing to anyone else any more than I can delegate my act of breathing. My sheer act of being is my most universal and critically important act. It is only within my unique and irreplicable act of being that my other acts, such as breathing, walking, talking, thinking and the like, do occur. And this act of being is mine and attributable in no way to anyone else. It is not at all yours. Not one whit.

Chapter 2   Strangers in Being

If I think my be-ing is even partly God's, I am into pantheism. I fail to honor the being with which I was uniquely gifted by God. This gift of being-at-all is given unconditionally. There can be no strings attached, no ties that bind. I can go to hell freely, abusing the gift entirely. Or I can receive the gift fully and thus enter everlasting bliss. It's my creature's choice. That choice is done *by* my be-ing *for* my being, in the grace of divine Love.

Tragically, as it is now, I find in myself an abiding unwillingness to accept *full* responsibility for my own *act* of being. This is not a responsibility for "having" it, or for the *fact* that I am at all. That "choice" was God's—whether to create at all and whether to create me. But having been so gifted, I am called to *receive* well and fully that gift. I am to *be* that being. Apparently, I have not done that perfectly, otherwise I would now be enjoying beatific life within God. A largely unconscious unwillingness to be is at the root of my estrangement from unqualified being.

Such original unwillingness-to-be comprises the originative failure that causes the wandering away of everyone who resisted, at least somewhat, in the very beginning, the unqualified goodness of being. This failure is so deep and so universal that it might be called the *originative* sin. And this primal, inaugural hesitation to be is the one that predisposes us for our daily failures, our daily hesitations.

This *originative* sin is far deeper than the original sin of Adam and Eve. Theirs was just its symptom. We, who are Christians, have been told that we are not responsible for the sin of Adam and Eve, but that we have inherited it from them and that they are responsible for it. That is true. But there must be something deeper that accounts for *why* we were conceived and born in their line and thus inherited it.

Just as we have long thought that God is responsible for our being rather than we ourselves, we are only too happy to think that the evil in our lives did not start with us personally, but that someone else is responsible for our primordial unwillingness to be. In this blaming frame of thought, we have been protected from the fullness of our ability—our *response*-ability.

Somehow we must be personally and socially guilty of our initial state of alienation from the gift of being and of being ourselves. Any Being who would really be infinitely good, infinitely powerful, and infinitely merciful, *could* not allow us to enter and suffer this world of great actual and potential anxiety, frustration, and torture unless we were in a certain, definite manner responsible for its being that way.

If any of us is a person innocent of an originative sin, God would have required our consent to be subject to the vicissitudes of this life. We would then be serving to help save those who are really subject potentially to losing out forever. We can, of course, ask ourselves if we are really here sinlessly to suffer the unjust arrows of worldly fortune for the sake of redeeming others who have sinned. But the question itself is almost an absurdity.

Even as Jesus walked the earth, children writhed in pain. Was he insensitive? Was he cruel at heart? Why did he not spare them if they were entirely innocent? Why did not his Father arrange for a different destiny, one proportionate to their innocence. Christians only know of two persons, Jesus and Mary, his mother, who are and were perfectly without sin. For our defective way of being, the rest of us must be really responsible in varying ways and degrees. In the spirit of the repentant thief at Calvary, we can say we are receiving justice.

Some of us may actually admit our being-searing sin; others may adamantly refuse. After all, it is so convenient to place the blame for the evil existing in the world on our first parents or on evolutionary cosmic laws. When we are unable, or unwilling, to think through the extent to which we are free and responsible for being here, a wistful determinism is a customary panacea.

Repressed Sin

Nonetheless, it is always possible that we might come to wonder whether we have been repressing something about the relevance of original sin. Inroads have been made in the 20th century toward understanding the role of repression in everyday life. Many, if not all, can understand how we tend to block out from our awareness the memories of past traumatic experiences. Pain-filled origins that are unwanted can be unconsciously denied.

This common phenomenon regarding shocking experiences might lead us to wonder whether this problematic life itself—filled with potential and actual torture and eventual death—is not the result of a much deeper, spiritual trauma that we have all repressed. We know

Chapter 2   Strangers in Being

how individuals are so ready to block out, both from themselves and from others, an awareness of certain repugnant happenings in their *temporal* past. So, is it not to be wondered whether the origin of evil and sin has been brought about by some vast social and individual fault, caused by ourselves at the durationless moment of creation *out of nothing*, and immediately repressed?

Could we have repressed our own personal act of being created—of *receiving our being* and of partially *failing* to receive it well? Could we not have done so as readily and even more effectively than we might do in repressing any merely temporal shock? Could it then be reasonable to suppose that each of us did then become, at least partially, responsible for the alienated state of the world in which we were conceived and born? And yet we still do not want to know about it?

After all, we have a quite difficult time knowing well the most knowable Being of all—our Creator. We wobble around trying to conceive the God who gave us being. The divine Being or Persons who created us are infinitely knowable. Yet we are largely numb and insensitive to their Being and to our own. Perhaps our reticence in admitting some of the simple but radical truths about the being of God and of God's act of creation is one of the prime consequences of our original failure to receive well the being with which we are gifted at the moment of creation.

Our Failed Super-Likeness to God

Consider some of the truths about the Creator and about created persons that are known through Faith and reason.

God is not simply the greatest and richest being that is. God is infinite Being: the "greatest" being that *could* be. God is not simply the greatest being, than which nothing greater could be thought or conceived. God is infinitely greater than the greatest object of any mere thought. Created persons are not even comparable to God. They are superrelated to God and like God, but cannot be *compared* to infinite Being.

When God says to each of us, with the act of creating, "Be, and be yourself," the meaning is infinitely powerful and unconditional. The Creating Person intends that created beings are absolutely in no way identical to the divine, even though there is a great likeness. Every created person really is wholly other than the Creator-Person *while remaining fully within the divine.* Knowing and thinking of oneself as *outside* the Trinity or the Unity is a prime consequence of failure to be who one is.

Everyone must be unconditionally like God in being. Uniqueness, otherness, withinness, and relatedness are important qualities of every being—created and uncreated. Of course, as we are counseled, "Be perfect as your heavenly Father is perfect," does not mean that we are being called to the same (infinite) quality or 'degree' of perfection, but that we should be *finitely* perfect. Each of us is a perfect finite creator and lover: fully unique and other-than-anyone-else, but at the same time fully receptive of every other being in the universe. The manner in which we are to be fully other, yet fully within, is finite, whereas the divine manner is infinite.

For Christians, at least, the divine Persons are unlimited: both in being Themselves and in the kind of being that they are. So we are, paradoxically, like God insofar as we are being ourselves perfectly.

At the moment of being gifted with being-at-all—a non-temporal moment—we were our own limited, unique kind of being, with perfect power to receive and be ourselves. (Being limited is not the same as being imperfect.) God gifted each of us with the perfect power to be and to receive fully the being that we are. But our way of *perfect* being is to be within others, to receive them within us, and yet be *other* than they are in a properly *finite* way. We are created perfectly in the "image and likeness" of God's perfections. God does not create junk; nor does God create anyone less than perfect.

So where have all the perfections gone? We must have said, in effect, less than fully *yes* in that perfect moment of being gifted with being. As God said, "Be," we said, "Maybe." Along with Adam and Eve and with all human persons who are sinners, we sinned and crashed in that originative moment of being, at once creating a spiritual unconscious in which we buried the 'deed.'

The sinful crash and burial ground for our sin did not occur in space and time. But it might be thought to have been, figuratively, a bit like the toppling of the towers in New York City on September 11, 2001. That horrific incident immediately resulted in the killing and burial of about three thousand people. The crash created the burial as well as the killing. Before the crash there was no burial ground. The crash created the killing and the burial ground, all in one 'act.' Similarly, our originative intention (about *be*-ing) actually created (caused) both the evil and its burial ground—our spiritual, emotional, and physical unconscious.

We *do not want* to know about the primordial crash of our being or even to think about the possibility. But there really is no other alternative in Faith and reason than to admit our failed response and to praise God's *infinite* goodness and *infinite* power to save us from ourselves, if we are truly willing.

Chapter 3

Crying for Salvation

We cannot deny it. We come into this world as strangers in a foreign environment. Insofar as we have sinned—by saying partially *no* to the gift of creation—our beingful otherness with respect to all other beings has become an outsideness, an overt estrangement. And our withinness is a kind of insideness or covert estrangement. We are like God, but the likeness has been contorted by our original *yes-no* to being-at-all and to being who we are.

In this alienated condition, we are not inclined to think about our profound likeness to God. Such reflection might bring us too close to admitting our responsibility for our own being and for the state of estrangement that we are in—even while we do not "remember" its cause. We much prefer to think that God created out of nothing the massively passive existence within us and around us. We do not like to think that the primordial chaos of *Genesis* 1:2 was self-made. That way we do not have to consider how it might be that all of the world's passivity is the collective responsibility of fallen humans including ourselves.

We have been trained to attribute all the good that we do to God and whatever evil we do to ourselves. But that is only said on the rather superficial and symptomatic level. More deeply, we can come to realize that God cannot do the good we do and still be God. God is responsible for *the good out of which we* create our own kind of created (moral) goodness.

Likewise, we are seriously induced to attribute the bad that we do to ourselves, except to say that its *origin* is somehow there in Adam and Eve and not in us. We seem to be satisfied to blame our first parents for the original evil that predisposes us for our daily sins.

Subconsciously, then, we think that God is somehow responsible for our being innocently afflicted with original sin and for our being subjected to the evolutionary laws wherein "evil is inevitable for growth." We seem to be unable or unwilling to understand that there is a protoconscious dimension of our being. In that deepest area of our being, we must have freely, if partly, rejected the gift of being-at-all. And this rejection has resulted in our primordial, personal estrangement from the goodness of all that is.

Due to the meagerness of our self-knowledge, consequent upon this personal and social "fall"—or better, "plunge"—we are hardly aware of our protoconscious act. But this primal dimension is an ontological reality, a non-temporal, non-spatial, strictly spiritual condition, in which we were originatively created. Therein we are engaged in the *act* of *be*-ing who we choose to be, right from the non-durational moment of receiving our being.

In that protoconscious activity, we establish our parentive attitude toward being. We give potential birth to all our moods, emotions, concepts, and intuitions. Like the nine-tenths of an iceberg below the water's surface, this singular, premiere kind of consciousness provides vastly greater weight and import for our personal destiny than anything else.

The protoconscious *is* our primary act of response to being. This prime act of *be*-ing who we are radically affects the structure of our whole selves—including the conscious, subconscious, unconscious, and preconscious dimensions that are delineated by psychology, philosophy, and theology. It is in our *protoconscious* activity that we are (or become) ultimately ourselves—for or against God and all being.

In protoconscious life, we said an immediate *maybe* (a *no* kind of *yes*) to the gift of being and to the Giver. As a result of the *yes* in our *maybe*, and unlike the angels of Lucifer who said absolutely *no*, we can be saved by God. We need salvation because of the *no* in our *maybe*. If we had said, in effect, fully *yes* we would have at once entered everlasting, blissful union with God. Gabriel, Michael, and multitudes of angels did just that. Perhaps at least a few, or even many, human persons did likewise and were really never in need of redemption by becoming children of Adam and Eve. (Adam is the father of the 'fallen human race,' the *fallen* human community.)

But we said *maybe*, and we need to "receive again" the gift of being and of union with God. Christians believe that the Incarnate

Chapter 3   Crying for Salvation

Word of God has come and has provided the base for our salvation, for our free *re*-reception of the gift of being.

Within the new view, Jesus has redeemed us from the guilt of our originative sin. That *protoconscious* sin was passed on to us in this life in and through the inheritance of the (historically) original sin of Adam and Eve. We inherited, *through them, both* their original sin (in Eden) *and* our own *originative* sin. We are assured that we will be healed eventually, if we willingly bear the pain, sorrow, and anguish of life in the cosmos and of any purgation that might come after it.

The Christian rite of baptism removes original sin and likewise its *roots* in our personal originative sin. But we still need to work out gradually—or abruptly at the moment of death—the promise of rebirth which the sacrament signifies and reveals. As a sinner, I need the critically infinite presence of Jesus. I must maintain, through Faith and good works, a conversion of attitude—a conversion in my total response to the goodness of being. But I alone make the final and effective determination. No one, not even God, can willfully receive salvation for me.

Dependence and Independence

Tragically, we come into this world skewed toward an attitude of serving ourselves more than anyone else. We are overwhelmingly disinclined to accept full responsibility for the way we are being and for our initial estrangement from the gratitude and joyous reality of being created out of nothing.

Further, as we are instructed in the meaning of our creation and redemption we are told that we are totally dependent on God. There is little practical distinction made between our relation to God in creation and our relation to God in redemption. We are given the idea that dependency comprises our *only* basic relationship to God—dependency both for being at all and for being saved. We also get the impression that created beings should be essentially dependent on one another.

And so, we might ask the question: Could any creature BE on its own without any dependence on other creatures? Traditionally, the answer is no. The only independent being is the divine Being. God is revealed as the supreme being, infinitely powerful and good. But, within that revelation, we still have not noticed that this infinite power and goodness creates *directly* beings who are *persons only*. These person-beings are so like their Creator that they are final ends in themselves, independent with respect to all other beings, even as God is independent. These persons are gifted to be independent-*with* God, not independent-*from* or *–of* God.

Sub-personal beings are solely dependent on others, and could not possibly be created *directly ex nihilo*. Such entities are intrinsically imperfect beings that are designed to support fallen human persons like ourselves, who botched their perfect finite being, as they were being freshly gifted with it.

As gifted with their being immediately by God, created persons—angelic and human—*are* their limited, finite selves: independently and fully. The *are* in charge of their destiny. God's act of creating them is absolute, final, irrevocable. We might say it this way: God could not make them cease be-ing even if God "wanted to."

Yet we are taught somewhat the opposite. The usual scholastic notion is that if God ceased to "think" of us or know us, we would cease to be. Despite the reality that this is an hypothesis contrary to possibility and that God could not cease knowing us and still be infinitely knowing, it would be better to say the reverse, if we still wish to play this speculative game. It would be better to say that, even if God were to cease to be, we would go on being and being ourselves. The infinitely creative act of God is just that absolute and powerful. We need to realize that every created person is much more like God than we have dared to think. So like God, without being God in any way.

What does this radical independence of all person-beings mean? Are all beings fundamentally unrelated? On the contrary, all are super-related. Every person-being, including the divine Person(s), is independent *with* others, not independent *from* or *of* others.

An example of relating to others through independence is the growth of a child into adolescence and then into adulthood. Only with maturity and adulthood can a son face his father as a friend. No longer is the father a functionary for the fulfillment of his needs. While a son is a child depending on his parents, he is hardly free to relate well with them in person-to-person friendship. But when he matures, the relations of fatherhood and sonship remain, and are enriched by the context of larger freedom and mutual independence

Chapter 3 Crying for Salvation

with respect to each other. Insofar as either or both of them retains an "essential relationship" of dependency on the other, their total relationship is weakened and unfulfilled.

Similarly, our relationship with God the Father is perfected as we become independent *with* him in being, just as He created us to *be*—directly out of nothing. If we continue to think of ourselves *only* as dependent on God, we surely are going to remain so. But multiple centers of independence in being are so difficult to think about that we quickly reject the suggestion that God and creature could be, in essence, mutually independent.

We have either never acquired, or have lost sight of, the original and everlasting intent of God. God creates with an absolute freedom and security of being. God said, "Be," and God means it. God creates only perfect persons with perfect freedom to respond fully. We could have said an immediate *yes* and would have been instantly free and rapturous persons forever. We could have affirmed and realized our being independent-*with* God and all others.

But, because of our immediate, fully free *maybe* response to *being* and to God, our Gifter, faith in the total goodness of God's gifting us with being-at-all is still wavering. We hardly even try to come to a beginning affirmation of our absolute freedom to be and of our full responsibility for this be-ing activity that we *are*.

Tragically, to the extent that we continue to regard God as the sole independent being—*confusing independence in being with infinity in being*—we make it impossible for ourselves, either consciously or subconsciously, ever to grow into the condition of friendship with God. We remain childish children, and our complete dependency impedes the maturity of friendship with our Father.

The 'Democracy' of Being

We need to recognize, and begin to live, the kind of 'democracy of being' in which we exist. Not only is it true that "all men are created equal"—all person-beings are created equal. All beings, including God, are equal, at least in their *being-at-all*.

Of course, every being has a unique degree and kind of power or function or "talent"; and in that way beings are not equal. No horse is equal to a human in quality of being. Nor is one human equal even to another human in their unique degrees of be-ing.

Moreover, no beings are equal, if being equal is equated with sameness. No being is the *same* as another. Every full being—every person—is uniquely who and what he or she is. But to be unique and to be at all——other than not to be at all—renders every being, as being, "eyeball to eyeball," so to say. Each one's "vote" counts.

We are instinctively ready to deny *any* equality in being with God. Traditional philosophers think that only God *is* Being, and that all creatures merely *have* being. But they are still laboring under the pains of latent pantheism. They are afraid to acknowledge that each created person *is* his or her being, primarily. God gifted each being uniquely and absolutely, without strings. They do not realize that we created persons who sinned "in Adam" are hiding from ourselves our denial of God's sheer gift and giftedness right at the originative moment of creation. Out of profound insecurity, we are "hanging on" to the unique being God gave us, instead of simply *being* it.

We are unconsciously trying to *have* a part of God's being as the only real *Being* that is—as the only independent being—instead of *be-ing* our own unique being with which we were absolutely gifted. We are compulsively unwilling to realize that all person-beings, in their very real and actual being-at-all, are "equal." We fear to think that each is in itself *not nothing, but quite something*, thanks to God's gift of creation *ex nihilo*. Each of us is totally unique—like, but not identical with, any other person-beings, including God.

Independence of Being

We need to make an *ontological* 'declaration of independence.' *Not* of an independence *from* God, nor *from* anyone else. But a declaration of independence-*with* God and with everyone else. Such avowal would be somewhat analogous to that political declaration more familiar to us—and would, incidentally, articulate the prime ontology behind the political one that constituted the American Republic.

We need to acknowledge that every person-being is created with certain inalienable rights, the first of which is the right to being-at-all—once it *is* by the free gift of God. And, in this right, each being is intensely related to all others, while being independent *with* them. Every person is beingfully *within* every independent *other*, and yet uniquely *related* to each.

Chapter 3   Crying for Salvation

In the preamble to renewal that is Christian or even theistic, such an emphatic statement of shared independence would be required. Theists are still inclined to think pantheistically when attempting to consider their relationship with *God*. They regularly fail to regard God's independence as a feature of *being*, not of being supreme. God is supreme by being *infinite* or *unlimited* in manner of being, freedom, goodness, power, justice, mercy, and on and on. We might even be secretly resenting that we are not infinite as are the (three) Person(s) who created us, and so we overreact by thinking ourselves helplessly dependent *in being* on God who *made* us. Such would amount to a very flat way of thinking about God's glory in *creating us out of nothing* by an act of infinite love.

In our everyday lives, however, it becomes especially difficult to recognize the 'democracy' that underlies the obvious dependency, need, servility, and even violence we experience on planet earth. We rightly view servility and violence as distortions of true dependency and need. But we do not seem to appreciate that even the need and the dependency themselves absolutely originate from the distortion we engendered in our primordial, protoconscious, being-with-Being relationship with God.

We not only affirm that these obvious conditions of dependency and need really exist, we also look forward toward these conditions being strengthened in order to lessen disorder and violence. We long for the lamb to lie down with the lion. We long to move from one-way dependency to mutual dependency.

The great truth of our need for redemption and for *dependence* on our Savior must never be overlooked. This reality can hardly be known and strengthened enough. But we readily miss an important paradox. We *need* one another, and especially do we *need* God, in order to come eventually to the realization in life and activity that we do *not ontologically need* God and one another. Lucifer does not need God in order to exist or *be* in hell, which is right where his own will embeds him. No saint needs God in order to *be* in heaven, which is right where his or her own will—*with* God's will—has led.

Amidst the jungle of theologisms and the conditions of great passivity within which we have been reared, we who are Christians recognize our genuine dependency on Jesus himself to heal us and to activate us. But we fail to glimpse the outcome of our inveterate dependency. The result of our deliberately choosing an authentic dependency upon our Savior will be the realization in thought, word, and act that we no longer are—*nor ever were originally*—destined to be ultimately dependent on him or on any other being, including ourselves. The choice to depend *fully* on Jesus will be made by us independently-*with*, not dependently-on, God.

Of course, we should accept, wholeheartedly and not grudgingly, the great network of dependencies in which we find ourselves thrust and enmeshed in this life. But the vigor and insight with which we engage in our redemption-needing condition could be much more enlightened than it is at present. We should be following the star of mutual independence-*with* God, while going along on our dependent ways in this world.

Philosophers and theologians have seemed to hold perennially that independence means separation, or lack of relationship. That false assumption renders us unable to affirm the mutual independence of persons with respect to the world and with respect to God.

Being dependent, of course, means being related. But being related does not necessarily mean being dependent. We could, at least, give good angels in heaven credit for being related to us without being at all dependent on us.

And we are grossly misled by the traditional theologism that while creatures are related to God, God is not related to creatures. Such an idea—though it is explainable in a technical way philosophically—amounts to, or fosters, a complete distortion of the relationship of God and creatures. While it is true that God is not *dependent* on us, this does not mean that God is not *related* to us. Who could be more related to us than our Creator gifting us to be out of nothing? If, as we have been traditionally taught to think, God is closer to us than we are to ourselves, we can be sure that God's "closeness" involves a super-relationship.

Communion and Communication

Reflective common sense can come to our rescue as well. We can ponder the meaning found in gift-giving and in the relationship of communication to communion. When someone I love presents me with a gift, including the very gift of friendship itself, I am grateful and feel superabundantly related to this person in and *through* the gift. I do not become preoccupied with thoughts of an obligation to

Chapter 3   Crying for Salvation

"pay back" the beloved one. The gifts of true friendship are given freely and unconditionally and are *received in that spirit*.

It is only with strangers or ordinary acquaintances that favors or gifts would seem to be occasions for a necessary reciprocation. In lesser relationships, there is often more dependency than there is in the relationship of true friends. The gratitude that consists in some kind of repayment—whether in relation to a fellow creature or to God—is a gratitude of dependency. Since we are sinners in a sinful world, we are within a condition of estrangement, and the gratitude of dependency is good and necessary.

But such was not the intent of our Creator at the non-durational, immediate moment of creation *ex nihilo*. And we can be sure that a gratitude of dependency will pass away for those who are finally healed within the image and likeness of the God Persons, who are infinitely independent with One Another in infinite Love—in Whom Christians believe.

The laws of dependency that necessarily steady us because of our originative *maybe* to God underlie the total field of communication. But they, along with the rest of the temporal world, will pass away as we enter into the mutual independence of communion.

Communion is not communication. Communication, on the one hand, is a giving and receiving of part of one's being, on condition that both the giver and the receiver have a similar ability, interest, or nature. These attempts at communion through communication do come in a variety of ways—whether by oral or written messages, whether through smiles, kisses, telepathy, and the rest. Communion, on the other hand, momentarily and partially conscious on occasion, is the unconditional giving and receiving of the total being of the persons involved.

The giving in communion is a *receiving* kind of giving. And the receiving is a *giving* kind of receiving. Only to the degree that the persons involved transcend "giving and getting" and the limitations of communicative activity can we say that they are communing.

Still, our communion with God and with one another in this world is terribly partial. Because of an estrangement from the fullness of being, we must communicate in order to work out our salvation, part by part, meaning by meaning. Communication is clearly functional; communion is celebrational. In communicating, we are tuned to the world of means-to-an-end; in communing, we are promised an end to all means.

Whether it is a communion or a communication, we find that those involved are both giving and receiving. In attaining the God-creature communion, of course, the principal activity for the Creator is to give and for the creature to receive. The Creator *gives* being with an intended response from the creature that this gift will be received unqualifiedly. But the creature *receives* being and responds, freely and immediately, by giving self—fully, partially, or not at all.

In the dimension of *communication* with the Creator, it is in giving to others that we receive from him and in pardoning others that we are pardoned by him. But it is still more true, from the perspective of *communion*, that it is in receiving from the Creator that we are *able* to give to others, and in our being pardoned that we are *able* to pardon ourselves and others.

A few moments of reflection on the "Prayer of St. Francis" may help to illustrate both the meaning of communion as receiving and the meaning of mutual independence between God and creature. According to the words of St. Francis, it is in pardoning that we are pardoned; and, in union with our Lord's prayer, it is in forgiving those who trespass against us that we will be forgiven our trespasses against our divine Father. Such is the truth from the standpoint of communication, wherein we are forced by our sin to understand and to work out our salvation by the sweat of our brow, piece by piece, meaning by meaning.

But it is not *exclusively* true that God conditions forgiveness of us on our forgiveness of others. Rather, like all of God's acts, divine forgiveness is unconditional from the beginning of creation. God forgives us by the very being of Infinity, even "before" our sin of failing to receive fully the gift of being.

The Infinitely Personal Act of Redemption

The issue remains basically whether we are *now* willing to become gradually aware of *infinitely* unconditional love. Will we really be like God and forgive ourselves unconditionally? This we can do by eventually receiving our being fully and unconditionally, as it was gifted definitively by our Creator. Such receiving is the most basic act of communion of which we are here and now capable; it is the

Chapter 3   Crying for Salvation

critically loving base for repenting of our *originative* sin. It is our side of the "interpersonal act of Redemption."

Because we are already pardoned or "fore-given," we are able to pardon or forgive ourselves and one another. There is no way we can do it without tapping into, turning toward, or even swimming in God's *infinitely* unconditional love for our *being*. Such must be enacted consciously or, at least, unconsciously.

Christians definitely believe that we have received *all* we are and have—right from the foundations of the creation-act. That would include the *redemptive* gift of God's only-begotten Son. Jesus as the Word of God was there in the beginning. In, through, and with him all was created. He comes as the second Adam, created to head the Redemptive Creation in and through the fallen world. He is God's forgiveness even at the beginning of the world of redemption—in response to our prime hesitation to *be*.

All was given in the beginning, and what is fully given takes on the character of redeeming us only "after" we have not *received* fully. Redemption will only "fail" if we refuse to re-receive well the grace of *absolute creation*—if we fail to accept the redemption and our salvation fully and sincerely.

Jesus was not given because, and after, man sinned. There is no special "bail out" act of God "after" the fall of man. We inevitably *think* of it that way because of our time-fixation. And, from the perspective of communication only, we are inclined to think that God's redemptive decision and action followed our sin. We project the gradually redemptive evolution of our vision onto the ways of the divine, as though Redemptive Creation was not quintessentially immediate, and, *as well*, worked out by God in time and space.

Salvation: the Fulfillment of Redemption

Our redemption has been thought to be primarily an act of God. Like creation, redeeming us is something only God can do. And did. But this redemption is essentially gifted to us in order that we attain salvation, which is quite another thing. The capstone of redemption for each of us is our being *saved* and entering everlasting glory.

Salvation is effected, directly and only, by God; *but* we ourselves are also critically involved. Salvation is the mutual activity of God giving and fallen humans receiving—actively, not passively. It is primarily the activity of God by reason of the totally gratuitous and infinite power of creation. But it is *also* crucially an act of human persons in their *receiving* their Creator and the gift of their being. The being that they receive is totally their own.

Redemption remains "incomplete" until our personal response is fully given. *This dimension of redemption* is called salvation: the finite will of the fallen person fully uniting with the infinite will of God. In redemption, God says, "I am saving you." We can say *yes*, *no*, or *maybe* to this loving intent as long as we are living in this world of (intended) recovery.

So, it is secondarily true that it is in pardoning others that we will be pardoned by God. But we would not even be able to think about forgiving others if we had not already, at least partially, *received* the forgiveness of God. It would be better to say, from the standpoint of communion—not excluding the pragmatic truth of the perspective of communication—that it will be in pardoning others that we come to realize we have been already pardoned by God and that it is this pardoning grace that makes it possible for us to forgive others.

When God is presented in Scripture as "threatening us" with hell-fire, it would seem to be a flaw in our communication that makes us passively accept this as literally so. True, God warns us. But there is no subtle pressure, no extortion, no threats, from God. We are the ones who really threaten with hell-fire. We threaten ourselves. We will experience unending frustration in the face of unqualified being if we ceaselessly refuse to admit the fundamental gravity of our primordial sin, and if we finally fail to work out our salvation in the presence of God who has already forgiven us. God has done the "100% infinite best" for our salvation, right from the beginning.

From our absolute (*ex nihilo*) beginning, we have received *being* and its power of self-rectification in case of sin. Like all of God's acts, the act of creating is an eternal act. We perfect, finite, and free persons are the result. Each of us was gifted with a being *like* our Creator's—our kind of personal presence or "participation" within eternal being, but not eternal in any way. We had a *beginning* in being; but we have no end.

Time is within eternity, but not identical with it. Time is our own "creation." We have been given everything—fully, absolutely, and unconditionally in the eternal creative act of God. But our *partial*

Chapter 3   Crying for Salvation

unwillingness to receive fully (what we have been given) actually produces the dimension of linear time in creation, along with space itself. Our being is all spaced out, doing time.

This very real and concrete condition of our being, the temporal and the spatial, need not ever have existed. If all human persons had received fully the gift of their unique, independent, and intrinsically relational being; if the Eve in us, the receiving power, had responded unconditionally to the gift of being-at-all; there would be neither solar time nor cosmic evolution with their attendant dependencies. As it is now, in and through our *ontological* sin of *maybe*-saying, *we* caused time, evolution, and dependency; we also caused the need for healthy moral choices in our present redemptive existence.

God did not create sin or any of its consequences. Rather, God created (finite) beings who were free to respond positively and fully to the gift. This finite creation entails the possibility of abusing that perfect freedom, the possibility of denying the goodness of being. And together with this finite capacity for being, God created, within each human essence, the ground for healing should sin occur. In the essence of the human person is the basis for time, development, and every other ministerial dependency.

Slavish dependency constitutes the original partial refusal to be a mutually independent being *with* God. But *ministerial* dependency necessarily serves to compensate. In time and its processes, there are found many slavish dependencies, often called "actual sins." These dependencies have their proportionate ministerial dependencies both in the sacral and secular realms, such as sacraments, rules, laws, customs, and, in general, communications of every sort.

Communications, time, space, and development have been the dire consequences of our originative estrangement. But, paradoxically, these also constitute ministerial dependencies or potencies. They are promises of recovery to those who are sufficiently willing to grow out of their primordial failure at the moment of creation out of nothing. The decisive work of healing and restoration—the process going from estrangement to friendship—can be accomplished for the individual prior to, and including, the moment of death.

For the human community, ongoing restoration takes place in the unconscious realm of spirituality, *as well as* in the process of cosmic existence wherein individuals and groups increase their personal and social interiority. Repentant people can move into higher and more perfect stages of consciousness, closer to God's original and abiding intent in his creational communion with us.

Now, we live largely as strangers to ourselves, to one another, and to God. Only once in a while, in a flash, is there any awareness of the goodness of being-at-all. For instance, within a cluster of friends sharing ideas on the ultimate meaning of life and death, there might come a fleeting moment of close and wordless communion. But if this communion of being-with-being can occur even for a moment, it can always become stronger and more sustained. Increasing and multiplying, communion can become the common state of the whole universe. *Shared independence of being-with-being can grow; and shared dependencies can be gradually reduced, making us ready to enter heaven wherein there is only communion—presence is shared as independence-with.*

We are each gifted with a unique and privileged responsibility to will our salvation to be an independence-with, concretely in thought, word, and behavior, and with a consummate attitude of gratitude.

Chapter 4

Beneath the Book of *Genesis*

Where is our *being* in the Bible? We are portrayed in the history of our redemption and potential salvation. But where are our roots in *being*?

The first chapters of the Bible do not really point to our beginning to *be*. They tell us something of how we *came* to be: the beginning of our be-*coming*, but not of our be-*ing*. They do not portray directly our absolute creation *out of nothing*.

The "six days" of creation, for instance, highly testify to a process. Process means that imperfection is involved, whereby conditions go from not-so-good to better, or *vice versa*. Nothing that is in process is whole or complete.

Taken *by itself*, *Genesis* conveys the sense that God's creative activity is imperfect, not really perfect. So, for genuine perspective, ontological and theological knowledge must be brought to bear.

During the six days or periods of time, either one of two things is happening. Either *this*: the one kind of being is coming out of (or *through*) other kinds of being (evolution-like). Or *this*: one kind of being is followed by higher kinds of being without any ostensible, necessary continuity (creationism). In either kind of process—the "smooth and long" or the "jumpy and short"—God is not being seen as a Creator, but as a Maker. A creator *gifts* being. A maker *works over* being.

St. Augustine in the fifth century offered a partial remedy for these disparate ways of seeing. He held that God created the world in one "day" or "all at once" with two kinds of createdness: actual and potential. What actually came to be known as "seminal reasons or natures" (the potential) was a way of saying that everything was created at once, including the incipient being of realities that would only mature later. Some first things were there completely. All the super-multitudinous others were like "seeds" of themselves. In that light, God could almost be known as the supreme Grower.

Other early Church thinkers, such as Gregory of Nyssa and the Venerable Bede held similarly more dynamic views of the world's origins. But, in general, the theistic tradition has overlooked some major implications of a creation truly *ex nihilo* (out of *nothing*).

Is God Merely a Maker or Grower or What?

The *Cause* of all created persons does not draw the various kinds of things to *be* out of other, more primitive things, as in evolution; nor does this *Creator* successively bring about the existence of different kinds of immediate "creations," as depicted in creationism. Such activities are rather the work of a Maker or a super-Artisan—gradually (step by step) forming a complete work. They are not the doing of an absolute *Creator*.

The *Creator* brings persons to be "out of" absolutely nothing. This infinite Gifter of being gives persons their being, whole and entire, perfect in every respect—including the *perfect freedom to receive immediately and personally* the being with which they are gifted. They are able to *receive* (not "get") the being that they are *by the act of that being itself.* This supreme, *non-durational, immediate* gift exchange between Creator and created persons underlies the *Book of Genesis.* It must be a necessary assumption—whether conscious or unconscious.

Faith-inspired reason can begin to detect this prime reality. Since sub-personal beings have no powers for receiving and for giving themselves as beings (having neither intellect nor will), they could not possibly be created directly out of nothing. They are inherently imperfect beings. Ultimately, but not directly, the effect of God, they are the direct result of created persons who failed to receive fully their own perfect finite beings.

Creation out of nothing can hardly be the same as creation out of something. The Creator as creator is not a Maker.

The Creator brings beings to be, perfectly and all at once. But a Maker works with or within already created forms so that something "new and better" can be fashioned. The Creator gifts reality with *someone* new, unique, finite, and perfect in every way. But the Maker works with *something* that already exists in an imperfect condition and makes it "better."

Chapter 4 Beneath the Book of Genesis

The Creator acts absolutely, in an *inter*-personal way, gifting finite persons with their be-ing, and necessarily receiving the free and full response of these creatures. Angels said either *yes* or *no*. Because of the double receptivity of their nature, however, human persons could say either *yes,* or *no,* or *maybe.* Their response to the immediate, free, inter-personal creation *ex nihilo* was as absolute as anything could be. And the response of those who said *maybe*—an absolutely indefinite response—left their beings in a real mess that needed the clearing and cleaning up known as redemptive creation.

By contrast, God as Maker acts relatively—and not necessarily *inter*-personally—in order to stimulate, fashion, and shape whatever already exists into higher and better forms.

The Two Creations

The difference between God as being Creator and God as being Maker-Redeemer has been largely overlooked by the main cultures of theism. Religious thinkers have conflated the two different acts of God's infinite love: the Creative act and the Redemptive act—the causing of *be-ing* and the causing of *becom-ing.*

We have then more or less settled our attention on the "process" of creation. God is thought to be a God of evolution or else a God of "dynamic stratification" (creationism). But God is rarely, if ever, recognized as the infinitely personal God who ever acts with infinite perfection, resulting in perfect persons *with perfect powers to love immediately in response.*

Theistic evolutionists—those who believe that God started and directs the path of evolution as the way of creation—draw on the same *im*personal attitude as so-called creationists. Both theistic evolutionists and creationists think that God is the Producer-Director of all created things without any *necessary, personal,* and *immediate* response from those "things."

But what has happened to the *being* of us created *persons* that we can conceive our Creator as so relatively impersonal? Something is missing in our ability to account for the very beginning of our be-ing.

We start talking about our response to creation as though it were a be-*coming,* and not a be-*ing.* But be-coming necessarily involves a process of one kind or another. And all process is a process *of* that which is *be*-ing. In order to become or come-to-be, a person must first be. There is no *coming*-to-be without someone *who* is there already *coming*.

Even for matters of growth in planetary nature itself, every *living* being comes to be all at once and then unfolds itself or becomes more differentiated. The whole being is there all at once—say, as a zygote—and only then becomes increasingly differentiated—more beautiful, mature, and (hopefully) not too lazy.

Only artifacts and non-living things can come to be or "become" gradually, part by part. They *are not* until the last "vital" part or piece is added. Living things, however, are totally what they are from the start, and the "parts" gradually develop as the whole of the living beings becomes more and more (functionally) what it already (naturally) is. A fertilized acorn, for instance, *is* an oak tree in its nature—if not in its recognizable functionality.

Such is all the more the case with beings who are persons created by God *ex nihilo*. They *be* all at once. But unlike the material, living substances, such as animal zygotes or acorns, these created persons are *perfectly whole* to start with.

Denial

When we confuse the *being* of created persons with their evident *becoming*, massive denial must be at work. We are denying the reality of our having been created perfectly by an infinitely perfect Creator. And we compensate, perhaps, by fixing our attention on the secondary, though critical, creation by God that is needed for our becoming (being coming back): for our redemption and potential salvation.

We unconsciously substitute the idea of God as Maker for the idea of God as Creator. We do not effectively appreciate the boundless difference. Only God can "make us whole," can redeem us. But that recovering, rehabilitating, and healing activity (of redemption and salvation) ought not be considered the same as God "gifting us whole"—gifting us with a completely free being at the durationless, immediate moment of creation "out of nothing" (*ex nihilo*).

We ought to wonder why we are so ready to deny what had to be our first and pristine encounter with God and with our own perfectly gifted being. Why do we keep hidden, from ourselves and the whole

Chapter 4   Beneath the Book of Genesis

world, our origin of origins, the *inter*-personal creation wherein God said, "Be," and we said, "Maybe"?

That *maybe*—that (ontologically) hesitant *yes-no* to our being—was a partial denial of the perfect goodness of being. By that denial, we must have absolutely shocked our own being. The distress would have been so totally traumatic that we buried it alive in the depths of our finite being. It would have created an ontological crater, now known as the unconscious, that is even taking its daily toll on our physical, psychic, and spiritual lives.

As a result, we cling merely to a restorative creation, and "forget" almost totally our absolute creation. So, we take the accounts of creation in *Genesis* as though they were directly reporting the origin of our *being*, rather than the origin of our *becoming*: our being *coming back* from a crash—from a profoundly deep sin within. We confuse ourselves and one another because we instinctively conflate creation of redemption—the creation out of something (*ex aliquo*)—with creation out of nothing (*ex nihilo*).

Because of this *unconscious* fusion or telescoping of two creations into one, we are unable to give a sound rationale for the world's evils. This inability is especially damaging to the credibility of our Faith, since we cannot really account for the evils perpetrated on innocent human persons, particularly nascent ones.

From the *Book of Job* to the "book of Kushner" (*When Bad Things Happen to Good People*), we cannot say *why* even apparently righteous folks are subject to getting bombed...as God "looks on." We would rather deny that God is *infinitely* powerful than admit that we are subject to receiving sometimes terribly painful treatment due *ultimately* to our *personally original* sin. Or, worse, we would be willing perhaps to protest openly to God about the "divine abuse" that we or others so apparently suffer.

Contemporary "protest theology" carries out unconsciously the perennial logic of thinking that God allowed, obviously unjustly, Adam and Eve to skewer us with their original sin—or, at least, with its consequences in the world of becoming.

We need to review carefully the "Adam and Eve problem."

Chapter 5

What about Adam and Eve?

Our first personal sin was not a temper tantrum in early childhood. Temper outbursts, little thefts, big lies, grand larceny, murder, rape, and so on are symptoms of the magnitude of the *originative sin* of all those who have entered the cosmic concentration camp called planet earth.

Even the sin of Adam and Eve in the Garden that has been known as the original sin was a symptom—a major symptom—of a crash in the original reception of our being. At the moment of creation "out of nothing"—necessarily an *immaculate creation*—the *originative sin* or *maybe*-saying of Adam and Eve (*and of all of us with them*) must have rendered us beingfully (ontologically) comatose.

By their originative freedom, right at the moment they were given being-at-all, Adam and Eve could *not* have been *confronted* with *both* good *and* evil. In their creation "out of nothing," they were faced *only* with the all-good gift of being and the infinitely good Giver. Simply, they were present with their own finitely perfect selves and the infinitely perfect love, who is God. There was no evil to "choose." Even the slightest demurrer before infinite Love would be necessarily devastating.

With God's gift of being, good-and-evil were not placed before them—only goodness. They themselves in that perfect freedom were entirely good, the sole effects of an infinitely perfect Creator's act. Adam and Eve, *along with all of us other created persons, angelic and human,* enjoyed complete, fresh, pure freedom to receive fully the gift of be-ing. They and we, who became their children, did not *choose* any evil at that originative moment of freedom; they and we *created* some evil out of the perfectly good gift of our finite being and *freedom*.

We were not tempted. God's best needs no test. We had perfect, untrammeled freedom to say *yes*. Our fully free act of lame response caused the 'temptability' that we have now *inherited from ourselves*.

That immensely real sin was not at all an historical event. It was a non-temporal, non-spatial *act* of *inadequately receiving* our perfect, immaculate being. And it could not then be *recorded* historically. It was "pre-memory." Because there was no time, there was no such thing as memory.

Amidst the energy-ruins of our originative freedom-failure, and obviously after immense preparation, God must have chosen the particular persons of Adam and Eve to be first in line for recovery from this originative sin. Their crashed beings were fashioned with functional bodies and souls and given a "test." As the result of their *originative* sin, they were tempted by the tree of the knowledge of good and evil that was planted 'right in their face.' The wiles of the serpentine spirit of evil were allowed to prey upon them.

Their response to temptation, however, seemed to be a foregone conclusion. God had said that the day they would eat of this fruit they would "die the death." God knew the result of the temptation and was allowing Adam and Eve to become aware—to awaken to—their own primordial condition of sinfulness that they had not *consciously* known. So, right after their first conscious, history-making sin, they were cast out of the Garden in shame and were accompanied by condemnations to servile work and to being the subject of social oppression. This first moral failure was a symptom of their ontological failure in *receiving* creation *ex nihilo*.

Immediately after the sinful deed, their shame of nakedness in front of each other, as well as their hiding from the presence of God, indicated that hitherto they were unaware of how untrustworthy they had been from the start in the Garden. The story of their having been created from the dust of the earth and a rib indicates also that *even then*—in the redemptive creation of *Genesis*—God was working with them in the *process* of recovery from a *crashed* condition, well before their first tragic *moral* experience, the one in the Garden. Adam's loneliness and the "added" creation of Eve also dramatized their less-than-perfect, sin-prone condition well before "the fall." It was not just Adam *alone before* Eve; it was Adam *lonely for* Eve.

Chapter 5   What about Adam and Eve?

The Wake-up Temptation

In sharp contrast to the pristine moment of pure creation, the *Genesis* story reveals the presence of a tree, an element that offered both good and evil. In the Garden, therefore, Adam and Eve are being portrayed as at least once removed from their originative freedom in being. They appear to be already in a *maybe* condition and situation.

Since their originative response to God's creating act had been *maybe*, which was inherently partly a *yes*, they were still graced with much perfection. But since it also had been partly *no*, they were distanced from complete accord and intimacy with God.

Perhaps God granted them a life within Eden to let them know how graced they were, but at the same time to let them be tempted. By the temptation, they were to become aware of how weak they had *made themselves to be*, right within the *interpersonal* activity of *originative* creation.

God had created them by a solo act—an act that God alone could do. And, by their own solo acts—acts that only *they* could do—they had immediately, but imperfectly, received themselves, all others, and the love of God. Their flawed reception had resulted in their immense self-determination to be and to live, somehow and to some extent, according to their own pleasure and measure rather than fully according to their own good.

The test in the Garden would then seem to be not so much a way of seeing whether they would succeed or fail to love God *fully*. They had already established *that*. They did not love fully.

The temptation was rather a way of making them wake up to their already self-weakened condition—a condition of being a less-than-*yes* to love. *Yes* to be-ing means "I love you." The less-than-*yes* meant "I think I love you."

In any event, they miserably failed the test. And God announced the poignant consequences: Adam was to labor by the sweat of his brow and Eve's desire for her spouse was to be frustrated by his domination over her. They were destined to live in exile, alienation, suffering, and with the inevitability of death. They were likewise destined to be redeemed and to be given a final opportunity to say *fully yes* to this redemption—a moment for salvation.

This "time," however, it would be the opportunity to say, "Yes, I repent fully of the sinful condition of my human personhood. I take full personal responsibility. I accept your supremely gracious offer of salvation and of total intimacy in the fullness of healed humanity. I love you with *all* my heart and freedom, my Savior and my God."

The Redemption Story

Genesis, then, is not so much the story of our *being,* as it is of our being-in-recovery. It is the story of how God's work of redemption got started. Without explicitly mentioning the dreadful *crash of our being, Genesis* depicts our origin in this world of fallen matter—a world of forsaken, yet recovering, *receptivity.*

A disaster in the originative creation had to have produced this world of cosmic dust. God is shown as fashioning Adam from this fallout, this dust, and Eve from a part of Adam. We can take the description as powerfully depicting some kind of "re-made" or "re-created" beings.

In other words, the making or shaping of the heavens, the earth, and Adam and Eve does not portray *directly* the originative act of God. The account is not specifically of the supremely first act by which finite beings *are,* but of the re-collective, recuperative, and incipiently redemptive act of God—therein giving fallen humans the functional, bodily prospects for salvation.

Nor do the thoughts and actions of Adam and Eve in the Garden necessarily depict *directly*, on their part, their original response to being. Instead, their actions in Eden portray their attempt to respond to God's "wake-up call" and they reveal dramatically their failure to awaken effectively.

The leading words of the Bible are challenging. "In the beginning God created the heavens and the earth" (*Genesis* 1:1). The beginning of what? Of our *being*? Or, rather, of our be-*coming,* that is, our *being* gradually *coming* out of the darkness of sin into the growing light of self-awareness and of God-awareness?

We have already indicated that *Genesis* implies a beginning before this "beginning." And we pondered the pristine condition of our being. By that primary beginning, God's infinite act causes one perfect whole creation of *all* finite persons.

Chapter 5   What about Adam and Eve?

Yet, in the accounts of the *Book of Genesis*, the creation of the universe of angelic persons remains grandly missing. Moreover, it is absurd to think that God originatively acts in serial fashion—first this, then that—as though time were God's chief workshop, even in creating "out of nothing." Only our shortsighted, egocentric point of view compels us to put God into a quasi-temporal framework.

Furthermore, the *Genesis* account reveals a creation of things out of *something*, rather than "out of nothing." The picture of the six-day creation and of Adam and Eve is one of "reconstruction" or of preparation for redemption of a once perfectly free, yet profoundly fallen kind of creature. Only by recovery and recuperation could this creature "return" to a glory unrealized.

By our originative failure, we had not fallen from *glory*, but from *freedom*. Perfect freedom. We did not enter upon *glory* from which to fall. But we did enter upon freedom.

Anyone who would maintain that the beginning spoken about in *Genesis* is *specifically* a creation "out of nothing" would seem to be admitting that God is a limping Creator. Though profoundly good as redemptive, *this* world of passive-reactive, opaque matter—from atoms to Adam and his descendants—is an entropic scene for the eventual dissolution of everybody and everything.

By any "impartial" observer, the whole cosmos would have to be regarded as a gigantic death trap—*unless it exists to be transformed by God, supernaturally.* God then did not create this cosmos "out of nothing," but out of something—something tragic that had left a primordial *void*. (*Genesis* 1:2)

The condition reminds us of something like the image of the potter in *Jeremiah* 18. There the artisan finds flaws and the pottery must be smashed and redone. One might say that refashionable pots are addressed until they are centered no longer in their own conceits, but in the mind and heart of the Great Potter.

Similarly, it would seem, according to *Genesis*, that God works to make the best out of a self-destructive, entropic creation.

But we earthly humans are not simply passive matter. We are self-flawed receptivity—self-distorted "pots," as it were. God works redemptively in this second creation by responding with creative power to the *yes* remaining in our self-disruptive matter. This divine response of love was critical to the activity of the vast energy—fragmented receptivity—that was processively being formed into the cosmic home for our redemption.

Original Sin and Originative Sin

In *Genesis* there is no real creation *ex nihilo*. Such a creation could not have been anything as impersonal and as functionalistic as God 'blowing breath' or 'fashioning from' a rib—whether taken literally or figuratively.

For Christians, at least, the absolute creation (*ex nihilo*) was an utterly Persons-to-persons activity, an activity of the Triune living God *willing* finite, perfect created persons to *be*—by the power of infinite love.

By contrast, the creation stories of *Genesis* are "process stories" that can also have symbolic reference to creation *ex nihilo*. But they mainly serve as accounts of the early stages of God's redemptive activity, reclaiming the *fallen* "human race" from destruction, and attempting to render "old creatures into new."

In this remedial, rehabilitative creation, all of the crashed, created, ontologically-comatose persons are virtually latent and inactive in being and becoming until conceived by a mother and a father. They are already created *ex nihilo*. But they are being created remedially *ex aliquo*, out of something (a rib, dust, *et al*.). Their individual conceptions within space and time happen *to* them as a dramatic beginning to their *functional* participation in their own redemption and potential salvation. Before that, their existence is virtually non-functional.

The whole of the Hebrew and Christian Scriptures seems to be directly concerned with *redemptive* creation. That activity includes the mega-process of bringing to restoration, in the Messiah, fallen creatures who are willing to awaken and to receive it.

Whether the life of Adam and Eve is taken literally, symbolically, or partially both, their original sin was literally history making. It was the sin that set off the immense train of progeny, conceived in sin—with at least two exceptions, according to the belief of many Christians.

But there again sin—like creation—is oversimplified. *Original* sin is not the same as *originative* sin. Along with all of us, Adam and

Chapter 5   What about Adam and Eve?   55

Eve, must have sinned originatively before they did so historically as our first parents, our progenitors in space and time.

Originative sin—the one committed by multitudes of angelic and human persons—is the uncaused cause of all kinds of sin and *cannot be the same as* the major symptom sin that has been rightly called *original* sin—original, that is, in space and time.

Only Adam and Eve committed the original sin. They and all of us, however, committed *originative* sin at the non-durational origin of our be-ing. But it is this *originative* sin at the moment of creation *ex nihilo* (out of nothing) that quite "naturally" has been spiritually and perennially repressed. It is individual and personal to each of us who said *maybe* to God's invitation to *be*. And like the roots of a tree feeding into its singular trunk, originative sins flow into the 'trunk of sin' that we call original sin. This trunk sin emerges in our consciousness through Scriptural revelation. But originative sins are there feeding it from below in our repressed spiritual unconscious.

Our First Act of Freedom

The spiritual repression of our originative sinning that was done in consort with Adam and Eve well serves our shame. We think of ourselves as victims of our first parents in order that we might deny that we were co-perpetrators. We have shifted the blame.

When thieves or other looters are caught, they instinctively find reasons to blame their consorts rather than themselves. This is very common, even with children. It should not be surprising then to realize eventually that we who are planetary partners are blaming others when we have obviously been caught saying to God less than fully *yes* for the gift of being. Our very partaking of this world of much woe and eventual death should make it evident.

Let us consider one way to express the basics of "the denial" of any personal, *originative* sin on our part, as it relates to "the fall" known as *original* sin. Some of the dynamics of how it could have happened rest on an emphatically Christian interpretation. But Jews, Muslims, and others might see applicability to their own beliefs.

At the moment of our creation, each of us was given a unique *act* of *be*-ing that was gifted to be entirely God-centered. (We say "was" even though we know that this act of creation did not transpire in time as such and could also be referred to in the present tense.)

This act of be-ing was and is our most important *act*. This *being* act is what we *are*, not just something we "have." I *am* my act of be-ing. You *are* your act of be-ing. Even now, as we are awakening from our defective exercise of that act—from our first response to God—we can come to realize that be-ing is an act that we *do*: like walk-ing, talk-ing, and breath-ing. Be-ing is our most *central* act.

Each of us is an unique be-ing, with an *individual* essence—not only a common essence—and many powers and acts. The act of our be-ing is like the roots of a tree. The act of being ourselves (our essence) is like the trunk. Most of our other acts, like breath-ing and think-ing, know-ing and lov-ing, are something like the branches stemming from the trunk and the roots. All of our multitude of acts of different kinds are branches from our essence and our be-ing.

In the gift of creation, we were given our own act of be-ing to *be* and to *do*. But, at that same non-durational moment, in our first act of *exercising* the freedom inherent in this gifted be-ing, we must have willed at least somewhat negatively. We must have refused partially the be-ing act itself that we were being given; we did not receive it fully. Paradoxically, we partly negated the gifted *act* of be-ing that we are—*by* that act itself.

This primal (*pre*-moral) sin was an ontological, being-restricting act. It was such a violation of pristine goodness, truth, and beauty that we repressed both the act and our profound shame. This first act of abusive freedom caused us to be in this world of *maybe*. Here we are in the thoroughly desperate condition of anxiety, disease, and death. In this "wake up" world, we come to realize perhaps that we caused the *possibility* of everlasting frustration.

Adam and Eve Within

The story of Adam and Eve can give us some indications of how our own signature sin could have happened. The literal or physical and historical level of interpreting *Genesis* could hold much truth. But to discern even literal events as clues the story must be taken symbolically.

Often, the realities of creation and sin are given a true, but merely two-dimensional, representation. They can be greatly enhanced by a careful attempt at rendering them three-dimensional.

Chapter 5 What about Adam and Eve?

The case is something like what happened in Medieval painting. The two-dimensional representation of figures with flat-plane effect finally yielded in modern times to the three-dimensional renditions of similar scenes. Painters learned how to paint in three-dimensional depth. Viewers who could appreciate the same scene in the flat, were afforded deeper perspective.

The point here is to discern whether the stories of *Genesis* might reveal a level of personal meaning that includes, but goes much deeper than, the usual one concerning our subjection to the sin of a primal couple.

So, let us attempt to consider Adam and Eve as symbolizing two correlative parts of each one of us in our *be-ing*. Adam would be the part of ourselves that is designed to *give* in a receiving, respectful manner. Eve would be the aspect of ourselves that is designed to *receive* in a giving, caring way.

Just as we are coming to know how the two lobes of the human brain emphasize different kinds of activity, we can similarly realize two "lobes" to the human person's spiritual life. Everyone is both Adam and Eve *within*. Men are both Adam and Eve within. Women are, too. But the manner in which "Adam and Eve" relate within a man is correlatively different from the way they relate in a woman.

At the moment of creation—in the instant we were first *be*-ing—we said, with all the power of our God-given be-ing, *maybe (yes-no)* to that gift itself. These inner parts (Adam and Eve) must have been critically involved. (For comprehensive treatment of Adam and Eve as 'archetypes of being' in all of earthly humanity, see *The Future of Adam and Eve: Finding the Lost Gift*, by Mary R. Joyce.)

Eve tends to symbolize the radical ability within each person to receive-oneself-in-being. By this power, we must have freely turned somewhat away from the gift of be-ing. Our capacity to "make ourselves at home" with God and with one another was willfully distorted. Right within this free act of less-than-total-receiving of the gift of be-ing—the receiving *power* of our be-ing would have been thus freely self-distorted. We must have willed, at least a bit, to be choice abusers, rather than to be full affirmers of be-ing. We had the perfect freedom to receive ourselves *fully* in being, but we did not *will* to do so.

Instead of fully *receiving* our be-ing, we partly rejected it. By this disaffirmation of our own unique be-ing, we were doomed to live in the passive (non-receptive, opaque) world of space and time, and destined eventually to die. Indeed, such a *maybe*-saying, right at the heart of who and what we are, would have helped to *cause*—along with the similar diffidence of multitudes of other perfectly free be-ings—the world of passivity *"par excellence"*: matter *as we now know it*. We crashed: from being face-to-face with the Trinity in freedom (not glory) to being prisoners of our own *tabula rasa* (the passive base of living and knowing).

Passivity really amounts to squelched receptivity. Receptivity is an ability *to do and not to be done to*. But passivity is the "ability to be *done to*"—and even to be "done in." Active receptivity is not at all the same as passive receptivity, that is, self-damaged receptivity.

By this originative self-negation itself—and from out of our God-gifted, purely active potency to love—we would have created for ourselves our own passive potencies, those abilities to "be done to" and to "be done in" as known in the classical philosophical tradition.

Purely active potency would become passively active—or perhaps we could say, passive-reactive. Passive potencies would abound as a kind of residual condition following the abuse of our purely active potency to receive our whole being and to give our selves to God and others. As a result, death would be a necessary effect of this original, if partial, *no*-saying.

Also, the *Adam* of our be-ing, the capacity within each of us to give-self-in-being, would have failed to give self to the *Eve*, the receiving capacity of our being. If we were to put it in terms of the *Genesis* Story, it would be as though Adam *could* have said in the Garden, "No, Eve, I will not eat of this fruit. I will continue to be a giving-self-in-being: I will be giving to, and with, God." Instead, it is as though Adam had said, "Yes, Eve, I will eat of this fruit. I will not give to God and to you the self that we are, but will try to give a self that we are not."

Eve, in effect, had said to God, "I will not receive fully this be-ing that I am. I want to receive something of the kind of be-ing You, the Giver, are. I do not want a sheer *gift*-being; I *want to be rather* an *infinitely* giving-and-receiving being, much as *You* are."

Chapter 5   What about Adam and Eve?

On the one hand, in other words, *Eve*, the receiving power of be-ing that we *are* and that we *do*—be-ing is chiefly an act, not just an "actuality"—said, "I *will* not to be a *purely* active receiving power of be-ing; I am *willing* to be at least a somewhat *passively receiving* power of be-ing: give me a be-ing I am *not*, or else I will *take* it."

Eve—the power to receive our be-ing in a giving way (to receive givingly, not just to "receive," to be passive)—freely said *no* to the *fullness* of self-being. By that very saying, through our inner Eve, we created, by abusing our freedom, a cataclysmic outsideness for ourselves. Right from within, our be-ings were immediately turned inside out, both individually and communally. They would remain that way forever, unless supernatural regeneration was being offered by the Word of God.

On the other hand, *Adam*, the giving power of be-ing that we are and do, in effect, said to God, "I *will* not to give fully this be-ing that I am. I *will* to give to self something of the kind of be-ing You are, a Creator-being. I am unwilling to give a solely gift-being; I want to *be*, at least somewhat, a Creator-being."

In other words, the giving power of be-ing that we are and that we do (our inner Adam) said, "I *will not* to be a totally receptive giving power of be-ing; I am *willing* to be an aggressively giving power of be-ing: I will give myself what I choose, not necessarily what I am."

By that radically free choice, Adam became *pro-choice on be-ing*. Adam, the power to give our be-ing in a receiving way—to give receivingly, not just to "give" performatively—freely said *no* to the receiving side of our be-ing, to the Eve. And by that articulation he freely created the hyper-kinetic frenzy of knowing things by fitting forms onto experience.

This condition entails knowing reality "from the outside" by habitually trying to fit the forms of our rational categories onto our experience of things that are known—an epistemic reflex activity compensating for our disjunction from reality itself. We would be in this condition forever, unless supernatural healing were offered by the loving power of God.

If the Adam and Eve *within our be-ing* had said fully *yes* to the gift of be-ing, we would *be* differently. We would not need to suffer imprisonment by our minds and hearts, as well as by our bodies, nor to endure disease and death for once or forever. We would be able to enjoy freely—timelessly and spacelessly—the beauty and goodness of our own gift-being and that of all others, and especially to enjoy the be-ing of the Divine Being-Creator.

Since we have somewhat denied the goodness of both creation and the Creator, we have changed our own being-structure. Not entirely, but emphatically. Changing entirely is beingfully (ontologically) impossible. Changing emphatically—radically—is quite a *beingful* possibility of *personal* freedom.

If We Had Fully Affirmed Being

What would have happened if we had said fully *yes* at the moment of creation? We would thereby instantly have fulfilled our power to be unique, dynamic, free acts of be-ing. Our freedom would have been fulfilled, and would not be even slightly distorted. We would have engaged in the sheer activity of the be-ing whom God gifted us to be, forever. You and I would have been uniquely pure act, sheer *do*-ing, *without limitation* in manner of do-ing or in capacity to *do the be-ing that we are*. Each one of us would be sheerly an act of praising God, finitely yet fully, forever.

Full-affirmers of being would be living in total intimacy with an infinitely loving God and with all the friends in creation who also said fully *yes*. The infinitely intimate, personal God would be the central, radiant personal presence in our lives.

In short, we would be what we even now hope to be after death: at home with God, living fully united with God's will, in supreme joy, peace, and love forever. We would be fully God-centered in mind and heart, and not centered even partly in our own wills or in the wills of our first parents.

Our destiny would not be as it is now: at best, to live forever as beings *healed* by God's saving power—healed of an originative self-inflicted wound.

In our present condition, we exist within this limited, cast-out, and *defective* world of space and time, of passive matter and motion. We are self-*centered*, not merely self-*concerned*. We are still far from becoming God-*centered* in thought, word, deed, and attitude.

All have been called to the supreme way of being: an everlasting happiness that we could have actively received from the moment of

Chapter 5 What about Adam and Eve?

creation, but did not. So, we are now in danger of losing it entirely. If we really refuse to repent and be saved, we will commit ourselves *forever* to frustration and despair.

Of ourselves alone, we can do nothing. Much less can we attain the original happiness for which God created us. We are not only limited beings; we are profoundly *defective* beings and doers, as we *caused ourselves to be*. And our limitations confuse us.

How Limited Are We?

We are limited in at least two basic ways.

Because we have sinned originatively, we are limited *by being defective*. We cannot act completely in accord with the powers God originally gave us. Our best efforts in thinking and in action are inevitably short-circuited to some extent. We can do much good at times. But we nowhere approach the fulfillment of our human potential. Our *first act* of freedom decisively wounded our being, ability, and freedom.

In the psychological world, claims are sometimes made that the human mind only attains about ten per cent of its potential. This is probably a gross overestimation, but who can measure it? The point is still a good one, indicating how limited we are in reaching our full potential in any area of life.

All fallen humans are afflicted with immense dullness of thought and action. We might think of it as a limitation, but it is primarily a special kind of limitation that might be called a *defection*. Defecting, even partially, from the gift of perfect finite being and freedom necessarily produces gross effects. This condition might be termed a *limitation of defectivity*.

The other basic meaning for *limitation* seems to come from the idea that we cannot do what God can do, or even what angelic beings can do, who are essentially above our nature. But that seems to be a radically different meaning for limitation and is not based in any defect on our part or on the part of anyone else. Just as I can never be you, or you me, nor a dog a cat, nor humans angels, and so forth, so too God cannot be non-God: the Creator cannot be simply and exclusively a creature, nor can a creature be the Creator.

In this sense, limit refers to the *uniqueness of identity*. One being cannot be any being other than itself. One *kind* of being cannot be, nor become, any other kind of being and yet be itself. But those conditions or limits are not really limitations as defects, but as specifications or identities—*limitations of identity*.

From the heart of God, however, every being can be "*un*limitedly itself." And that is not a limitation at all. Just as God is a pure act of *unlimited* being, each creature could have been simply a pure act of *limited* being: purely and "unlimitedly itself." To be a created person is not a limitation—although many persons subconsciously want to be God.

The problem is that no being in the cosmos, as we know it, can be functionally itself unlimitedly. Every being in space and time is dysfunctional relative to its potential. With a couple of exceptions, every such being does not simply *be*, as being by the act of God, but as the result of originative sin—an act of the *self*.

God creates pure acts, each of which is *like* God, but is not God. By the structure of sin, the creaturely pure act of be-ing is made into an impure act—known commonly in the tradition as a mixed act—having passive potency.

To Be Limited Is Not Necessarily To Be Imperfect

If we had not committed an originative sin, you and I would *be* and be *perfect*, without having any essential limitation other than the "limitation" of be-ing created, of being our unique selves, and of not being the Creator.

But it is *not a defective limitation* to *be* what purely and fully you really are. It is, however, a gross self-limitation (*self-defect*) to think that it *is* a limitation to be what you *are*.

Unfortunately, many philosophers and theologians in the Christian West have generally thought quite like that. They have traded on the idea that we are not pure acts. They have taught that only God is a pure Act of Being. All other beings are thought to have a mix of act and passive potency, meaning that they are not, by their very nature, pure acts.

But philosophers and religious thinkers throughout history have not taken into account the reality of an *originative* sin. They talk about the principles of being as though an originative sin had not occurred. As a result, they study, reflectively, human beings who have already emphatically, if not fully, restructured themselves by

Chapter 5 What about Adam and Eve?

deformation of their own self-betrayed freedom. They study a world that not only has been created, but has been created definitely out of something: out of the mess resulting from the grave self-harm of originative sin. From *cosmess* to cosmos, this world exists in a process of being recovered.

Cosmic creation is a crashed creation of persons undergoing an attempted recovery. All human persons who originatively failed their initial freedom of being thereby grossly twisted themselves. By *that* response to their be-ing, they *added* massive imperfection *to* the absolute perfection of their God-like being.

The original God-gifted perfection of being was not taken away; the self-wrought distortion was added. They were then *both* perfect *and* imperfect beings. By their originative sin, they were responsible for causing the elements of cosmic dust and the need for *subhuman creaturehood* that would aid in their redemptive recovery.

As a result, we *maybe*-sayers are largely dysfunctional compared to what we could have been had we, as fully free beings, said fully *yes* to our whole being. If we had, we would have been perfectly and purely free forever in God.

Chapter 6

A Defect in Traditional Theology and Philosophy

Evil in *this* world started by sin in the Garden. But this world itself was started by our *originative* sin, within the heart of God. *Original* sin remains *rooted* in the *originative* sins of Adam and Eve, and of each offspring. Philosophers and theologians have failed to account for the absolute origin of evil.

Religious thinkers have been doing their theological reflections using concepts taken from philosophy. The basic ideas of nature, essence, existence, substance, and the others are transported into theology without sufficient realization. But these terms are coming from a philosophical perspective that does not account for the *effect of sin on our very concepts* and on how we go about analyzing and theorizing.

Christian philosophers have rightly noted our own intellectual inabilities to conceive things well, due to the effects of *original* sin. But since *that* sin was not considered a *self*-decimating one—and was regarded as basically an inheritance from Adam and Eve—the "laws of nature" *seemed not* to be affected intrinsically.

The common idea of philosophers and theologians, holding that created persons are *not* pure acts, but are acts intrinsically limited by passive potency, comes itself *from the heart* of our *originative* sin. Religious thinkers did not even conceive of a *pure act of limited being* because they confused a *simple act* or *perfection* with *infinite* perfection. Another indication of an unconscious desire to be God.

Traditional philosophers of being are fond of saying that "act as act is unlimited." But they have seemed blind to how that "unlimitation" was merely the unlimitation of being oneself or of something being-itself. What that apt metaphysical phrase should have meant was that every being in its sheer actuality is "unlimitedly itself," not that it would have what might be an "unlimited beingness." Act *as act* is *perfect*; not necessarily unlimited.

Metaphysicians seemed to think that an unlimited act (with no passivity about it) had to be the unlimited Being (God), rather than simply an act "unlimitedly itself," an *un-sinful* person. (A "limited act that is limitedly itself" is, of course, an absurdity, unless the expression signifies a defective way of *doing* the being that it *is*.)

Philosophers of being were defectively limited in understanding. The idea of limited perfection did not seem to them compatible with absolute perfection. They were confusing "limited" with "defective." They were not allowing for the "limitation" of any being—of God or creature—to be the limit of the being itself and not of any other being or by any other being. Even God is limited being in that sense. God cannot be you, any more than you can be God. Each one is unique and "limited" to one's own identity.

God can even be said to be "limited"—limited to being God, the unlimited being. Even an incarnate God is still God and does not become non-God, ceasing to be God. There are many things God "cannot do," but that is neither a limitation nor a defect in God. God can bring to be anything that is intrinsically do-*able* and not sinful— anything that comports with God's very being and goodness.

Can God even make a square circle? Can God make something so heavy that not even God can lift it? Making a square circle violates the principle of being that says nothing can be other than itself. *A square is a square is a square; and a circle is a circle is a circle.* Similarly, making something so heavy that God cannot lift it "cannot be done by" God because it cannot *be*. God is infinitely powerful and does not do anything, as God, by *lifting* physically. Lifting is a strictly creaturely, material action. Christians, of course, believe that Jesus lifted things as incarnate God, but not simply as divine. Thus, God cannot *be* simply and only a creature. And only creatures that are confined to space and time can, strictly speaking, lift physically.

People who seriously ask these kinds of questions misunderstand God and the structure of being, based on God's essence. They might as well ask, "Can God sin?" Indeed, that is what thinkers in the contemporary "theology of protest," actually claim. They do accuse God of violating the victims of the holocaust. And they call on God to repent. They try to bring God down to "our size."

Chapter 6 A Defect in Traditional Theology and Philosophy 67

Since we really *cannot be* God, at deeply unconscious levels we seem always *inclined to make God into a creature.* A compensation?

Our new perspective, however, lets us see *why* we are disposed this way. By originally saying *no* (albeit partially) to our be-ing, we refused to be limited. We hesitated to be a mere creature and chose to be our own "God." We rejected the 'limitedness' of having a perfect *created* identity.

By act of will, going against the very being that we are, ironically we *really* became limited *defectively*: by our own agency. This kind of limitation was a *defection*, a grand impairment of the beautiful being we really are. We became self-*limited* be-ings—limited by our *self*. Only God then could save us from our "self" and from this freely wrought self-limitation or self-defection. We surely could not.

Traditional philosophy speaks much about *passive potency*: the ability to be "done to" or to be changed and determined without free cooperation. Such a condition must have come into be-ing by means of the original, partial *no*-saying—within our original *maybe*-saying.

God can create *out of nothing* only acts that are pure. If any acts are mixed with passive potency ("clunkiness of being"), they result from creaturely self-deformation. By creaturely self-abuse—by self-distorting our original freedom to be unlimitedly who we are—we *caused* passive potencies of all kinds in our own be-ing. Passive potency resides in the be-ing of any person who freely chose to "be other" than the purely actual be-ing that is given at origin. Passive potency and all sub-personal being result from originative sinning.

The kinds of (passive) potency—all of the multitudinous ways of limiting the pure, actual being of which we are gifted—from essence to substance to potentials for activity, can then be thought to stem directly from the way we freely and immediately began our being: by an originating, self-limiting act of denying, however partly, the goodness of our pure finite be-ing, our pure act of *be*-ing.

The Heart of the Self-Infliction

Our poor reception of the gift of be-ing at creation means that we were not entirely willing and pleased to be who we are. We caused ourselves—freely and immediately—to be "what we are not." We did it by thwarting our own God-like, magnificent freedom that is now largely repressed.

We were free to affirm the be-ing we were given in creation. But we willed, *by that very be-ing itself*, to be a different being. And, *in* so willing, we *self*-distorted. We engaged in a *dis-self*-ing activity that turned our being "inside out," as it were.

This dismembering act of be-ing we can call our *originative* sin. By choosing even slightly against who we were—whom infinite love willed us to be—we necessarily caused the need for the second or redemptive creation, as described figuratively and/or literally in the first two chapters of the *Book of Genesis*. The subsequent, historically relevant drama of Adam and Eve in the Garden of Eden actually confirmed in that time and that space the *now thoroughly unconscious* spiritual act of negation at the heart of our being.

For us, who sinned originatively, creation by God *out of nothing* led to creation by God *out of something*—out of passive matter. This passivity is symbolized by references to the dust of the earth and the rib of Adam, as well as to the void and darkness over the world.

The Importance of Wondering Well

In considering this root supposition about believing in personal responsibility for some kind of originative sin, we will naturally wonder about the consequences for the whole of our life of belief and practice. But before reflecting on some of the consequences, we need to be clear about what we are being asked to acknowledge.

The main question, first of all, is not *how* originative sin happened, but *whether* it happened. We can know *that* something is *so*, without knowing much about *what* it is or how it originated.

If, all of a sudden, you were to hear right now a huge, booming sound, you might wonder *what* it is and *how* the sound came about. But you would not wonder *whether* it is. You would not wonder *whether* there was a sound.

Similarly, we are being asked whether we actually know *that* we committed originative sin—not of *what* it consists in detail, nor *how* it exactly occurred. Without knowing many details, we can know, by way of holistic reasoning *that* personal responsibility for *originative sin*—not for original sin—exists in our lives.

Even in the case of the loud sound, you not only know *that* it occurred, but you know something of *what* it is—a sound, and not a

Chapter 6 A Defect in Traditional Theology and Philosophy

feeling, nor a flash of light, nor an idea, and so forth. You know it was a *loud* sound, not a soft one.

And you also know something of *how* the sound happened—at least negatively. You know it did not occur by means of impacting two feathers together nor simply by the vibration of human vocal chords. Similarly, perhaps, we not only know *that* we are personally responsible for originative sin, we also can know *what* it is and *how* it happened in some (negative) detail.

For instance, many Christians claim to know, through faith in Christ mediated by his Church, that *original sin*—not originative sin—is inherited historically and that all people suffer from its *real* guilt that must be removed if they are to be eligible for entry into a Godly life forever. Christians believe that all human beings on earth inherit this sin from Adam and Eve and that it entails a primordial weakness and proneness to sin, right within human nature as existing in the space-time world.

Besides, Christians claim to know, in part, *how* this sin occurred. It entailed an act of disobedience to God's express command and did not occur as a surprise burden placed by an infinitely just God upon the first ill-choosing couple. Adam and Eve were *personally* guilty. We also know that a "third party" was involved: the Evil One, the deceiver, adding a profoundly social dimension to this disobedience by created human persons.

These truths and others about the *what* and the *how* of *original sin* leave us free to find new interpretations of their implications. We are privileged to be able to participate in the discovery of the origins of our existence in space and time, *and* in be-ing itself.

Knowing Originative Sin

One of the "details" marking our concern about the *original* sin in Eden is *whether* we—as well as Adam and Eve—could have been personally responsible for an *originative sin* that the Bible does not write about directly. May we reasonably infer from what we do know about human nature, Scriptural Revelation, and creation *ex nihilo* that this unique kind of sin *did* occur even though we have repressed it and we are now, for a variety of reasons, unaware of committing it?

Does an *originative sin* explain better the whole of Christian belief in particular, and theistic belief in general, without taking away the mystery of good and evil, God and creation? Does this belief help us to go more deeply into the mysteries of creation, sin, and redemption and in what we have been taught to believe?

Right from the start, I have stressed the importance of belief in God's *infinite* goodness and *infinite* power, and that our God-like human freedom had to have been perfect by God's activity *ex nihilo*. Keeping their minds and hearts immersed in these truths, common to most theists, readers are invited to explore some of their own deeper meanings in light of the Faith hypothesis of personal responsibility for originative sin, and to stop unconsciously, if not consciously, blaming Adam and Eve as the main source of their troubles.

Behind the Words of *Genesis*

Whatever happened at that originative creation, the results leave us with Adam and Eve at the head of the line of those who "fell" or "plunged." From among all human persons who said *maybe*, Adam must have been chosen to be the leader in the reclamation story.

If so, the lonely Adam then became paired (with Eve) for the sake of recovery from sin—for the sake of his own redemption and for the redemption of countless others along the temporal trail. At the absolute moment of their creation—originatively—humans in their likeness to angels would not be created *necessarily* for pairing. But each one might be regarded even originatively—perhaps unlike angels—as more feminine or more masculine in be-ing, thereby bearing the potential for the act of pairing (marriage) should they require redemptive generation.

Only humans—the kind of persons who *could* say *maybe*—would have the potential for *actual* pairing, were they *actually* to say *maybe*. *Human sexuality* is their ability to *be* who they emphatically are: either masculine or feminine. It includes a pairing potential; but

it really has nothing *necessarily* to do with *human genitality*, which is indicative of the potential to procreate offspring.

Genitality and sexuality are quite different. Genitality presupposes sexuality; but sexuality (being either masculine or feminine) does not presuppose genitality. We comprise *sexuality* in our *likeness* to God, as man and woman. But we have genitality (being either male

Chapter 6 A Defect in Traditional Theology and Philosophy

or female) through a common, functional need for redemption: the begetting of offspring, persons to be redeemed from originative sin and thus from original sin and its effects.

At any rate, Adam, like the rest of us, did not originatively give full assent to *be*-ing.

Did God then create a place for the hesitant Adam, where he could be paired with the hesitant Eve, and put on trial? Was this place a "paradise of incorruptible matter," not existing in this corruptible (cosmic) world? When they failed the test, were they cast out of their paradisal state into the cosmic condition where they could be redeemed?

Whatever the actual story, we know the general outline and the Scriptural indications.

Moreover, by sheer faith and careful reasoning, we can come to know that God must be an infinitely pure creator of finitely perfect beings who are completely free. So, it would seem reasonable to hold that *Genesis* can be taken as simply *presuming* this "prior" supreme creation *out of nothing*—the *immaculate creation*.

The idea of a creation *out of nothing* did not come easy to Jews and Christians. Gerhard May indicates an initial firmness developing in that belief around 200 A.D. because of Theophilus of Antioch and others (May). Some scholars might demur.

In any event, the Scriptural accounts of creation speak specifically of a *making*—both of things and of humans. The accounts imply a making even where the word for "creation" might be used.

The first account refers to the creation of the cosmos—day by day from darkness to light, from non-life to life, and from animals to humans. The second account concentrates on the making of Adam and Eve. The two versions, however, seem enmeshed in each other.

The announcement of banishment from the Garden because of disobedience is an effort to make us realize how this sin is one of *personal* irresponsibility. *Through* this *original* sin of Adam and Eve we are made slaves to the awesome *impersonal* forces of the cosmos as we know it.

Indeed, all points merge into the *being*ground, the background of all backgrounds. Therein we can come to acknowledge our pre-

Genesis beginning. This *beginning of all beginnings*, was/is God's infinitely free and loving act of creating us "out of nothing." This absolutely interpersonal and immediate activity of God's infinite intimacy with us is merely implied in *Genesis*. We must actively receive the messages from our hearts and from the depths of our minds.

At the absolutely first moment of creation, there is no *medium out of which* to create finite persons. And there is no "buffer zone" of sub-personal process. There had to be *infinite* love and intimacy offered by the Creator and directed *toward* the creature.

On the part of the free creature, however, there is simply a *primal opportunity to respond* by an activity of complete, free, and loving intimacy with the Creator. The failure of at least billions of human persons to respond fully and freely to God's intimacy makes the "subsequent" account of *Genesis*—the account of the beginning of redemption—profoundly meaningful.

Part II   Where Did We Come From?

Chapter 7

The Roots of Being

In his book, *Roots*, Alex Haley described a search for the origin of his family in Africa. He wanted to know where he came from in order to learn more about his personal identity. In the search for his temporal background, he confronted the tragic history of slavery that had separated him from his family of origin.

Roots fascinated millions. The book and also the television series prompted many other Americans to trace ancestors deep into their countries of origin. Learning about *where we came from* and *how we got here* makes us feel more at home in the world.

But when we start searching for *who* we are—not just *where* we are *from*—we must go deeper than history and geography. This *being* who we *are*, this radically personal identity, is closer to us than any of our earthly beginnings. *Who we are* is within us—in our own body, mind, soul, and spirit. But basically the relation is the reverse. *Who we are* includes *within it* our body, mind, soul, and spirit.

If we go deep enough, our roots might even reveal why and how we, as essentially free persons, came to dwell at all in this cosmic world of evidently less-than-wholesale freedom. Our fascination with our various geographical, historical, and cultural *backgrounds* comes unconsciously out of a deeper wonderment. Our primordial concern revolves around our origin in *being*, our *being*ground.

The story of our background in *being* begins with our creation "out of nothing." From nothing-at-all to *everything* we are. This absolute *be*-ginning is not the same as our beginning-to-be-at-some-particular-place on this planet, in whatever month of whatever year.

The *difference* between absolute and relative beginnings seems to have been realized by the mother of the Maccabees as she ardently encouraged one of her sons to be a martyr. "I beseech thee, my son, look upon heaven and earth, and all that is in them: and consider that God made them out of nothing, and mankind also" (2 *Maccabees* 7:28). Being an insightful mother, she knew that her conceiving and giving birth was not the origin of her son's being-at-all, but simply of his coming to be in *this* world. The way she speaks might not fully indicate *creation ex nihilo* (creation out of sheer nothing). But, if not, it borders on it.

The absolute beginning of our being-at-all is *not dependent* on our ancestors or on any conditions of space and time, nor on anything that might be seen as "prime matter." In this fundamental beginning *to be at all*—the background of all other backgrounds—we find our deepest roots.

Fracturing the Freedom to Be

Over the centuries, philosophers and theologians have alluded to our most profound origins. But the story is still virtually untold. We somehow know—unconsciously at least—that God had begun by creating humans who were *perfect creatures*: not gods, but flawless persons. We fail to appreciate, however, that, by the very act of God creating them, human beings have received the perfect *ability* to be *immediately* intimate friends and lovers of God forever.

The prime creation is, so to say, an *un*timely event. No time is involved. God gifts us with the necessarily perfect power to love: immediately, unconditionally, and forever. How could we really expect anything less from the gifts of the heart of God?

Given the perfect potency to love ecstatically at once and always, created persons had no *need* for *time* and *space*—no need to *develop*. They could have "had it all" from the start.

But, just for the sake of argument, let us suppose that created human persons did *not* have *perfect* freedom at the moment they were gifted to be. Assume that they received a less-than-perfect gift of being. Then we really would have to say that God is not *both* infinitely loving *and* infinitely powerful.

God would then be regarded as either unwilling or unable to create a perfect human creature with perfect human freedom. But God's "*integrity*" is *infinite, unlimited.* God's *infinite power* makes it possible and God's *infinite goodness* makes it necessary that every

Chapter 7   The Roots of Being

act and effect that is *solely* of God be perfect. Both the *act* and the *effect* of the act are perfect. The act is infinitely perfect; the effect (the *created* one) is finitely perfect.

God is *infinitely free* "to create or not to create." But if God wills to create there is no "choice" to create *either* perfect *or* imperfect being. The absolute creation of "an imperfect being"—directly "out of nothing," solely by the act of God—is a contradiction in terms, like a square circle or a sinful virtue.

At the point of primal creation, the new person's potential to *be* an intimate friend of God is a perfect ability or power. It is not, as it is now, an imperfect potential, full of "maybes." We cannot reasonably attribute to that condition of pure freedom the present characteristics of freedom. We are now recovering from a crash—particularly a crash of our freedom.

In our present circumstances, every day we seem to say, "*Maybe* I will choose this God-centered course of acting," or "*Maybe* I will choose this me-centered way of acting," or "*Maybe* I do not care that much." And we complacently regard *this* as our "human, personal freedom."

Maybe is an imperfect *yes*; however, it is also an imperfect *no*. Our present "potential" results specifically from the originative *maybe*. It is, therefore, fraught with imperfection: a self-imposed imperfection in our *ability (our freedom) to will*—self-imposed by the ratio of *yes* and *no* at the moment of creation out of nothing.

Imperfection exists in our being; but that could only be because of a radically imperfect act of *be-ing* on our part that constricted our freedom and caused our *maybe* condition. One result is the space-time *manner* of being: the *existing* and the kind of *choosing* that we are undergoing now.

The restlessness of our existence had to have come from us. A supreme *maybe*-saying on our part must have caused our God-given perfect beings to become *may*-be-ings: beings that are indecisive and rather indifferent with respect to who and what we are. There is no way that this imperfect manner of being could have come from God. And infinite Justice would not allow other creatures to impinge upon our pure freedom without our having been originatively unfaithful *to being* and to the God of *being*—or without our permission, if we had not sinned at all.

We human persons are not angels, although we are quite *like* them. Lucifer and other angels caused—by their finite, but absolute, *no* to God—an everlasting fracture in the angelic community. But what about us human persons who turn up in the cosmos and yet who are "a little less than the angels"? We must have caused, by our *maybe*, the partial separation of our beings from our fellow persons—from both the angels and the humans who said fully *yes*.

We dampened our prospects for receiving God's glory. And we totally *repressed* what we did. Our originative, partial *no*, moreover, placed us squarely under the dominion of Lucifer and his cohorts. Once we faltered in being, we were "fair game" for the influence of evil spirits. And we come into this world conditioned to repress or deny that we failed to say fully *yes* and that our present state of being is already *self*-afflicted. We are quick to deny that *we* did anything wrong from the *start* of our *being*.

By saying *maybe* to the gift, we made a mess of our being. Only now, in this relatively ordered, rehabilitative universe, are we *on the way* to serious recovery. Our final success depends on becoming freed from the forces of Satan and his powers by allowing God to free us *from within*. Freedom from without will not do.

Levels of Perfect Being and Freedom

God's being and freedom are infinite—freedom to be and be and be. God is *unlimitedly* free to be. The Personhood of God is free and infinitely other than the limited (yet perfect) freedom intrinsic to *created persons*.

God does not have "alternatives" in the divine freedom and way of Being. God is unlimited perfect freedom. Any "alternatives" would be conditions of limitation.

The being and freedom of created persons is finite—freedom to be fully who they are gifted to be by infinite freedom. Angelic and human beings are *created perfect*, but their perfection of being is not unlimited.

Even so, this finite or limited perfection is *not defective*. The being comes with limits of being that naturally yield alternatives. The very being is *able* to will or not to will *to be*. And that is the prime "alternative."

Chapter 7 The Roots of Being

Created persons are able to receive or not to receive the *gift* of being. If they fail to receive (welcome) the gift, they still "have it"— they still *are*—but miserably so. The resultant defect in their nature comes from the self-deformation they exercised upon their particular kind of perfect, limited freedom.

There is no defect in being a limited being. But to *will defectively* constitutes an entirely different kind of limitation: a constriction of the freedom-power itself.

Angelic and human persons originatively do not *have* or *get* their freedom. They really *are* their perfect *finite* freedom, even as God *is infinite* freedom.

Philosophers and theologians who think that to be one's essence— or even to be one's being—would be "to be God" fail to appreciate God's absolute *gift* in creating us. All created persons are gifted to *be* the being that *they are*, and not at all simply to *have* their being.

There is no question of created persons being "all the being that is." They are given a *being* that they *are*. In this, they are *like* God who *is* the infinite Being. God is *not* being. God is *infinite* Being.

A terrible confusion has infected traditional thought. Contrary to many claims, God *is not* identical with *being*. God is identical with God's (*infinite*) being. God is *God's* being: unlimited in kind.

Nor are we being. But we *are* our perfectly gifted finite being. We do not simply "have" it.

We finite persons, however, differ in the *kinds* of limited being that we are.

Angels are persons with *receptivity* (the *ability* to receive their *being*) *simply* in an *unqualified* way: either all or nothing. Their receptivity is more like God's than is ours. Yet, unlike God's, their receptivity is limited, allowing for the *possibility* of willing badly.

Human persons are different from angelic persons. Human persons are also receptive beings. But their receptivity includes the *ability* to receive their *being* in a *qualified, as well as unqualified way*. They are able to receive willingly their being. But they can do so fully, not at all, *or* only somewhat.

Such created being is a lesser kind of being than that of the angels. By being receptive on more than one level, human persons are, so to say, one step below angelic persons.

In responding to God originatively, angels *willed* either to be or not to be themselves *entirely*. Angelic persons are simple, whether viewed from their being-at-all or from their kind of finite essence.

Human persons, however, besides willing to *be* their freedom, like angels, could also *will* to *be* their finite selves *more or less*. Angels "could not." Human persons are complex in that they are able *both* to *be*-at-all *and* to *be*-what-they-are. They are specifically *duplex persons*: receptive with respect to both their *being* and their essence.

The reality of being able to will the good (or the bad) initially and absolutely is properly a feature of created freedom: perfect finite freedom. Only we who are *created persons*—angelic and human—could or would *be* uniquely finite freedom.

Simply to be, but not to be Being Unlimited, means that one must, as a created person, acknowledge whether this gift of *be*-ing that one is *doing* is good or bad. Every kind of created *person* necessarily exercises this freedom of self-determination. The question is: What *kind* of *individual* be-ing do I *will* to be? Good or bad?

But the ability to determine or "choose" *how* good or *how* bad one's being really is: that was the "prerogative" of humans, not of angels. The initial freedom of any human person is a lesser kind of perfection than that of the angels. But it is a created *perfection*, not an imperfection.

While the angels, by their nature, could "only" say *yes* or *no*, we humans could say, in effect, *yes, no,* or *maybe*. Our less-than-angelic nature involved matter; *but it was not the present, cosmic, passive kind of matter that we know now.*

We were created to be *celebrationally* one with God. Our matter was not functionalistic: it had no functionalistic powers such as consumption, assimilation, processing, and elimination. There was no reason or grounds for food intake or for waste disposal. Ours was originatively a substantial, but "transparent" form of matter. It could almost be called a spiritual matter; and it could certainly be called a *purely receptive matter*.

Chapter 7   The Roots of Being

This matter was gifted into *be*-ing by the sheer act of God *and of nobody else*. So, this characteristically human, receptive power (matter) was supremely festive—a good in itself—a perfect *ability to receive* fully *who we are* as a gift. *Not* a *passivity* at all, but a distinctive kind of power to *act*: a pure *receptivity*. *This matter was a pure power to receive, to be supremely active in receiving the kind of being we are given.*

This pure matter or receptivity—the intrinsic *mother* principle of *be*-ing who and what we are—was far from what we know it to be now. To our originative (receptive) matter, by our *sin*, we "added" passivity: the kind of functionality that we observe in the cosmic processes. Present matter is quite *impurely* receptive; and it is not essentially celebrational. It is mightily functional—and redemptively so.

How we *appeared* physically at the moment of pure creation is not in question.

For one thing, we did not have the passively functional kind of matter (body) we now have that would make "being looked at" possible. There was nothing to "look *at."* *We* did not have a face, head, torso, and limbs in the way we do now. We had no corruptible body at all, with its necessary organs of assimilation and nutrition, as well as of detoxification and elimination of wastes—organs such as liver, spleen, intestines, and bladder.

Our originative matter must have been perfect, *organless* matter—neither tangible nor imaginable. Yet quite intelligible (intellectable) in itself. Our present, opaque condition of matter, in contrast, is self-obscurant and yet immensely functional.

Together with the body as a whole, all of our organs *exist* for the purpose of rejuvenating our *being as a being*. This complex body is a quasi-placental part of our being-in-recovery-and-rehabilitation.

The angelic persons, however, *with whom* we were created had no matter at all. They were *a simple receptivity for the gift of their own being*. Their essences were unique, but utterly simple, and without ontological (beingful) parts or principles. They could "only" say *yes* or *no* to the gift of being. They could receive or not receive who they were *as a whole* immediately.

Like us, angels were perfect, whole beings; but they were more God-*like* than we humans. They could either receive fully or reject totally the being and nature they received. There was no capacity in their essence—no matter—for their being to be received *possibly* in a *more-or-less way.*

But *our* receptive capacity included this other level of receptivity that has been known as the material dimension. Besides being able to receive or not to receive our being-at-all—to say *yes* or *no*—we were capable of receiving the *kind* of being we are. We were able to receive our own *essence fully* or *not so* fully. We were able to receive to *a greater or lesser degree, or not at all.*

We could determine what *kind* of a *human* person we would be, and to what degree. That ability represents a level of perfection less than that of the angels. But it is still not an imperfection, since it is primarily a freedom to say *fully yes*. We could say specifically *yes* to the *human* person that we were gifted to be.

We were *able* to say *yes*—both to our being-at-all *and* to our being fully human. Some humans might have done just that and entered the glory of heaven immediately. Others might have said *fully no* and thereby frustrated themselves completely forever. (They refused to *receive* at all.) Such is the perfect human *freedom* to fulfill—as well as the *ability* to distort.

We humans who are now in space and time did not say fully *yes,* but faltered *to some extent*. Many hesitators would have said *yes* more firmly than others. We might then be regarded as doing our *being* diversely and in degrees. The stronger our originative *maybe* was on the *yes*-side, the more perfection—both of humanity and of individual selfhood—we effectively would have allowed ourselves to receive. Of course, the stronger our *maybe* was on the *no*-side, the greater would have been the intrinsic consequences of our relative *unwillingness* to be and to be *who* we are gifted to be.

Due to our uniquely free be-ings, the *originative* intensity of *yeses* and *noes* would vary. Yet within our present existence no one could possibly judge, despite *supposedly obvious cases*, the comparative strength of originative *yeses* or *noes*.

The angels had a power more God-*like* than we. It was simply a willingness to be or not to be. Of course, in willing to be, they did not "make themselves to be." They simply co-affirmed with God the

Chapter 7   The Roots of Being   81

gift of their being. Or, in willing not to be, they did not annihilate themselves. They absolutely determined themselves to be enemies of God and of themselves *forever*.

We humans had not only a "choice" to be or not to be—that is, to receive or not to receive our being and our nature. We also had a "choice" of the degree. We were able to "state" the degree to which we would be who we are. Such "additional" freedom is not really an "added perfection" in our nature, but an indication that our freedom of being is more complex than that of the angels. Our freedom is "less like" the simple, *unlimited* freedom of God.

God's freedom is simply unlimited. Originatively, the freedom of an angel is limited, and the angelic willpower is simply an "all or nothing" prospect. The originative freedom of human persons is likewise limited, and it admits of degrees or kinds. But the human willpower is complex: *both* "all or nothing" *and* "all or something." We "chose" the *something*—neither the all nor the nothing.

Originative Matter and the Sunlight

Originative matter is the sheer receptivity within human essence, having no passivity at all. By the act of originative sin, however, we activated our prime matter (receptivity) distortedly and damaged its nature—its disposition to receive. From being gifted as purely active receptivity, our prime matter became passivized.

We need to appreciate the effect of our *ability* to distort our nature. Perhaps we can illustrate by considering a figurative example of our originative matter: the light of the sun.

Sunlight is clear and pure when considered *relative* to the things lit up by its "rays." And although we might think of this physical light as being "spiritual" and unseeable by us, it is truly material. The things illuminated by sunlight are matter, but so is the sunlight itself.

Similarly, our originative matter was, as it were, pure and fully able to receive whatever it "illuminated." Our receptive *matter*—together with our essential nature—is not at all the same kind of essence as that of angels, those simply spiritual persons whose essence is simply "matterless"—having no receptivity of essence, and no need for it.

Our *originative* state of matter is a perfectly receptive principle of essence. By our very *be*-ing, we are able to, and must, *receive* our own essence, right from within, however well or poorly we may do so.

But the nature of this matter was corrupted by our awesome failure immediately to live it out in its capacity for receiving our essence. The nature of our matter imploded and congealed—caved in upon itself, as it were—so that now it can be compared relatively to the "things lit" by sunlight, rather than to the sunlight itself.

Sunlight is, as it were, spirit-*like* without being spiritual. Similarly, originative matter or receptivity-in-the-essence is *like* the essence of an angelic person without being such in any way. We are angel-*like*, but fully human, matter-persons—essence-receiving persons.

By our failure in first freedom, we became also persons who were *passive-reactive* in their matter, their receptivity of essence. We rendered ourselves impervious to our magnificently gifted original essence—a perfect essence that *remains, yet is largely blocked from our self-awareness.*

Originatively gifted *human* persons are still not "purely spiritual" beings. On the contrary, we are gifted to be purely *human* beings. Our beings *are*, in our essence, free of any *passivity* in the matter, that is, in the receptivity.

Our God-gifted essence is *what and who we are*. Our nature is the disposition of that essence to *act* according to itself. But in our first act of *being*-our-being we clogged the nature—the disposition of our immaculate essence—by being *unwilling* to be *fully* our essence. We were *unwilling* to be a sheerly receptive-giftive (that is, matter-form) human person. We failed our essence by partly twisting our nature in its very first act.

Human persons are, originatively and essentially, totally material as well as spiritual. But *material* means *perfect receptivity in and of the essence*: the kind of essence that receives *itself*, as well as its being. Unlike angels, human persons are *receivable* within their essences as well as within their being as a whole.

Again, this receivability of human essence is symbolized perhaps by the diaphanous character of physical light. Light is, of course, matter. But it is a kind of "receptive" matter. Relative to the things lit up, the light itself is other than, and receptive to, those things. Light itself cannot be "seen," but it is that *by which* we see and

Chapter 7   The Roots of Being

without the power of which we see nothing. If light were to lose its receptivity to things that are lit up by it, vision and action would become blocked. And that is what happened at the very moment of *maybe*.

Individual human essence, then, by its matter—by the intrinsic principle of receptivity—includes the *possibility* of badly receiving the essence, correlating with the *possibility* of badly receiving sheer being-at-all.

In the *de facto* faulty reception of the gift of be-ing, multitudes of humans—we among them—caused their own *being* to become *more or less* the essence it was gifted to be. Thereby they created passivity with respect to both essence and being-at-all.

Angels are quite different. By his essence (Gabrielity), the angel Gabriel said simply and fully *yes* to his being-at-all. By his essence (Luciferity), Lucifer said simply and fully *no* to his being-at-all. By *our* essences as individuals, we said somewhat *yes* and somewhat *no* to both our unique human personhood and to our being-at-all. By the "more or less" attitude, we assaulted ourselves.

In summary, God is not simply "freedom itself." God is *infinite* freedom. And each *created* person—angelic and human—is directly created to *be* simply a unique *finite* freedom that the creature *is* and that God *is not*. *Human* originative freedom is a "bit less than" that of the angels' by being a double, rather than a single, *receptivity of being*.

Humans, moreover, were not created "a little less than *God*," as some contemporary translations would have it in *Psalms* 8:5(6). The being and freedom of God are *without limits*. Created persons cannot be *compared* to infinity, however much they are intimately *related* in likeness.

We readily overlook the *infinity* of God. And we tend to assume that our super-likeness to God implies some kind of partial identity or, at least, comparability. Such is another consequence of dimming the light of our being.

Chapter 8

The *Unlimited Being and Freedom* of God

Divine being is not complex, but perfectly *and infinitely* simple. God does not "have" the created ability to say *no* to the goodness of being, nor even to choose between good and evil. God wills only the good, *both* freely *and* necessarily. God's kind of freedom—eternal freedom, without beginning or end—is *infinitely* deeper than the most perfect and profound finite freedom.

Of course, we created persons who are defective might be said to "have chosen" between a *yes* and a *no* to *being*. But this *ability to will affirmingly or negatively* is really being-bearing or ontological, not merely moral and rational.

And we *fallen* human persons now also choose between good and evil *actions*. Our choosing between options of activity is specifically a moral ability based on *moral, rehabilitative* freedom—a freedom that is reparative, not originative.

God does not "choose" at all, even though we talk as though such is the way of God with us. God *wills* purely, simply, and infinitely, without the limits of choice.

Created persons simply could not *be* infinite freedom—as God is. If created persons were to be at all, God had to give them—as perfect beings (persons)—the *ability* to say *yes*. So, they were given the *freedom* to affirm—including the *ability* to deny—the being they were created to be. They were created free to be determiners of their own destiny—in *likeness* to God, who is the determiner of all the *gifts* of Being.

Many seem to think that they are *free* to do evil as well as good. But the very idea is the result of our abuse of freedom. Freedom is rooted in goodness and has nothing *essentially* to do with the *ability* to abuse one's goodness and freedom.

We created persons were gifted with the *freedom* to do what is good. In being finite, we were *able*—not free—to do evil. We were created to fulfill our God-gifted essences through *good* willing, not bad willing.

Our "freedom" to do evil is rather an *ability*, not a freedom as such. Our careless consciousness allows us to speak of the "freedom to do evil," perhaps because we are not concerned enough about the difference between good and evil, and about the difference between choices that are self-fulfilling and those that are self-abusive.

God's freedom is transcendentally real. God is *infinite freedom*. Any finite freedom that could *be* and could be *known* would have to come by the activity of the infinite and eternal freedom, which is unlimitedly perfect freedom.

Insight into being yields recognition of only one way that there could be freedom in creation. God, the ultimate source of all being and freedom, would have to be *necessarily* free. Nothing or no one could ever be free, except ultimately by the *act* of infinite freedom itself. Without warrant in infinitely perfect and "necessary" freedom, finite freedom could not *be*.

Like being, freedom is an absolute. There is absolutely no finite *being—originatively—*without infinite Being that brings it freely to be. Similarly, there can be no finite *freedom* without the infinite Freedom to cause it freely to be.

Any absence of freedom in creation cannot come *from* God. Nor can God be *arbitrary*, having characteristics of the fallen that is abusive. In God, freedom goes together with harmony—not caprice. *Infinitely so*. Everything God *does* and *is* is the best that *can* be. Only our self-centric minds can suggest any other possibility for God. (Perennial debates about whether God could have created a better world reveal a void in understanding the infinity of God and our sinful response to creation *ex nihilo*.)

God is not dynamic. God is transcendent power and grace. Our notion of "dynamic" is of something that is opposite to static. But neither *dynamic* nor *static* can be said of divine reality. Nor can it be said of any originatively created reality and of the powers that abide in us even now that actually come from our condition as created persons immediately *ex nihilo*.

Chapter 8 The Unlimited Being and Freedom of God

We are quite distinctive in our God-likeness: neither in constant motion and change nor in a static fixation ("contemplation") on a Platonic set of forms. We are *be*-ing, even within our existence and becoming. (Existence means to *ex-sistere*, to stand outside ourselves as *be*-ing in need of be-*coming*, that is, "coming back" to itself.)

Tragically, in our latent arrogance we use our own standards of logic and cosmologic for God's *infinite* acts. We blithely assume that God's causing someone to *be* necessarily renders the person dependent in being.

We fail to realize that *infinite* causality is not a production or rendition, but an *absolute gifting* of a whole unique being *to* that being to be who he or she is: God's *friend*, not para*site*. We are created as *friends* of God in the grace of creation. We are free to embrace our creation in friendship, but we are *able* to distrust it.

Our originatively gifted agency of freedom is, quite like God's, an essential freedom. But it is an essential *finite* freedom *as gifted*. Our actively distorting it, when *receiving* it at creation—that is, *as we received and exercised it*—made our freedom, as it were, *less-than-fully functional*.

Our *functional* freedom remains now, after all, not necessary; it is contingent and can be rendered totally void by our own free doing. We are *able* to act unfreely. We can "freely will to be unfree." And those created persons who *fully and freely will* to be *functionally* unfree become—by *that* willing—necessarily unfree. And that is hell.

People who end in hell do so by distorting their freedom to the limit. They willingly let themselves slip even beyond the scope of finite *cooperation* with infinitely loving redemption. God respects forever the *will* of the created person.

At the moment of creation, God can "only" *will* to be good and do good—infinitely—and cannot will to be either good or bad. God's freedom is to be *infinitely* who and what God is as the ultimate and unlimited gifting source of all freedom.

Our Relationship to the Freedom of God

Unfortunately, we are inclined to treat *God's* being and freedom "on the same plane" as *our* being and freedom. We *say* that God is infinite freedom. But then we think that we can only be a part of (or take part in) God's freedom. We regard ourselves as "participating" in God's Being and Freedom.

Some believers then get the idea that we have no real freedom of our own. They assume falsely that we are given a share in the *divine* freedom and that we "have a part in" *God's* freedom.

Our "participation," however, in the being and freedom of God is quite different from *the necessary participation that we must do in our own being*. What we do *essentially* is to participate in the utterly unique (God-*like*) freedom that is *ours* and *not* God's.

This freedom is God's absolutely free *gift* to us. Divine freedom and created freedom are different in kind—infinitely so.

We are *not* infinite freedom—even "in part." There are no "parts" to infinity. Nor is God's freedom simply finite freedom, writ large—larger than all finite freedoms taken together. God's freedom is absolutely and exclusively *God's*: unlimited in being and scope and in nowise somehow "partly" ours.

Reciprocally, our freedom is fully and exclusively ours. In our originative state, we *are* our own finite freedom, and we are not even a part of God's infinite freedom. God gifts us with a perfect finite freedom *of our own*. Because God's freedom is infinite, *God can create out of nothing a unique gift of being and of freedom for each created person—unique to each one*.

Our primary participation in freedom, then, is a "taking part in" the freedom that is *our own* and that is our very *being*. Our being is our freedom and our freedom is our being. Our originative exercise of that freedom determines whether we participate fully, or not so fully. But the freedom in which we participate is essentially *our* freedom and not at all God's. Our finite participation in our own God-gifted freedom is *essential*.

But *co-essential* with this personal participation in our own being is our "participation" in the being of others, most critically the Being of God. We participate in our own being in the *presence* of God. In that way, we share in the presence, power, and freedom of God.

But this sharing in the being of our Creator is not a "taking part in." There is really no such thing as the "whole God" in whom to participate or take part, because God is *infinite* being and *infinite* freedom. Every "whole" is *finite*—whether it is a quantitative or a

Chapter 8 The Unlimited Being and Freedom of God

qualitative whole. The idea or estimation that infinity is some kind of a "whole" or "fullness" is self-negating. A "whole" without limits (an "infinite whole") is a contradiction.

Unfortunately, many philosophers and theologians have treated God as the "fullness of Being," in whom every creature "has a part." The created person is then affirmed to "*have* its own being" from Another and not to *be* its own being. Only God is thought to *be* being. Created persons are said to *have* being (*habens esse*).

But that way of thinking amounts to a subtle form of pantheism and says unconsciously and curiously, "We are a part of God." Such an interpretation of our participation is, of course, convenient. It blocks awareness of our originative sin—our pristine faltering in *be*-ing and *will*-ing. We are regarded as unable to *be and do* the gift of *being* that we *are*. And so we cannot be thought to be responsible for *it*. But, in reality, we are the ones who *made* us so.

Tragically, the gifting Creator is thereby seen as Self-*possessive* and other-*possessive*. We are thought to be the subtle possessions of God. This condition entails necessarily, but perhaps unconsciously, the practical impossibility of ultimate *friendship* with God. No one who is either possessive or possessed can really *be* a friend. That is why Adam and Eve, as we come to know them in *Genesis,* were God's conversationalists more than friends.

Even before they had sinned in the Garden of Eden, Adam and Eve "participated" in this possessive tension as the result of their own *originative* sin. They had been offered, had refused, and had repressed the prospects of *full intimacy* with unlimited Being and unlimited Freedom.

Chapter 9

Intimacy Offered and *Unreceived*

The supreme creation was a creation of *persons only*—angelic and human. Like the angels, human persons could freely receive being as a gift by the powers of what we now call their intellects and wills. They were *not partial creatures*, like animals and plants, unable to know and love their own being. They were person-creatures, free to respond immediately and intimately to the Love gifting them to *be*.

Human beings were given the *powers* of love and intimacy and the freedom to express them fully and immediately. They were endowed with *total freedom to receive and to enjoy* the particular human personhood they were gifted to *be*.

At the moment of supreme creation, each created person received, by the gifting of God's infinite love and infinite freedom, a *unique* being. Consequently, these perfectly love-able creatures were not "overwhelmed" by infinite love. Real love never overwhelms the beloved, but acts to unite in genuine freedom. The Creator's gift of being was given to each creature: "out of nothing," "from within," and perfectly proportionate to his or her uniqueness in the freshness of being.

The created person was called to receive—to receive God, self, and all others. These were three, quite different kinds of receiving, but they were mutually proportionate. We receive others, even now, in ways different from, as well as similar to, the way we receive ourselves. And if we had received God directly and fully, all the other ways of receiving would have been proportionately fulfilled.

At this moment of potential wedding with God, freely and forever, we did not "fail the intimacy test." There was no such "test." There was an opportunity given for entirely *beingful* "closeness."

The "testy ones" are we human defectors. We freely retreated from the familiarity of freedom that God offered. By our semi-receptive act of *self*-contamination we created the false security of freedom-and-intimacy-impaired.

Intimacy comes in and through the abilities to know and to love. With these powers (intellect, will) at the primal *be*-ginning, human persons could willingly know and love in one of three very different ways.

They could fully know and love. They could fully know and hate. Or they could fully know and partly love, partly hate—as in the case of us freely, yet partly, defecting human persons.

The first of the three ways fulfills the gifted intellect and will. The second way functionally mangles these powers of intimacy. And the third way severely damages and weakens them.

Our potential for intimacy that was severely impaired right at the receptive moment of creation can be appreciated figuratively even now in our fallen, broken world. Of the people we newly meet, relatively speaking, some seem to know us instantly and are warm and loving in their acceptance. Others treat us with suspicion or indifference. Still others are guarded while they are getting to know us. We might say that some potential friends are "yes" friends, others are "no" friends (no potential for friendship), and still others are "maybe" friends.

But what happened in the virginal relationship with our Creator? How is it possible to conceive of a created person actually having *any* reservations about the Creator, who is *unlimited* goodness and love? A basic response to this question will always bring us into the depths of our God-gifted, pure *freedom* that we have so decisively diminished and repressed. We are bound to have difficulty *knowing* this freedom as self-distorted—and *admitting* it.

We were purely gifted with real freedom of *be*-ing: freedom to *be immediately*—with no time involved—*who and what we are*. At that originative moment of our be-ing, we did not literally "choose" who and what we are in a merely rational manner, deliberating among alternatives. We immediately willed—with the pure and perfect freedom of our being in that immaculate creation—how we would receive both the gift of our being and God the Giver. So, we caused

Chapter 9 Intimacy Offered and *Unreceived*

the "consequences" or effects within our being—both the self-conferring (good) effects and the self-inflicting (bad) effects.

We find it difficult to understand freedom, love, and intimacy. But that is because we have denied and *repressed* what we have initially *done*. We now cover it by *projecting* our way of relating in this highly damaged world *onto* the pristine, originative relationship from which all the damage stems: our original, flawed response to God. We think freedom must have always been the way we know it now.

So, in our self-centeredness, we inevitably think of God's way of originally creating us as similar to the way *we* create *artifacts*. But our productions cannot help but be as we make them: unfree. God's creation is totally *person*-all and *free*-for-all.

We ought to cease engaging in escapist projections. Instead, we should try to do the best we can to let ourselves be purified by God's infinite ever-presence—at every moment.

We can be gifted with much more understanding of how *we* cause *things* and also come to think afresh how *God* causes *reality*. The way we cause things, including relationships—especially in loving people and in making friendships—is a bit *like* God's. But God's way is not our way at all. The infinite way is not *like* finite ways.

By a free act, we determined ourselves to be, at least partly, self-centered in our being—rather than fully God-centered. This act was an exercise of our *originative* freedom. We had absolute freedom—freedom for the utmost intimacy with the Being of God. God's gift of the freedom to be and to be ourselves necessarily involved the exercise of the maximum in our power of self-determination.

By God's infinite power to gift us with perfect freedom, we were *able* to love God, ourselves, and all creation. Had we fully received the gift that we were given, and the Giver as well, we would have confirmed ourselves as completely in Love. We would have lived, as of that moment, the ecstatic life of glory, that "...God hath prepared for them that love him" (1 *Corinth* 2:9). Instead, we freely diminished our *yes* to the gift, thereby causing our destiny as the "poor banished children" of Adam and Eve.

Three Basic Attitudes

God *always* acts with unconditional and unlimited love. At the moment of originative creation, Adam and Eve, *along with all other persons*, angelic and human, had an absolutely perfect opportunity to meet and unite fully with God. And, as human persons, they were as able as they *could* ever *be* to embrace one of three fundamental attitudes toward *being*.

God proffered unique and supremely God-like gifts of being to Adam and Eve and to each one of us. What must have been our first, immediately knowing, and self-determining response? Three key possibilities suggest themselves:

1. "I adore you and love you, forever and ever, most intimate Gifter and Lover of all being."

Such receivers of being, at the very moment of their creation from nothing, would fully confirm the covenant of intimate love offered by their Creator. Their full *yes* would create in them an ecstatic oneness with God. Entering heaven immediately, they would never have any need for redemption. There would be nothing to redeem. They would be "home free" *both* by God's infinite love in creating them *and* by *their* finite, but perfect, *receiving* of that love.

2. "I never asked to be created. I'll do things my way now that I'm here. I will decide, freely and exclusively, what kind of being *I* will be."

Such deniers of the *gift* of being would exercise their freedom of will by a firm stance of rebellion against their Creator. This full and total perversion of mind and heart would thereby constitute hell. There would be no hope for redemption. There would be nothing to redeem. They would be self-exiled by their finite, but *total*, rejection of the infinite love given to them as they were loved into being "out of nothing." They would have lunged back "toward nothingness," without being able to "be nothing again"—as they would desire, once the consequences of their self-willing took effect.

If Adam and Eve had responded in this way, what would have happened to us? Would we, too, have gone to hell with our "first parents"? And have been "procreated" there? Not if God creates us as essentially and personally responsible beings. We humans are not a swarm like bees, nor a collectivity of common workers like a

Chapter 9 Intimacy Offered and *Unreceived*

communist camp. We are a community of persons with a common nature that allows the full autonomy to each individual within that nature. Such persons are *able* to unite with, or separate from, all other humans forever.

3. "I have not decided how to respond to this gift of being you are giving me. I will have to think about it first!"

Before their disobedience in Eden, Adam and Eve acted as if they had already hesitated in this way. At the instant of their creation, they must have wavered by freely questioning the being they were given and God who was giving it. They did not say fully *yes*. They did not say fully *no*. Each of them must have said *maybe*. "Maybe I will receive this being fully, maybe I won't."

Adam and Eve were companion doubters of being, *along with us*, before they were chosen to be "the first couple."

After our common crash—theirs and ours—they were selected to be the first in line for "awakening." They led the way in a generative procession of multitudes down through the ages. All of these fallen humans needed to be revived from their self-caused "slumber of being" and their repressive unawareness.

Energy for Recovery

Moreover, by originative sin, Adam and Eve, along with countless other human *maybe*-sayers, would have caused a fractured actuality within their *being*. The *fracturing* of being would have produced *energy*, the capacity to do work—the work of recovering.

Energy was created by the infinite goodness of God interrelating with the *maybe* response to absolute creation. It is not God's energy. There is no such thing in God as energy, the power to "do work." Only power and grace. But energy comes from the effect of the ontological crash that *we* caused, even as God acted with infinite love upon us in our plight of needed redemption.

In its *cosmic form*, this energy must have emanated from God's acting on our originative response. It is the consequence of both the partial *yes* in our *maybe* and the partially passivizing *no*. By our *no* we occasioned a "cosmess." But by our *yes*, we were immediately ready to attempt the reactive recovery under the power of God's redemptive love.

We said *maybe*. God's infinitely compassionate being was at once faced with the massive mess. God's immediate response was to provide abundant resources for the potential recovery. God then would be the primary cause of what we know as the *cosmos* of redemptive matter—a creation *ex aliquo* (out of *something*).

This redemptively creative activity is suggested by the work of the "days" reported in *Genesis*. We, the multitudes of *maybe*-sayers, had caused a "being-bang"—one that diminished our own God-gifted receptivity. And this ontological or being-based crash would have involved, as well, what has come to be known eventually as a physical "big bang."

As a result of the "big bang of our be-ing" (our originative sin), we left ourselves languishing: a comatose human community. God then worked with, and directed, the resulting energy into higher and higher actualities, leading even to the threshold of conscious human recovery. By the divine activity the ground was laid (*Genesis* 1) for human persons to be conceived and to grow in space and time.

When the time was right, God drew Adam, the first recovering human, out of the passivized human receptivity—"the slime of the earth" (*Genesis* 2:7). Adam and Eve and all their progeny thereby attained the prospect of developing an eventual consciousness of their weakness in being and of the need for a Redeemer.

Adam and Eve, then, as "a couple of humans under a tree," were never at home with themselves. They had been created originatively in wholeness, freedom, and perfection of being. They were created to be at home immediately and forever with God and with the entire community of finite persons.

But their personal *response* was not fully receptive. A completely new, immediate creation was required: a redemptive one.

Their *partial* reception of the gift of being—right at the originative moment of creation—was not a moral failure. It was a pre-moral failure. This free faltering in *being* was not yet moral; not really a moral choice between *good* and *evil*. There was only good in being. But this hesitation to *be* was an absolutely pure act of finite freedom done badly—entirely from within, and without any evil present to tempt the created persons. By their very first act, Adam and Eve and all the freedom-failing human receivers had turned their God-intended actualities into "fractualities."

Chapter 9 Intimacy Offered and *Unreceived*

Part of the active matter (the ability to *receive* one's essence) within their being was changed so profoundly as to cause itself to become passive-reactive, and in a *sub-personal* manner. This part constitutes the most ontologically repressed area of their personal being. It has been known as prime matter in classical metaphysics.

But, together with God's infinitely redeeming power, this passive-reactive part generated the impersonal base, the redemptive cosmos and its space-time environment, *through which* fallen persons might *eventually* be conceived on their way to potential recovery.

Beginning with the *sub-personal* matter of the cosmos, God began fashioning everything in the "six days of creation." All those to be redeemed were destined to appear in this cosmic setting: a kind of *temporal* home for their originatively perfect human nature—now also imperfect. Theirs was a *placenta-like existence* as an imperfect, but vital, part of the reach of their whole being for salvation.

Thus, the totally-personal matter of Adam, Eve, and their eventual offspring had fallen *from receptivity largely into passivity*. Infinite Love, however, worked immediately to begin recovery.

The eventual result was the *cosmic* (ordered) world of passive-reactive matter. Fallen persons would be eventually conceived in this whole world of space and time to which they had personally contributed. By being conceived in this world, at their own moment of conception, each would receive a kind of functional human leverage. These fallen persons might then begin to recover and to rise toward the integrity that they had missed.

So, the *Genesis* story is, at first, about a couple already fallen at the level of *being*, and not yet fallen at the moral level. Their first significant *moral* choice was the choice to eat the *fruit* of the tree: to know by *ex-perience* good and evil. This choice stems from their "root-choice." Not their "fruit choice," but their "root choice," wherein lies their prime failure to receive fully the gift of being. By their first *moral* choice, they originated the "trunk" of the tree of fallen human freedom in space and time.

Genesis elaborates on this beginning of the "trunk" of history. But by careful reflection, we can be drawn deeper. We can discover the "roots" of the *being* of Adam and Eve, and of our own. These roots are grounded right within the creation of all persons—angelic and human—"out of nothing" by the infinitely intimate heart of God.

Our *maybe*-saying caused the necessity for the long duration and assimilation involved in the recuperation of our being. Time and space were fashioned by the loving power of God, out of our fallen actuality. They critically minister to our potential recovery from the originative sin.

At the common roots of our being—where we all together, as well as singly, failed to be fully who we are—we find, in a critical sense, who we *really* are. And we become somewhat aware of *why* we are *here and now*—definitely all "spaced out" and "doing time."

We ought to appreciate the deepest roots of evil. They are found within the individual agents or doers, not only in the "first couple." Attention solely to the sin of Adam and Eve, as the *origin* of *our* evil, tends to cut the trunk off from the roots of revelation about good and evil.

The originative sin of Adam and Eve, and that of each one of us completely free persons, emanated from *Adam and Eve and us*. The supreme power of freedom was *absolutely given to us* by God and *immediately exercised* (or put into act) by us. Our response was an ontological, "being-bending" act of freedom—partly de-structuring our own being.

We were perfectly God-like persons, who had been created as free, structured-to-be-intimate friends of God. But we gravely forfeited the intimacy by self-contorting our *ability* to love.

We were left with needs for redemption, contrition, repentance, forgiveness, restoration, and salvation. These needs have come not simply from our relation to Adam and Eve in the historical past. They cry out *from within us*: from *our common roots with the first couple* in the heart of Being, the intimacy of God.

Chapter 10

The Roots of Becoming

"Thou hast made him a little less than the angels, thou hast crowned him with glory and honour" (*Psalms* 8:6). So the Psalmist sings. But millions of us still think that we started out as human zygotes. We regard our absolute beginning as that of tiny organisms here among the animals and plants in the world of becoming.

Yet, right from this beginning in the world of coming and going, everything is changing and becoming different. *This* kind of life seems to have little in common with the angels.

We develop not only physically, but mentally, emotionally, and spiritually. And as we grow, we gradually realize that the way we come to know things at first tends to be the opposite of the way those things are existing.

We come to know the lesser things before we know the essential. We know, for instance, the green of leaves before we know the chlorophyll process. And only very gradually do physical priorities yield their place in our minds to more substantial priorities that are mental and spiritual.

Our meanings and values are also subject to a kind of process. In our childhood, for instance, we know and desire the physical and emotional presence of our caregivers. But later we come to know and deeply appreciate the motivation and spirit that emphatically *caused* their loving attentions. When we become fifty or sixty years old, we know our parents so differently from when we were five or six.

Even philosophical and theological meanings can do a reversal. The whole world looks different once we seriously see ourselves from the perspective of God's act of creating us "out of nothing."

God's act is no longer viewed as "mega-magic." Nor as some kind of serial exercise of a Great Artisan in "making things be."

God's act of creating can become appreciated as a unique activity whereby all created persons, including the highest kinds of angelic being, are brought to *be* in one and the same instant—within the non-durational moment. Creation can come to be acknowledged as the integral result of an infinite activity.

So, when we become aware of ourselves changing, we are then challenged. We must attempt to understand how the growth and the development is part of our be-*coming*, but not of our entire be-*ing*. Be-coming is only part of our be-ing. And we *are* much more than we come-to-know of ourselves.

Our be-ing has been originatively compromised. We do not simply *be* and *be-with* God, as we were created to be. We *are*; but we are also "outside ourselves."

We *ex*-ist. Moreover, our *ex*-istence—our being-cast-out-into-this-world—has roots. These roots are living and growing from our need to be-*come*. Our *being* needs to *come back* to its originative self.

The roots of our be-*coming* are surrounded by our massive fixation upon our egocentric plight in space and time. These roots grow from our condition of self-estrangement. *Where we are and how we can make the most of it* preoccupies us. Compulsive concerns impede an awareness of our total *be*-ing.

However, in the light of our *be*-ing—of our being related person-to-Person with God—we can even examine the roots of our *cosmic existence*. These roots were developed within the vastly impersonal world of space and time. Here we are *be*-coming: trying to become (*come* to be) the person we *already* really are—as pristinely gifted by God.

How in the World Did I Begin?

My life in *this* world began when a sperm from my father met an ovum from my mother. These two cells interacted as mutual *causes*. Their mutual effect was *not* I. I did not *start* to *be* then. Their effect was *my existence-in-the-world*. By this particular effect, I started *ex-isting functionally* in the world of passive matter and motion, known as space and time.

Chapter 10 The Roots of Becoming

Existence is not the same as *being*. Ex-istence is a *way* of being—a manner of being alienated from self and others while still being somewhat connected. But neither the event of my conception—nor any ensuing embryonic development—gives any evidence of my creation from nothing. The creation of my *being* is obscure.

By contrast to my present position, originative creation is simply a causation that is done by God alone, strictly *out of nothing and not out of something*. It is known only by means *other than* sensory observation and emotional connection. My zygotic or embryonic beginning, however, is known directly by empirical means and is not an originative creation.

Furthermore, what "decision" could I possibly have made at the moment I came into life as a single cell? Or, while I was gestating in my mother's womb, how could I have said to God *yes* or *no* or even *maybe*? I was definitely "out of it." Even as a little postnatal child, I couldn't say much more than "Dadda" and "Mamma." How could I say, "I receive the gift of being with gratitude and love"?

If conception was really the moment of my supreme, fundamental creation, where was my Creator? And where was the personal *love*: God's and mine? Where also was my response to the gift of being?

We are confused about conception. We think of it as the moment we were given the gift of *being*. But it is the gift of *existence*—a *manner* of being. Our existence is our beginning to be brought back to a lost wholeness.

Because it is so relatively impersonal, conception could not have come directly from the activity of the infinitely personal God *alone*. Conception came as well from the impersonal laws and serendipities of Nature. Even if I had a twin brother or sister, our relationship in the womb would have been less than consciously interpersonal.

Nor could my mother and father relate *interpersonally* with me at a practical level. I was, of course, *naturally* a person in the womb. But they could only respect my life and wait for me to be born and grow to be more *functionally* a person.

Many human embryos die. (Thankfully, we did not.) These tiny beings perish, apparently without ever having a conscious thought or making the slightest choice—in *this* world.

Where is God's perfect act of creating them with infinite love "out of nothing"? They would seem to be but accidents of the impersonal forces of Nature, even though they are within God's providence. At least, that is the way it would seem to be according to our merely ordinary consciousness.

Human creatures at their earliest stages of life in this world are fragile, unfree, and critically undeveloped. They are like people in the earliest stages of an attempted recovery rather than in the pure wonder, joy, and ecstasy of receiving direct creation by God. They seem more like people trying to regain consciousness, staggering at a crash site—wobbling around precariously.

Being conceived in space and time is definitely not the same as being created. Instead, if conception is some kind of a beginning, it is the definite beginning of a person's restoration. Besides being a good, powerful, and wondrous event, conception is involved with the shock and disorientation caused by a wrong turn in *being*.

Conception as the starting point of *becoming* is connected with the necessity for the redemption from sin and from the immediately devastating effects of sin on our *be-ing*. Christian teaching says it, at least minimally: we were *conceived* in sin. The prophet David weeps over it in the Psalms. (*Psalms* 50:5)

Conception itself is good and should be understood as occurring in the service of one's potential recovery. But, at least according to Christian teaching, the ones who are conceived are themselves in a condition of sinfulness. Adam and Eve are regarded as initiating the train of sin in space and time.

Apart from that issue, however, all three theistic traditions might consider whether we are denying our *personal* connection to this original sinfulness. Is the chain of historical sin, initiated by Adam and Eve, simply a kind of symptom-sin? If so, what caused all these symptoms throughout the ages, including the original one in Eden?

God must have intended that our *being* itself be *the gift*, both perfectly given and perfectly received. God gifted us with the glorious opportunity to unite with our Creator immediately, fully, and freely. In the instant of being created, God willed that we would freely accept an ecstatic (finite) union with eternity.

Chapter 10 The Roots of Becoming

Instead, by our even slight deformation of freedom, this "instant" that would have initiated an immediate union with eternity had to include a "*time* out"—a process of struggle with good and evil that we call *time*. Both time and space are obscure and frustrating ways of relating with the grace of being-at-all and of being-with God.

What God intended to be a creation "out of nothing" embraced by a full *yes* was a creation "out of nothing" received by a *maybe*. Time and space flow from this failing response.

Within the womb of time and space, there occur eventually, as we well know, *human conceptions*. Each conception initiates a process of individual human growth and development. This process is destined for delivering the self-inflicted person's final response to *being—yes* or *no*.

Creation "from nothing" is a solo, interpersonal act of God, and it is *not* a process. God's activity is in no way time-conditioned. At one and the same non-durational moment, so to say, God gives unconditionally to each person a unique being. And, in that same instant, each one *receives*. God says *be*, and the created person says basically *yes*, *no*, or *maybe*.

Primal creation is an interpersonal activity in every respect. *There can be nothing passive and impersonal about it.*

Conception, however, is the beginning of a process—a process of promise. This effective process transpires within a dark and dismal *latency* of *lost and ineffective being*, that had immediately resulted from the crash caused by our *maybe*-saying.

As a fallen circumstance in the cast-out world, this condition is neither reincarnation nor incarnation. Just a coma-like state of being, awaiting rescue through conception by parents. The processes, both a languishing before conception and effectively growing afterward, are supremely conditioned by passivity.

One can even speculate about the *preconscious* meaning of the prophet Jeremiah when he represents the words of God:

> "Before I formed thee in the bowels of thy mother, I knew thee: and before thou camest forth out of the womb, I sanctified thee, and made thee a prophet unto the nations" (*Jeremiah* 1:5).

Since God can be said to form us all in the womb from conception onward, could it be that Jeremiah and each one of us was known before we were conceived—known *not* as a "possible being," but as a real one, in dire need of redemption and salvation?

In any event, through conception, my life begins to unfold from the obscurity of unconscious existence into the dawning light of consciousness. I slowly, but eventually—if I live long enough—become somewhat aware of who I am.

How in the World Will I End?

Most of me, however, even as an adult, is still in oblivion—like the largest part of an island below the surface of a body of water. I know little about the preconscious and unconscious content of my own mind, heart, and soul.

Nonetheless, I am now developing. I am moving from conception to death—perhaps destined to suffer afterward in another purgative, recuperative dimension of my being.

Many Christians believe in purification *after* death. This purgation comes once the person, at death, accepts the dominion of God by a final *yes*-saying and is likewise *willing to suffer* whatever is required to *receive* salvation. The suffering may be required not in order to "merit" salvation—such is impossible—but in order to express his or her *sincerity* of *be-ing*—and to "prove" it.

Anyone can *say yes*. "O God, you are my Savior." But do they *mean* it? Life in this world and in any further purgatorial existence affords us the opportunity to say *yes* with our *being*—at the same core level by which we issued our *maybe*. In a post-mortal process, we are afforded the opportunity for our *maybe* finally to become a *fully mature yes*—if it has not become so in the brief purgatory of *this* life.

Whatever our decision is at death: *that* determines our destiny forever. A decision that is basically *yes* will likely require in most of us considerable maturation of the *yes* in order to become perfect enough for graceful entry into the all-holy presence of God.

Many seem to think that salvation simply comes from saying *yes* at some point during earthly life. But the question of insincerity and the depth of the ability to *deceive ourselves* must be addressed. If we are *authentic* in our acceptance of salvation, we will be determined

Chapter 10 The Roots of Becoming

to receive whatever pains and suffering are due to us for our sins—and especially for an originative sin.

Like creation, our *redemption* is effected whether we will it or not. But *salvation* requires our personal acceptance of the redemption. Salvation can occur only by co-operation of our free, independent will with God's will. Nothing is forced.

Not one whit of salvific grace can be *earned*; it is *all* a free gift of God, even as our *creation* is. But every bit of *our will must be purified*.

To think that God does our work for us—either the work of saying *yes* or even the work of purification—is to take away our own responsibility for failing to *receive fully* creation *in the beginning of our be-ing*. We would be reinforcing our originative sin and would thereby betray a latent, intransigent lack of gratitude for *being* and for *being-with*-God.

Sincerity in *receiving* is not a matter of "earning," but of *burning*: a profoundly personal burning with love for God and creation, far beyond a merely logical *yes*. The *genuineness* of one's faith is shown through suffering, wherein faith, like gold, is tested by fire (1 *Peter* 1:6-7). People can be self-deceiving. As Jesus once put it, "Not every one that saith to me, Lord, Lord, shall enter into the kingdom of heaven: but he that doth the will of my Father who is in heaven, he shall enter into the kingdom of heaven" (*Matthew* 7:21).

Similarly, we can be virtually certain that not everyone who says, "I'm saved, I'm saved," will be saved. Such a one might not really mean it *in the core of his or her being*. It might be meaning by lips, not by being

The gift of God's saving and healing life cannot be merited. But our acts of receiving that gift result in degrees of authenticity that can only come *from us*. God cannot be "sincere" *for* us, without being "insincerely God."

At any rate, most Christians and many others believe that life-before-death *itself* involves plentiful purgation. Within that life, the honesty of our *yes*, once given, can be brutally tested. And the test is of us, not of God. Even with the *infinite* love of God, the way to everlasting life is rather *narrow*; and the way to destruction is *broad* (Matthew 7:14). Our sincerity is defectible and our ability for self-deception is immense. That realization should bring us to our knees regularly.

Being conceived, then, in this world of space and time promises a definitive beginning of a cleansing transformation. Some may have a short time of it. Others, a long time. Many perhaps do not make it. Through bad choices here in this life, their *maybe* can become a *no*, certified at death.

There are many people whose early death or mental handicaps offer no real opportunity for significantly *conscious* choice. These persons would be ending their journey with a *yes* or *no* that might have to depend on the character of their originative *maybe*, when he or she had perfect freedom. Was it more *yes* or more *no*? If more *yes*, their final response is more likely to be *yes*; if more *no*, it is more likely to be *no*. We observers in space and time have *no way even to begin to evaluate, in particular cases, what that originative act of protofreedom would have been.*

At the *moment* of death, besides, there may well be flashes of opportunity for the spiritual self—somewhat independent of its largely passive bodily and spiritual condition—to accept or to refuse the love of God. Even those persons who are undeveloped because of their brief bodily existence may be the beneficiaries, upon dying, of a moment of salvific opportunity in the depth of their spirit. That kind of momentary presentation of divine Love to the self could also be happening even at the death of everyone.

Somewhat like the moment of primal creation, one final flash of an invitation-at-death to receive the saving Life of God might be given each of us.

In any event, the process of life within this world ends in either a freely chosen *yes* or a freely chosen *no*. That determination cannot be made *for* us in any way. God cannot force us one way or the other, much less do it for us. The decision is as fully *ours* as was our originative *maybe*. In making the basic decision for or against being-saved, of course, we can be genuinely helped by the prayers and sacrifices of our spiritual companions and we can be supported by the protective powers of the good angels, as well as hindered by the militant forces of evil.

Everyone now living in space and time still faces the ultimate decision. This decision of our destiny is not God's; it is ours. So, in

Chapter 10 The Roots of Becoming

view of our essentially personal *freedom*, it does not seem likely that every person would finish in the final *yes* of heaven.

For us, the moment of death is as sharp as the moment of supreme creation. Death takes us back to our roots in *being*. We are given a *final* occasion in order to rectify our originative willing—an ultimate opportunity to reply *as positively as we can* to the infinitely tender and loving invitation of our divine Savior.

Chapter 11

Where Is My Oneness?

The mystery of the relationship between our being-*created* out of nothing and our being-*conceived* within space and time begs deeper understanding. But the theistic traditions need much more awareness of the difference and unity between the supreme creation ("out of nothing") and the redemptive one (out of something freely fallen).

Since the theistic culture tends to conflate and to confuse the two creations, customary explanations about human self-identity are dualistic. The expositions incline toward treating every human being as somehow divided into two.

The idea seems to be that at conception God creates directly the spiritual soul, and infuses it into the body that the parents cause. Practically speaking, God is seen as directly causing the soul; and the parents, as directly causing the body. God seems implicated as strictly a captive of the processes of space and time.

In such an interpretation, where is my unity? How can I regard myself as one whole, singular person—body and soul? How can I avoid thinking, at least unconsciously, that I am an anomaly, like a centaur or a mermaid?

In the way we understand the relationship of the human body and soul—at least, regarding their beginnings—we are accustomed to seeing ourselves as somewhat like these fictional composites. We think of a corruptible body being united to the soul as a spiritual (incorruptible) principle.

Nature appears to "give me" a body. Yet, cosmic nature cannot produce the spiritual, human soul. I seem to be backed into a corner where I am forced to think of myself as an in-tandem product of God and Nature. But neither God nor the human person is honored well by this way of thinking.

Soul and Body Dualism

Dualism means thinking that the human comprises two different kinds of being—and not just one kind with different dimensions. Thomas Aquinas, the greatest of Christian theologians, defended the unity of the human person *against* dualism.

Yet, Aquinas fell into a dualism of his own. He seemed sure that the soul *separated* from the body at death, and that it continued to exist, as an *incomplete* substance, until the personal resurrection. And within the Christian creed, worshippers profess belief in "the resurrection of the body," which is *commonly interpreted to mean* that the immortal soul "reunites" with the body from which it had been separated.

This kind of relationship of *separability* between body and soul has merit *figuratively*. But not literally. The new view provides a different analysis.

At the deepest levels of being, my conception and death are not to be seen necessarily as acts of "joining and separating my body and my soul." They can be understood, instead, as *critical events within* my *whole unitary being*. These events take place in the process of redemption. By this process I can recover the opportunity for a full *yes*—an opportunity that I missed by saying *maybe*.

Christians and others can still be faithful to their commitments by re-conceiving—and not by changing—the *data* of Faith and reason. Concerning body and soul, we can see the relationship in a light quite different from Thomas Aquinas and many other theologians.

A new view would go like this. God creates directly—*ex nihilo, "out of nothing"*—my *whole* being, including my essence, form, matter, and the *active* potencies to receive and to give. But the question of soul and its reciprocal principle, the body, is a different matter.

Traditionally, when we speak of *soul* and *body* we are using terms more appropriate to our space-time *existence* that belongs to the derivative creation known as redemption. *Soul* and *body* are names for the *remedial dimensions* of my essence that *originatively* is constituted by my *form* and *matter*, and not by soul and body.

We let ourselves be deceived, therefore, when we identify our form with our soul and our matter with our body. And it "looks" as

Chapter 11 Where Is My Oneness?

though soul separates from body at death. But the cadaver (a hunk of multifarious non-living matter) is not my *living* body—the only kind of body a living being can have. *Nor ever was it such.*

The corpse only *looks* like my body *for awhile after death*. Really, it is matter that was expelled from my living *being* at the moment of death. By dying I separated from empirical connection to the world of space and time—but not from either my body or my soul, my (ontologically) wounded matter and form.

The question, then, "Where is my body *after death*?" cannot be answered on empirical grounds, since nothing of the living body then can be viewed or touched. The "remains" are super-multiple substances, such as carbon, nitrogen, water, and the like: a hunk of disparate material substances, of inanimate molecules. That is all that is "left." So, we can be sure that my body is *not* its physical *remains* that are to be buried and become food for worms.

Once death occurs, neither soul nor body is perceivable. But this does not mean that they no longer exist or *be*. We must resist the temptation to think that something does not exist *because* we do not *experience* it. "Me no see, it no *be*" is bad epistemology (philosophy of knowledge).

Even now before death we do not strictly *perceive* the *substances* of things in this world, including body and soul. But we definitely *conceive* them within our perceptions of their manifestations. Only by intellect do we know the principles of being—including the substance of material beings. By the senses alone, we would know nothing of the *essence* or of the *substance*. Nor would we even know the modifications of substance: *the accidents as accidents or as modifications.*

Dogs and cats, for instance, know sensorily the colors and the contours of a tree: its accidents. But they do not know its accidents *as accidents* any more than they know the substance (tree) *as a substance*. Only by intellect can substance and accidents be known.

Once *human* death occurs—affecting a whole being, not a partial being such as a tree—then body and soul are no longer *directly discernible* by intellect. But if we analyze their relationship in human persons even before death, we can infer something critical. Body and soul are *redemptive extensions of form and matter*—of the powers to *give* and to *receive, within and by* the *essence* of our being. Hence body and soul belong together forever—'for better or for worse.'

God does not create persons in parts. "Part body, part soul." Only a mere maker *produces* things in parts. Such an agent can put these parts together and either let them pull apart or "hold" them together.

God's supreme act of creation, however, causes a perfect being: a *finitely perfect being*. There is much confusion about the difference here between finite and infinite kinds of perfection. Many thinkers, consciously or unconsciously, regard being-finite as equivalent to being-imperfect. But there is nothing imperfect about being-finite— unless it is thought subconsciously that the one who is finite "ought to be God." Being finite or limited is *not* the same as being defective or imperfect.

I have been created perfect and whole, form-and-matter at once— as *purely active* form and *purely active* matter. My substantial form and my prime matter are *celebrationally inter*-related. When I said *maybe*, I partly frustrated my nature, the disposition to act according to my essence as a human person, with the perfect ability to *give* (form) and the perfect ability to *receive* (matter). Originatively, form and matter were not *functionalistically* related, as they obviously are now. They became so for the sake of the recovery phase known as our *becoming* and they are now often thought of as *soul* and *body*— the compensatory and *functional* dimensions of form and matter.

Neither my form nor my matter was gifted to be as it is understood to be now, as soul and body. At present, neither is perfect, as is my originative form and matter gifted directly by God at the moment of originative creation. At this moment, my form and matter—what are now *called* my soul-and-body—must have been perfect; they were magnificently different from what, as a result of an originative sin, they are *known as* now. *Neither my form nor my matter involved the slightest bit of passivity.*

But my conception in space and time ultimately occurred as the result of *both* my originative sin *and* the original sin of Adam and Eve. God is ultimately the cause of why we *are and are good*, but not ultimately of why we are in the "here and now" and imperfect. We made God's loving redemptive activity necessary. God *could not* "freely" refuse to redeem anyone who *could* be redeemed as the

Chapter 11 Where Is My Oneness?

result of having said a less-than-full *yes*. Eternal love is *infinitely* unconditional.

In the divine dispensation that provides a means for healing my whole being, my eventual conception in my mother was a critical point. I was conceived because my being was self-diminished. I needed a process of recovery from having said *maybe* to the *gift of being*. At the moment of creation *out of nothing*, by my own ill-willing, I crashed and damaged severely this incomparable gift.

Prior to being conceived in my mother, my whole *being* was quite dysfunctional. By my "signature sin," I had made myself completely unconscious. My whole being (still giftedly perfect, yet receptedly imperfect) was structurally disarrayed—by an act that caused me to have *an unconsciousness*. I could only "hope" for conception, that is, the kiss of orientation into this world of *functional consciousness* and of be-*coming*.

The Events of Conception and Death

Having been conceived, I am now *actively in recovery*. But I am in this state that is critically impaired, compared to the pure unity of my originatively created being. Death will happen to me, just as conception did.

At death, my soul—my partly dysfunctional, yet reparative kind of form—will not separate from my *body*—my partly dysfunctional, yet reparative kind of matter. Only the *space-time dimension* of my bodily participation-in-existence will cease. My rootedness in this world will terminate. I *will separate* from *this* world and its physical connections, but *not from my body and soul, nor from my form and matter*.

The creation-dimension of my body, my reparative matter, will survive with the whole me. The originatively pure receptivity in my essence—my matter, including its now externalized, "expelled from Eden" condition that we call my living body—cannot be taken away from my *being*, despite how self-damaged or dishonored my *being* might be. I *am* my body, even as I *am* my soul. That is, I *am* my failing, yet reparative form even as I *am* my failing, yet reparative matter.

At death, my corpse will be buried as an "afterbirth," as a once-serviceable "placenta" of my wounded nature.

Strikingly, at my *birth*, the placenta-part of my whole living body died and the remains were cast away. Similarly, at my death, all of the *visible-functional part* of my whole living body—the part that immediately rooted me in this "cast out" space-time world and that we commonly call "body"—will die. Ceremoniously, its remains will be confined to the earth.

But that "separation" will not be a fragmentation of my *being*, nor of my *essence*, nor of my soul and body, the reparative dimensions of my essence. While I will die because I am in need of redemption, I will go on living as a whole being, in the creation-dimension of my *wounded* matter and form: my body and soul. I will be ready or be readied, it may be hoped, for the healing of the deepest rooting of all: my rooting *fully* within the heart of God.

My whole being, including the matter and the form—now known practically through body and soul, the 'essential effects' of my originative *maybe*—was created "before" conception. (It was not strictly "before," but rather in another, non-temporal dimension of my being. There is no "time before time.")

I had to be conceived only because I had crashed at the moment of originative creation. In my resultant condition—a coma-like manner of being—I needed a process of awakening and of healing. Only God could effect it, through the secondary (redemptive) creation: one that calls for my eventual cooperation in order to be saved.

By my initial personal crash, I was self-submerged in ontological darkness for all the preceding periods of time, along with the other billions of *maybe*-saying humans. (When scientists speak of "dark matter," without knowing it, they may be speaking symbolically of some of the results of the crash.)

I was "waiting" to be conceived in order to start on my way to a prospective awakening and repentance. Within the depths of my being, I unconsciously longed for an *opportunity* to attain eventually a promised union with God.

The "before" and the "waiting" are terms taken from our temporal perspective. They do not mean, however, that there was some "pre-existence" of any *formal* kind, such as is thought to be happening in reincarnation. There was a "pre-existence" of an informal kind in which we lay fallow as self-maimed, created persons of God. But we are conceived only once in this world of space and time.

Chapter 11 Where Is My Oneness?

The conception event happened *to* us, while we were languishing in virtual oblivion of *being*. This comatose condition had resulted from our fundamental indecision about *doing* our *being*.

Stubbornly, our present consciousness is now *locked into* a space-time framework. So, we find it *almost impossible* to understand how conception is *not* our beginning to *be*, but our beginning to be-*come*. The egocentric fixation on "things being the way we first understand them" prevents our appreciation of conception as *not at all* the beginning of our *be*-ing, but strictly of our *becom*-ing.

While not being eternal entities ourselves, we have a beginning *within* eternity. Therein God's infinitely personal and perfect act of creation freely loved us into being.

In addition, each of us *crashed* humans has a *formal* beginning *with* time, and as the result of the common crash that caused the *existence* of time. "Before" conception, we ex-isted feebly until we were able to be conceived and to receive our *particular formal and functional* beginning *within* time—at a definite point in the cosmic process. This second beginning—functionally a temporal one—was *our moment of conception*.

These beginnings—*originative* creation and *conception* (our first restorative moment of creation)—are critically related, but they are no more the same than are eternity and time, *according to which* they occur. Time is within eternity for those persons who *need* time. And the restorative creation is *within* the originative creation, not "after" it.

The roots of our prime *becoming*—of our redemptive creation—are distinct from, yet inseparably united with, the roots of our *being*—of originative creation. In the midst of God's unconditional love, we are now struggling to *become* who we were gifted to *be* originatively.

For further perspective on soul and body in relation to substantial form and prime matter, see these terms in the Glossary and in the next Chapter.

Chapter 12

Being Conceived and Being Deceived

Even adults can be easily deceived. They can behave like children, who are apparently innocent and naive.

We can receive well the gift of divine revelation. But then we start to interpret the gift. And misunderstandings multiply.

One critical "miss-take" for almost everyone is the idea of dualism in the relation between body and soul. But another is the idea that human persons are, in any serious or even partial sense, animals. A third is thinking that this world was caused by the physical "big bang"—an explosion of matter—without any reference to the "big bang of *being*."

The big world of becoming—of mega-processes seemingly going somewhere—is ever bending our being into many distortions. These deformities of meaning are evident in the conflations and confusions about what we see or *think* we see.

Still, we can remedy our misconceptions, at least somewhat, by developing our ideas beyond our present fixation on the space-time framework. So, let us continue by examining some quite common misunderstandings.

No Reincarnation

Being-conceived is our *functional* beginning in this world. It is a major happening within our "natural" second beginning: *redemptive* creation.

Conception is neither incarnation nor reincarnation. At conception, I already have a body and soul (a wounded matter and a wounded form). This conception *happens to me* in order that I might receive a sort of "lifeline," and that I might reach for support for my being and its impaired matter and form. By rooting into the ground of spatiotemporal, redemptive existence and by participating in it, I gain leverage for "coming back" to the completeness of originative *being* that I have already momentously missed.

At conception, I do not "take on a body." I do not incarnate. I *am* already a bodily being in somewhat chaotic stillness, resulting from my *maybe-ing* response to primal creation. My being had a collapse.

Conception affords my wounded kind of being—with my *soul and body*—a critical *opportunity to awaken*. I can then realize my need for the redemption—through contrition, repentance, and penitential *existence*. Conception is the beingful (ontological) breakthrough on the way of becoming actually redeemed and potentially saved.

A popular notion in both the East and the West is that we have been, and will be, incarnated again and again. Reincarnation is the idea that we serially take on more than one bodily existence in the spatiotemporal world.

But that way of thinking only magnifies the usual dualism of body and soul. It suggests that I am really only my soul and that I can change bodies as my soul processes throughout the ages. I then would have to think of myself like a centaur's head that changes bodies, while remaining the same centaur-head. But already I can experience and know more integrity of being than that.

Reincarnation, however, does suggest an important truth: that in this life we do undergo what we deserve from something "past" (*karma*, in the Hindu tradition). This doctrine, however, as usually conceived, denies the integral character of my essence, of my *matter* and *form* or, as they have been known through a largely empirical, remedial perspective, my body and soul.

Christians and other theists, therefore, cannot really believe in reincarnation—wherein body and soul are *intrinsically* separable. The human person in this world is one whole person. The soul intrinsically manifests itself in the body. Every person's body is a kind of sacrament of his or her soul.

And Christians also believe that, in Christ, even the Divine relates bodily to us in this world. Yet they can recognize belief-concerns common to both Hindu and theistic traditions.

Before my conception within the trajectory of space and time, I must have existed as the same *being* I am now. I was being the same perfect person that God originatively gifted me to be. But I was self-

Chapter 12 Being Conceived and Being Deceived

blocked and totally unaware. I was a perfect creature *imperfectized* by my first act. (Again, my first act of being *added* imperfection *to* perfection; this malreception of being did not destroy the God-gifted perfection, but imperfected the whole. To the gifted pure form and pure matter, my originative sin called for an added remedial factor, the redemptive gift of soul and body.)

My receptive *imperfection* was thereby an *ontological addition* to God's gifted *perfection* of my being. Hence, I was responsible for the reality of the ontological twists involved in the soul and body flowing out of the perfect (purely active) form and perfect (purely active) matter.

Before conception, I existed in a self-crashed, feeble precondition. Right within myself, I was "cast out" *from* my perfect form and perfect matter, with which I was gifted at the primal creation. I was blocked by my own originative sin—blocked from any measure of further self-determination of my *being*. I had begun *existing* pre-functionally: having a quite non-functional being that was destined, by God's grace, to become functional formally in space and time.

Conception was an event that happened *to* me and was part of a divine design to rouse me to become aware of my self-disoriented *being*. That *being* is intrinsically independent of *time* and *space*—even though now *functionally* quite dependent on these dimensions of healing recovery.

This world *of time and space* will pass away. But my immortal *being* will not. It will pass into one of two final conditions. I will be forever within either heaven or hell, according to my free response to the saving power of infinite Love.

Conception and death demarcate my definitive participation in the redemptive process of this *space-time* world. But these dramatically crucial events do not define my being. Nor do they determine my soul and body.

My self is not a soul with a body, or a body with a soul. I do not *have* a body as I have a suit of clothes. Nor does my body *have* a soul as the earth has an atmosphere. My body is not merely a sign of my soul; nor is my soul merely a glow of my body.

My exercise of the *created* unity of my original matter and form was greatly weakened by a being-wrenching sin. The result is what I now call my body and soul—my responsive weakness in respect to matter and form. But I still *am* my body, and I still *am* my soul.

I know this quite clearly if someone steps on my toes. I might say, "Hey, you stepped on me!" And that means all of me, including my toes and my soul. I am a whole *human* person, from the moment of creation *out of nothing*: with a matter-form that, at conception, was revealed darkly through a body-soul or a soul-body—a being, form and matter—in need of healing.

Matter and form are, strictly speaking, dimensions of my God-gifted essence as a human person. *Body* and *soul* are terms that tend to bespeak this matter and form as revealed in cosmic *nature*—the essence as disposed toward *functional* activity. By the originative sin, my nature became ill-disposed to flow freely from my essence. My soul and body form the troubled face of my God-gifted perfect essence (form and matter).

Both Eastern and Western cultures suffer severely from the idea of some kind of split between body and soul. Hinduism in the East and Cartesianism in the West, for instance, are massively conditioning us even today to deny what we somehow suspect: that we humans are a singular kind of being; that we are an indivisible unity within a great complexity.

Though we are *like* both animals and angels, we are neither. Not a single cell of our bodies is an animal cell. Nor is our nature simply spiritual—spiritual in an angelic way. We are complex because we are *essentially* both matter and form as one person.

Dualism and a split personality might show up in our self-concept and in personal activity. Thereby dualism might seem to account somewhat for much of our *behavior*. But it does not explain the inner *sources* of that behavior: our nature, essence, and being.

Like two really different sides of the same coin, soul and body here in the cosmos are surrogates of my originative form and matter. They are essential to my *fallen* being's destiny. I learn about *all* of me when I learn about my body—both its internal and external dimensions. I learn about *all* of me when I learn about my soul. I learn about my soul when I learn about my body. I learn about my body when I learn about my soul.

Body and soul fully *represent*—in our fallen condition—the two correlative sides of the *essence* of a single self, the *matter* and *form* (the *receptivity* and *givity* of our personhood). (In Chapter 17, I will reflect further on the meaning of this matter and form by means of terminology that is quite positive.)

The "Rational Animal" Deception

Among all the kinds of being in space and time, a human person is *essentially* unique. To be human is to have the quintessential ability to know what things are and to be concerned in a self-reflective way. Even a *fallen* human person can come to know self as self and give self lovingly to family, friends, strangers, and God.

This cosmo-centric human being is fully a *person* in *every* part of himself or herself. Every cell in my body is the cell of the whole *person*, not of an animal or of a plant. Every bit of my energy is human energy—person energy.

I am not a thinking (rational) animal, any more than an animal is a seeing or hearing (sentient) plant. I am a human person in every one of my parts. And so are you. Even when, at times, we wake up and "feel like a bear," or "eat like a bird," or "swim like a fish," or start "acting like a bull in a china shop," we are persons, not animals. *Likeness* is not even a partial *identity*.

When we think of ourselves, even as partly animals, we make a momentous, age-old mistake. We tend to assume that what is first in our perception—our animal-*like* structures and functions—is what is first in significance. But this common error of identifying what is first in our knowing with what is first in being really locks us into a distorted self-concept.

We ought to free ourselves from reductionism—from thinking that we are basically animals (animalism), as well as from thinking that we are basically angels (angelism).

Why, for instance, do we often say that humans are like animals, as though animals were the standard for understanding humans? Why are we not alive to the much greater truth that animals are like humans? Even though it might somehow be true (figuratively) that God is "like" humans, it is far truer (analytically) to say that humans are like God. We are basically persons and *as such*, like God and *unlike* animals. Only secondarily are we *like* animals.

Perhaps, in this fallen world there is a law of intellectual gravity. This strong tendency in our mind pulls us down to following the lowest, easiest common denominator, instead of recognizing the dignity of our own nature. Such a law would have been instigated at the absolute beginning of our be-ing by the very degree to which we willed negatively concerning who we are. Our *maybe* dragged us down and *keeps hanging on.*

So, some say that human nature came into being on the planet *through* the development of subhuman nature (evolution). Others are convinced that it came into being separately (creationism) with or without a prior evolution of the subhuman.

In any event, *what we are* is essentially superior to *how* we came into existence on the planet. Human nature should be, therefore, a transcendent measure of meaning and value for the other living things in this world—things that *minister* to fallen human nature.

Unfortunately, the law of intellectual gravity pulls us away from our true selves. We find it exceedingly difficult to establish a more centered standpoint. The negative "self-concept" that we had given to ourselves by our response to the first creation—out of nothing—haunts us from within. Hence, we need to become liberated from our instinctively egocentric, self-complacent perspective. Only then can we hope to recognize a more insightful way to evaluate ourselves alongside the creatures of earth.

And, of course, the better way is just the opposite of how we are first conditioned to view things. So, we must try to see that the main likeness is not of higher forms to the lower, but of the lower forms to the higher.

Plants, for instance, are somewhat like non-living things. But they are essentially superior in their *way* of being. Plants can grow and engage in self-repair and produce flowers and fruits thoroughly from within themselves. They are not subject merely to accretions or to external additions and subtractions, as are rocks, raindrops, and all other inanimate things. Vegetative substances have their own integrity and vital force. Therefore, we can more reasonably say that non-living things are like plants, than that plants are like non-living things.

Animals are like plants, but are essentially superior. Animals can grow, do self-repair, and reproduce like plants. But they can also

Chapter 12 Being Conceived and Being Deceived

feel and express pleasure and pain, and can move by crawling or sliding or walking or leaping. Though both are true, it is still truer to say that plants are like animals than that animals are like plants. No one, then, should think that an animal is basically a plant "with some difference." An animal is essentially an animal. It is nothing more, nothing less.

Similarly, humans are a little like animals. But they are essentially superior. Humans can grow, do self-repair, generate offspring, feel pleasure and pain, and move by crawling, walking, and running like animals. But humans also have the *natural* capacity or power—even though not all have the *functional* power (babies, the senile, and so forth)—to know and respond to the *meaning* of stimuli, and to create new languages and arts to express this *meaning*. It is truer to say that animals are like humans than that humans are like animals. Why, then, do we think that humans are basically animals, or even partly so?

Humans are essentially human—an unique kind of being, similar to animals and to angels, but quite radically different from both. We would raise the meaning and value of both humans and animals by affirming that animals are like humans, though they are not at all—even in part—human. We would raise awareness on humans and angels by affirming that humans are like angels, though they are not at all angelic.

Part of our cultural problem seems to come from making a mistake about the familiar teaching from Aristotle. This primary philosopher in Western civilization taught that every living thing has a soul: plant, animal, or human. He defined the soul as the principle of life in that which has life.

Among other things, he meant *or implied* that only an animal soul could be the ultimately structuring principle for an animal body—including its cells. A plant soul could not. So, too, only the human soul could be the ultimately structuring principle of a human body—including each of its parts. An animal soul could not.

Yet, Aristotle has been generally interpreted to have defined the human to be a *rational animal*, as though a rational soul could, at least partly, be the ultimate form of an animal body. But by the expression *rational animal* he meant, of course, that a human being is a rational living *organism*. Yet he failed to realize that the human being is, first of all, a *person* and, in this world of matter and motion at least, an organismic person.

Though he advanced well beyond Platonic dualism—the human as a soul somewhat imprisoned in a body—he retained a kind of false monism by insisting that humans are primarily living organisms. He overlooked their being primarily persons. And he was, of course, unacquainted with how they could be (originatively) *purely and solely active* in potency.

Whether we believe in evolution or not, we can recognize that humans are quite different from plants and animals. Whatever the *manner* of humankind's "entry into" the spatiotemporal world, the substance or essence of the human person is *not* primarily *of* this world. Nor is human nature *specific* to it. (It might be said, however, that this world is *specific* to *fallen* human nature.)

Yet every bit of this physical world, even unto the galaxies, *is necessarily related* to the human being. By virtue of flowing from our originative *yes* and *no*, this world is both naturally formative and chronically disruptive, respectively.

It may be true that humanity is a part of cosmic Nature. But it is even truer to say that the whole of cosmic Nature—including the myriad of galaxies—is a *part* of humanity. Cosmic Nature is larger than humanity, quantitatively and spatially. By its essential human *personhood*, however, humanity is immensely "larger" than Nature *qualitatively and essentially*.

At least billions of human persons now find their nesting grounds in cosmic Nature. This natural world of passive matter and motion had resulted from two prime sources: from the exploded receptivity of human nature caused by primal sin and from the essential activity of God in the rehabilitative creation of be-*coming*.

Along with strictly spiritual powers of the redemption, this cosmic condition helps to form the basis for a potential recovery from the human crash. And according to the basic *Christian* understanding, the eventual reclamation includes historical events in the process, particularly the conception, death, and resurrection of Jesus, the only Redeemer of fractualized humanity—whether recognized or not.

Chapter 12 Being Conceived and Being Deceived

The Big Bangs

In our times, an impressive convergence of thought underscores a "big bang theory" for the origination of the cosmos. Scientific investigation will always be constricted. Any theory essentially tied to strictly empirical matters is liable to suffer inevitable changes and even eventual dismissal. This theory could lose its "bang."

The new *being-based* perspective, however, is not at all decisively dependent on empirical observations or on any scientific theories. So, we can only suppose the "big bang" theory to be valid for now. And if it is valid, part of the new *being-based* view would express itself in terms such as the following.

Cosmic Nature itself and the cosmic big bang would have been the result of a *being*-based explosion—the *maybe*-saying of the first sin. *Maybe*-saying persons refused to say fully *yes* to God at creation, so their admirable *natures* virtually collapsed. *That partial negation* of the gift of *be-ing* created an explosion of passive-reactive (*no-yes*) energy, *out of which God created the cosmic universe amidst the severe resistance of fallen human willpower* that is reinforced by the complicity of demonic spiritual powers.

At the moment of pristine creation, this "pull-back" by multitudes of human persons injured their own pure natures to the core. The shock would have produced, from the distorted activity done by their purely active receptivity (active matter), the relatively passive, yet reactive, kind of matter we know as cosmic energy and its materialization into physical parts. This matter is passive due to the *no*-saying in the *maybe*; but it is reactive due to the *yes*-saying.

To our saying *no-yes*, God responded with creatively redemptive love. Nevertheless, cosmic energy, along with its expression in the forms of physical matter, is one of the major negative results of our originatively indifferent, *interpersonal* interaction with God.

In short, the "big bang" *of being* (our originative sin) would have caused a comparable explosion of our originative matter—the gifted receptivity of our essence. In this *being* bang, the power of willful human reservation in relation to the Creator instantly generated the reactively passive condition from which God could draw forth the explosive, yet redemptive, energy of the second creation.

From that self-afflicted condition, our distorted willpower emitted an *alienated*, expanding, fragmenting, scattering, and struggling kind of expelled *human* matter or receptivity. In the redemptive creation, this matter constitutes the subhuman *cosmos*. That "star stuff," as well as the micro-world, is human. It is fallen, fragmented, totally dysfunctional human *freedom*: gone awry, yet standing by in mute witness, supporting our "return" to originative *being*.

The six days of creation recounted in *Genesis* do indicate God as first working from the big void (*Genesis* 1:2). God is then seen as progressively giving order to this visible material universe.

The account suggests that God gradually shepherds higher stages of matter and motion from within lower ones—whether rapidly or slowly. God seems to be working with all these vulnerable degrees of energy so that they are finally suitable as conditions for *hosting*—from within—the *fallen human* community that is in dire need of awareness and repentance.

Divine power thus broadens human creative power—originatively gifted "out of nothing"—into redemptively co-creative energy, the actual power to "work at something." The redemptive cooperation with God is seen clearly in the eventual generation of offspring. Procreation serves as a kind of co-creation with God—*redemptively* speaking.

The human procreative drive is one of the many obvious motions of matter toward the goodness of human personhood. All human energy naturally harbors its own teleology, its own intrinsically patterned drive for higher perfection in the restoration process—powered partly by the *yes* from our originative *maybe*.

Adam and Eve—along with us, their eventual offspring—are the banished creatures whose primal *maybe* had caused both a spiritual and a material *void*. The form-matter *vacuum* (void) caused by us was apt "matter"—passive matter, passive potency—for the creation depicted in the *Genesis* story. Out of this void and primeval chaos God fashioned the redemptive universe.

Here in this world, we suffer a catastrophically reduced ability to perceive who we are. Therefore, *what* we *first* come to know *in this world* about cosmic Nature and ourselves tends to be the opposite of the way it really is.

Chapter 12 Being Conceived and Being Deceived

We think and talk first about the cosmic matter all around us. But this fragmental world of passive matter and energy in which we are immersed, as well as the matter-energy we know as our space-time bodies, must be a partial restoration of originatively distorted pure receptivity—of pure freedom. *Energy* (frustrated receptivity) was *not* originatively meant to *be*.

At present, we suffer immensely from all of our defective ways of conceiving and of interpreting things rationalistically. Under such a weight, we can barely *intuit* the original actuality and power of our *be*-ing.

We failed originatively to respond fully, and thereby our exercise of freedom yielded the impaired form of actuality that we now call "energy." Concerning its base, philosophers often have referred to what they call "prime matter."

The new view, however, regards creation "out of nothing" more seriously than is done through the usual cosmic perspective. In view of the *immaculate creation*, this *matter supreme* ("prime matter") can be understood as an *originative* dimension of our *perfect* human being.

Contrary to traditional notions, this originative matter was *purely active receptivity*—the active power or *potency to receive who and what* we are. It was not—originatively—the passivity and passive receptivity delineated by Aristotle.

Along with a perennial trail of philosophers after him, this Greek philosopher was a beacon of refined common sense. Nonetheless, in his cosmic-centered philosophy he had acknowledged only the kind of matter that had once resulted from our beginning sin. He was functionally unable to recognize such a sin and its *consequences* that are now structured into our world, both material and spiritual. He had no way to conceive of *purely active* matter—matter without *any* passivity. Pure freedom to receive.

This pure or perfect matter, the originative matter, was not the already-skewed matter and energy directly producing some kind of cosmic detonation that has so enamored empirical scientists in our time. Originative matter was and is our intrinsic *capacity to receive* our human essence *from within*, purely *as gifted*. Anything less represents some level of our failing in freedom and love.

Out of the Depths a Human Zygote Cries unto Thee

We can come to know this originative prime receptivity—this prime matter of our *being*. But our attainment comes only gradually, through an integration of reason and Faith. We carry within us many hindrances to understanding.

For instance, as an unique individual being, I am *both* one with *and* radically other than the passive matter of the cosmos—from the inter-galactic to the intra-molecular. Cosmic passivity will include my eventual cadaver that will constitute the specific remnants of my functional oneness with the cosmos.

Neither dualistic nor monistic thinking will suffice. I must accept *both* difference *and* oneness in my ways to relate within myself and with everything else.

By understanding myself as two separable "parts"—as body and soul—I make it difficult even to suspect what my creation "out of nothing" was like. But I know that an unlimitedly perfect Creator must have created a *whole* person, not part of a person.

And the creation was *complete*. It is only my own faltering first response to originative creation that could have brought me into this flawed, sputtering, inertial world that this first response itself had a critical role in causing.

When a particular sperm and a particular ovum of two individual persons met in space and time, there occurred my conception. This event marked my direct, functional entrance into the process of spatiotemporal recovery. This conception happened *to* my unique personhood that was already there: the whole, but primarily self-frustrating personal being.

At the moment that the sperm and ovum interacted, they *died* as sperm and ovum. They gave up their gametic lives—not that I might live, but that I might live *in this redemptive world*. They co-caused me to enter *here and now*.

Sperm and ovum were never potentially I. They were simply potential *causes*—causes of my *ex-istence* in *this* world. The result of their causing was that I—all of me—could *begin* the process of awakening from my super-traumatic *slumber of be-ing*. I could then *be-gin* moving toward the resolution of my originative *maybe* into either a full *yes* or a full *no*.

Chapter 12 Being Conceived and Being Deceived

The zygotic part of myself comes from somewhere deep in my *whole benumbed being*. This tiny growth, rooted in becoming and redemptivity, emerges out of my own deep passivity. *By* the activity of father and mother—and *by* the instrumentality of their gametes—*in and out of* the passive potency of *my* afflicted prime matter (*my* supreme ability *to be done to*) comes the new organic life that is now so critically recognizable as mine—the one by which I am punching away at this computer.

As a single cell of my earthly beginning, the zygotic part of my being has roots sunk in the darkness within me that I alone could have caused. Gradually, through wondrous physical and emotional growth, I reached the "age of reason."

At that point, my reflections about the human condition began in earnest and increased. By much continued education and personal meditation, I started to feel my roots below the surface of the cosmic world, and I began to see vaguely into this darkness.

As an adult, I am becoming more conscious of my true beginning. I acknowledge that my presence in the space-time world comes out of the self-wrought darkness and repressive effects of my incipient *maybe*-saying to God. While being a magnificent human person—*essentially, even if not functionally, independent* of the world's passivity—I am now thoroughly rooted in cosmic existence for the sake of making a commitment to full recovery.

The roots of my entire *being* began to *be* by the infinitely creative activity of God. The roots of my *becoming*, however—roots of body and soul as found here in space and time—must have begun to be co-creatively. These temporal roots are the result of *both* the re-activity of my *may*-being (my originative *maybe*-saying) *and* the *infinitely responsive activity* of God toward me within my *maybe* condition.

Nevertheless, they are roots, too: the roots of my coming-to-*exist*, my *be*-coming, in the world of the *where* and *when*. With at least billions of others, I co-initiated this world of space and time through the *implosion-explosion of my being* at the moment of creation "out of nothing."

The world of space and time, of passive matter and motion, is then grandly placenta-*like*. The whole cosmos acts like a "service organ in common" for the awakening of our stunned, numbed *beingful* selves, of which we are here-and-now barely aware. Our gestational condition within this world of *where* and *when* was originatively caused by a strictly inconceivable, yet utterly real, crash in our God-gifted be-ing. This breakdown or semi-collapse *within originative creation* was the failure of our quintessential freedom.

The matter and the forms of all the particles of the whole cosmos have come to be out of the crash of *maybe*-saying human persons. Energy and existence arose from the collapse of our God-gifted freedom.

Part III   Contemplating Our Condition

Chapter 13

What Happened to Friendship?

In earthly life, almost everyone has experienced a lost friendship. Perhaps as a child, you related with someone who you thought was your friend. But, all at once, the "friend" started to keep a distance from you. This former companion no longer phoned you or visited, nor even returned your calls.

You might have been shocked, wondering what you had done that turned your friend into a foreigner, if not an enemy. You suspected that the former companion's alienation was not due to what he or she did—although it could have been that—but to what you did or did not do. Despite your efforts, you simply could not think of how you failed in the relationship.

This feeling of estrangement from what might have developed into a rich, rewarding, and lifetime friendship can serve to remind us of our present relationship with God. Although we might not *feel* it, we know God is real, and with infinite love wills to be our friend. We *believe* God's integrity and fidelity are inviolable—and not like our experience with an immature friend's fickleness.

But where is God when we need a friend? And where is infinitely loving intimacy, such that this world's troubles vanish in the divine embrace? Where is the unification actual, and not just promised? And why not union now? Why must we wait?

What has caused this stark alienation or immense distance from our divine Friend? Is it something that we have done or not done? If a friend in need is a friend indeed, where is our Creator-God in the darkest hours?

We do ask with many others, "Where was God at Auschwitz?" But we also ask, "Where is God this very moment as billions starve for food, shelter, and meaning?"

People are wandering here in the world-womb of space, time, and myriad motions. Millions come and go, live and die, without any apparent meaning that is interpersonal, intimate, and without threat of ending. Perhaps, if they knew more about the condition they lost when they were totally free and failed, they could better see through the density of the cosmic condition.

In characterizing the *origin* of our plight, however, millions of believers have gone from one extreme to the other: from "original curse" to "original blessing." But God is, first of all, our Friend. A genuine friend never curses the innocent, nor lets the guilty cover over their failed responsibilities by using rhetoric about "blessing." How, then, is God our Friend?

Ecstatic friendship with God—even by saints—is rarely found in this world. So, we might try simply to glimpse the goodness of the friendship we lost. We can begin by trying to look through the tiny opening of genuine, if halting, human friendships in our present, awakening lives.

Freedom and Friendship

Every true friendship includes unconditional, affirming love. This love says, "Be and be yourself. Let us share who we *are*."

True friends will give each other expanding room for growth in intimacy. But they also will allow freedom for diminishment and departure.

Friendship, as such, is not possessive. Genuine friendship is *self*-fulfilling, paradoxically by being *other*-centered, *other*-enriching—and by *not* being *self*-centered, *self*-enriching.

Our friendship with God was intended to be *pure, perfect,* and *other*-centered. We were created to be God-centered, God-praising. Paradoxically, by embracing the Other, we would have affirmed ourselves as gifted-to-be by the Other alone. A marriage of God and created person that would be One with one, and One with all, forever.

Chapter 13   What Happened to Friendship?

Revelational religions have at least touched upon the idea of God as friend.

The Islamic tradition of Sufis, a mystical practice of the *Quran*, included those who held that friendship with God was an animating purpose for their spiritual union. This prospect of spiritual intimacy was initiated by God, their friend, who can lead human persons from darkness to light (Burrell, 182).

Some contemporary philosophies and theologies in the Jewish and Christian traditions emphasize the import of an I-Thou relationship with God. Martin Buber, Gabriel Marcel, and others speak hopefully about establishing this intimate dialogue with God.

Saints and mystics throughout the ages have communed with God, at times with interpersonal rapture. Holiness heals wounded love.

But theistic people seem to be unaware that this relationship is one that *we* personally have quite freely *blocked*. At the interpersonal moment in which we were created, we failed in friendship.

Nevertheless, we have not completely lost the potency for this communal relationship. The dialogue we seek can be understood as an attempt—by means of a quite radical change in attitude toward everyone and everything—to regain the lost power to be a created person in full communion with the Creator.

Christian believers can speak freely of the call of grace *in Jesus*: the friendship with God. In his life on earth, Jesus exemplified the divine friendship. He told his closest followers that they were not merely servants, but friends (*John* 15:14-16). And he laid down his life for his friends—*all* who need redemption.

When he said he would give his Body to eat and his Blood to drink, many of his "friends" walked away. He immediately asked his closest companions if they, too, would leave him. He did not back down on what he meant, and he gave them the freedom to walk out of his life.

Near the end, Jesus was so friend-conscious and other-centered that he called his betrayer "friend." Jesus received the kiss of Judas with a lament. But he affirmed in his betrayer a radical *potential* to be a friend, yet a profound *freedom* to "do what you will do" (John 13: 27). He made no effort to take possession of this "friend."

Beyond Dependency

Even though they call others their "friends," many people do not share deeply who they *are*. Most folks have some good relationships, and they depend on their buddies and companions for mutual support and enjoyment. But that is not the same as friendship.

The *attitude* we hold toward others and ourselves is critical in establishing true friendship. Many are not so much into friendship as into friend*shop*. They are "shopping" for self-fulfillment. They are hurting for friends or, at least, *a* friend. But they seek *acquaintances*, and they are quietly asking in their hearts, "Are you the one for me?"

They are *me*-centered, rather than *be*-centered. They do not relate well with the *being* of others—or with the *being* of themselves—and so they try to compensate by possessing the unpossessable. They endeavor to *get* a friend, more than to *be* a friend. They base their desire for friendship on their dependencies.

Friends, like buddies and companions, depend on one another with respect and trust. But friendship is something more. Unlike simple companionship, mature friendship is the gift of just being together and sharing deeply.

Loving human friendships are basically relationships of *shared independence*, not shared dependence. All human relationships on the planet include dependencies. But the core of any of them that would qualify as a genuinely loving friendship is not dependency. While the best of friendships includes dependence of each person on the other—especially emotional dependence—reliance on each other to help fulfill needs is secondary.

Dependency for the sake of fulfilling basic requirements of life originates in passivity. And *all passivity* is the result of our first refusal fully to be and to be entirely a friend. When we balked at being created, we dropped from being purely active to being acutely passive. We "co-created" our *need* for ancestors, for first parents, and for God redeeming us from our own partaking in "the tree of knowledge of good and evil."

Only our passivity makes us dependent—on others, and especially on God. If, at the non-temporal moment of being purely active, we had said fully *yes*, we would be neither passive nor dependent.

Chapter 13 What Happened to Friendship? 135

Christians, for instance, can find revealing the redemptive love of Jesus. He did not really need our love, but we desperately needed his. Independently—not dependently—he offered his whole being for us, his friends. He "depends" on us to respond positively to his independent love.

If we respond well, it is decisively because of his *independent* love that we are thereby saved; it is not because he "depends" on us to accept redemption. If we refuse, he will still love us, independently of our hatred. Jesus tells us to love our enemies, and he showed us how by his life and his death.

The Independence of Friends

When we begin to think—as Jews, Christians, or Muslims—about the prospect of being *friends* with God, we have to develop our meanings for dependence and independence. On the relationship between God and created persons, the many traditional theological interpretations tend to assume that our dependence originates with God. We are inclined to think that God could not create us except as dependent on the Supreme Being.

The idea is that God is the cause of all created being, including the relationship itself. Therefore God is independent of created persons, but we are totally dependent on God. Since every effect is dependent on its cause, in the essence of our relationship with God we are thought to be totally and exclusively dependent.

Such an approach, however, is good specifically only in respect to God's restorative creation—the creation of redeemable beings. Such creation, however, is *not* "out of nothing," but out of the condition of emptiness (the "nothingness") that these creatures had made of themselves in failing to receive fully their originally gifted being. That *failure to receive well* has to be regarded as an act of *poorly willing* created persons—acting *independently of* God. God could not at all do it *for them*. The act was theirs alone. And they exercised this gifted independence *badly*.

Besides, those who did *receive fully* their gifted being—such as the good angels—would have had to do so *independently with* God, but not *dependently on* God. If we had to depend on God to do for us *our* initial—or even final—act of receiving, it would not really *be our free act*.

If *we* had *received fully*, we would have done so *independently with* God—not independently *of* or *from*. Nor would we depend *on* God for the *receiving act* itself. God could not *do* the receiving of *our* being *for* us and we still *be* who we are gifted to be.

The idea of being *independent with* God might strike us, at first, as foolish and blasphemous. But that might be because we have only one basic meaning for independence. Our notion of independence is derived from the relation between causes and their effects in our space-time world, wherein *dependence* is necessary.

To us, anything that is dependent can be thought to be *that which cannot be without something else*. As we commonly say, *an effect cannot be without a cause*. So, we reflexively think that whatever is *independent* cannot be truly an effect, and that an independent being would have to be something that can *be* without anything else.

We take, rather directly and simplistically, our understanding of cause and effect, *as it is experienced in this crashed world*. We then project it onto our *originative* relation with God.

This projection is done because we never consider admitting an *originating* sin that made all cause-and-effect to be the way we *experience* it here. We think this world's way is the *only* kind of cause-and-effect relationship that is *possible*. Such an assumption is an ego-centrism writ large.

But further light can help us to see another possibility. Even in the present world, and to the extent that we exercise our capacity for *unconditional* love, we and others can begin to realize our deepest relationships. Insofar as we are deeply friends, we are mutually *independent with* one another. We are not simply dependent *on* one another. Nor are we independent *from* (or *of*) one another.

We might well feel—all or most of the time—either hopelessly dependent on or hopelessly independent *from* (or *of*) one another. Some people do. But it does not have to be so.

We can delight in the *being* of other created persons. And we can delight in them not simply as good-for-*us*, but as good-for-*them*-in-themselves-along-*with* all others—no matter how badly they act at times.

Chapter 13 What Happened to Friendship?

We can enjoy others from our capacity to affirm their *be*-ing in an unconditional way. We love them in and from our power of being independent-*with* them.

If *we* can *give* unconditional love like this, how much more so can God? Infinitely so.

Being, the Gift of Affirming Love

In our own highest moments of love and friendship, we are called to see what we are experiencing. Then and there we can begin to appreciate something significant about God's *infinitely* unconditional love, as it was and is in the act of creation. *Even as we can give love in this world, at least in part, without at all rendering the beloved dependent on us, God can give us our being without rendering us dependent at all.*

In ordinary life, we can *affirm* another person by acting with our receptive powers of listening or by gazing lovingly. Such activity is not rendering this person dependent. The person is being received as he or she *is*—and as being delightful.

This *kind of causing* gives the other person his or her being, as it were, and allows the other to be larger and richer for himself or herself. The affirmed person receives from the affirming one that deeper sense of *independence*—not *necessarily* dependence—with respect to the giver (the cause, the affirming one).

In the *originative* creation, an effect (the created person) *could* not be dependent on its cause (God). Therein cause-and-effect is simply Giver-and-gift. The gifting relationship is totally prior in excellence to dependency. Cause-and-effect in the immaculate creation means shared independence with respect to being and to being good: the Creator is unlimited, perfect Love; the created one is limited, perfect love, potentially and immediately—not "perfect dependence."

The divine Sharer is infinite, even as the shared one is finite—sharing in his or her *own* uniquely finite way. Infinite person(s) and finite persons sharing *as mutually independent beings*: such is the peak condition for intimacy and bliss.

In the originative creation, to be an authentic effect is to be *gifted with* being and to *receive* it fully, actively, with the independence of being-*with*-being. When we regard that *prime* relationship with God as being one of dependence, wherein we "owe" God something, or even everything, then we are somewhat refusing to be *responsible—we unconsciously reject our freedom in God.*

Thinking of ourselves as *essentially* dependent on God is likewise profoundly egocentric. The very thought violates the creative act of God because everything about creation is fully gifted. God gives us our be-ing as *our own*, not as a loan.

By regarding our *principal* relationship with God as being one of dependency, we would be insisting on maintaining our mentality of servile one-upmanship. In thinking passively like that about God's *gift* of being, we would be treating God as having to exercise a "one-upmanship" attitude toward *us* in being our cause, since that is the only way *we* would do it if we were God.

We project—onto the act of creation—the essential dependency involved in any cause-effect relationship that is found in this cosmic concentration camp of our own making. We attribute to the giving-of-being in absolute loving creation the *same kind of relationship* as we experience in the servile world of self-affliction. We misconstrue the principle of causality. We project the meaning of causality in this world onto creation itself. Our ego-centrism would seem to be boundless.

In space and time, it is true that every effect is dependent on its cause. But the *principle* of causality can be understood to be simply that there *is* a cause for every effect, not that there is a dependency. The relation between non-spatiotemporal effects and causes is not *necessarily* one of dependency.

In being created *out of nothing*, we were *gifted* with *being*—not granted it. God does not "dole out" entities, as typically passive interpretations of creation would have it. God *gives* all to all. Our functional deficits—in us and about us now—did not come from God or God's agency.

Christians, for instance, can miss the point in Jesus saying, "Unto whomsoever much is given, of him much shall be required...." (*Luke* 12:48). The *originative* gift of being was not relative, but absolute and perfect. We were all given the perfect power to love God with whole heart and mind.

But that does not mean that we are the same. Each one of us is *uniquely* perfect. The idea that we are anything less than perfect

Chapter 13 What Happened to Friendship?

within ourselves came from us, not from God. We were gifted, perhaps, with different levels of perfection. *But these were not levels of imperfection.*

In being created, we did not *get* anything. *We were gifted.*

Because of our present defective condition of being, we are faced with the challenge of *receiving*, not of acquiring. Because of our own initially willful resistance, we are ultimately required to *receive what we have not yet received.* Receiving can be neither getting nor letting, but rather *being-with* the Creator, who infinitely gives to us throughout our participation in this empirical, miserly world of "give and take."

Receiving and Getting

To be created as a *person* is to be *able* to *receive* one's be-ing: immediately, freely, and fully. This perfect *receptivity* means the *ability* to welcome anything that is good, without the least resistance to it. Wherever there is *perfect* reception of *being*, there can be no passivity or dependence.

But our ordinary meaning for receiving obstructs us from this understanding. Our meaning for receiving usually fails to notice the distinction between receiving and getting—between utterly non-possessive receiving and the possessive, even clutching, kind of "receiving" that is really a getting, an acquisition.

A Zen Buddhist concept regarding enlightenment might begin to suggest the difference between receiving and getting.

Suppose you want to drink a glass of water. You naturally look for an entirely clean glass—free of stain or residue from substances like salt or milk or lemon, left over from previous uses.

If there is even the slightest taint of another substance in the glass, water is not received well as water. The water will not taste like itself; it will be flavored with the suggestion of salt, milk, or lemon that was not cleanly removed before the water was poured into the "receiving" glass.

In the Buddhist tradition, the condition of being-enlightened is likened to the way a glass receives water when the vessel itself is utterly clean. Water can then, be received, so to speak, as water in an uncontaminated way. Similarly, reality can be received as it is—by the *pure or purified consciousness* of the receiver.

From a theist perspective, we might then say that in doing the drinking of water we have a partial image of our receiving activity at the moment of creation "out of nothing." At creation, we must have let our own being receive itself *tainted by itself*, instead of being free of even the slightest of self-centered contamination. We partially centered on our self as receiver, rather than fully on God as Giver. We failed to be fully receiver *as receiver* and tried to be a *receiver-and-giver* of our being.

Such is a bad act of receiving. And it is also a bad act of *being-a-gift*. Our being that was entirely *gifted* by God was not entirely *received* by us. Rather than being fully *gift-receiving*, we were more or less *self-receiving*. We are therefore *self*-infected beings.

This portrayal has limits. Any example that our matter-mentored minds take from the material world contains inherent constraints. Passive matter weakly reflects the profound depths of the spirit.

But we try to do the best we can in offering material clues for transcendental meanings. And further analysis of the meaning of *receiving* taken from the physical world might reveal still further intimations of a being-with-being attitude.

For instance, another look at how fluid is received by a container exemplifies an Aristotelian principle. The time-honored statement is that *whatever is received is received according to the mode of the receiver*, and not according to the mode of that which is received, nor according to the mode of the giver.

The idea is that whatever is received, say, a liquid, is received according to the way the *receiver* exists. Water is therefore received not according to the water's own manner of being, but according to the nature of the container. So, a sieve "receives" water like a sieve, letting virtually all of it go through. And a regular cup "receives" water solidly, holding the liquid in place.

Receiving is something that is done *by the receiver*, not at all by the giver. Nor by the given as given. Such a principle seems obvious when pointed out. But the flow of experiences can swamp it. Gross miss-evaluations of what is going on can result.

Chapter 13 What Happened to Friendship? 141

In *responding* to our *being* as created, then, *we* were the ones who were doing the receiving—*not God*. We were receiving our whole being. And we were doing that receiving *by that very gifted being itself*. The receiver and the received were the same *in being*. The receiving was *intra*personal.

The Giver was also received; but not in the same way as the gift. The Giver was being *received* by the created being—in a different, *inter*personal way.

If our being resulted in any *dependency* on God, that dependency really occurred because we did the receiving impurely, imperfectly. It could not have come because of any dependency-rendering aspect on God's part as infinitely perfect Giver.

God's gift, our *being*, is received according to *our* free reception, not according to God's infinitely free intent in giving. So, we can freely and effectively block God's "best intentions." Even *infinite* goodness will be interpersonally received defectively by the freely, but self-pollutively acting, finite *receiver*.

From Dependence to Independence

Traditionally, we sometimes seem to think that in heaven we will be completely dependent on God. Finally. We assume that, since there will be no independence "from or of" God, whatever is left is complete *dependence*.

But we are suffering from misunderstanding. We are confusing "being related" with "being dependent." In heaven we will be—as we could have been right from the moment of primal creation—more *related* to God than ever. Fully related, in fact. But in order for that fullness of relationship to *be,* we will have to come into a condition of *non*-dependence—a non-possessive, non-self-tainting relationship.

We are here and now dependent massively on God and on other creatures. An almost inevitable result is that we miss how causality works differently in the world where *redemption* is *not* needed.

We ought to begin to see how truly and thoroughly dependent on God we redemption-seeking persons really are. We must come to realize that this dependency is to be acknowledged, received, and affirmed. Such affirmation of dependency is done by repentance, obedience, penance, and sacrifice. Nevertheless, we are living our vital dependence upon God the better to grow, paradoxically, ever more emphatically, into the *eventually*-shared independence, that is, *independence-with* God.

In other words, we do truly *need* God. But we need God in order to come into the condition of *not needing* God. This condition was originally intended for our very *be*-ing. God gives being originally "without any strings." We do not "hang" on God's being, unless we reject at least part of our completely endowed being and *thereby* create the dependency. The measure of originative rejection causes the degree of dependency.

The traditional philosophy and theology that see *only* dependency between the effects and their cause might subtly be working from an egregiously defective assumption: that this material world of space and time is the model for how realities can come into *be*-ing.

This world of largely passive matter, however, is not a world of *being* so much as a world of *becoming*. The way things are caused in the world of becoming is not necessarily the way they are caused in the world of being. To become is to be, but to be is not necessarily to become. The laws of becoming are not sufficient for the laws of being. But you and I are rooted in *both* becoming *and* being.

We chronically confuse the way our present world works with the way God's world works. God's ways are lumped together with our ways. Thus the usual theological concept of heaven may unwittingly amount to thinking of our everlasting happiness as an unending or final addiction.

We are thought to be dependent in heaven—completely dependent on, and possessed by, God. But addiction and possessiveness never characterize pure relationships because addiction and possessiveness are necessarily based on *dependency*.

Mature relationships are founded on *shared independence*—shared independence in *being*. Theists are not called to be God-addicts any more than they are called to be self-addicts. They are called to be fully *with* God, within God, yet utterly other-than-God—forever supremely intimate friends and grateful lovers of God.

Shared Independence

The notion of a sharing kind of independence strikes most people as foreign because they think independence involves some kind of

Chapter 13 What Happened to Friendship?

separation or separability. Instead, independence does not have to involve separation at all.

If independence necessarily meant separation, Christians could not affirm that God is three independent Persons in one, harmonious nature. According to the doctrine of the Trinity, the Father is related infinitely to the Word and to the Spirit, and *vice versa*. But, in these relationships, none of the Persons is dependent. In each One, there is infinite freedom.

Even in the fallen human world, we can somehow come to know that there is a difference between being dependent and being related. We know that to be dependent is to be related. But to be related is not necessarily to be dependent. To be related can also mean shared independence: freedom to be, to be oneself, and to be *with* God and *with* others. Our potential to be a true friend reveals itself.

There is both good and bad independence. Good independence is the condition whereby we can freely give and receive love. Insofar as some dependence is involved, we are necessarily, to that degree, less free and less capable of love and of lasting intimacy. *Insofar as we would be dependent upon God, we could never be completely intimate* with the Divine.

Dependency blocks mature intimacy. We are now living with a self-conscious dependency-complex. This disorientation inevitably obstructs our attributing infinite *goodness* to infinite activity. We grossly "underestimate" the *infinite* power of God to give created persons independent being—their very own (finite) being that is not at all a part of God's Being.

Perhaps nowhere are we more confused about our relationship with God than when we think that God *could* annihilate any or all of created reality—so "powerful and masterful" is God. In reality, by our tyrannous thoughts about relationships and power, we project onto God's activity our sinfully conditioned notions.

Perhaps more prayerful reflection might remove our presumption. God would not really will any being to be annihilated because God "could" not do it—so absolute is the Word of God in gifting created persons with their own shareable autonomy. Everlasting heaven and hell derive from God's infinitely loving act of gifting persons *to be and to be themselves unconditionally*. Such includes *their* making of decisions of destiny.

God receives far more glory from the freely given love of an *independent* creature than from the partially free love of a *dependent* creature. In thanksgiving and joy, independence *with* God—the full harmony and mutually autonomous accord—is the essential opposite of independence *apart from* God in rebellion and denial.

We are so habituated to the world of becoming, of passive matter and of motion, of space and of time, that we still might ask questions such as, "Is it really desirable not to need God?" And the response would have to be frank. "If we had said fully *yes* to the gift of being, we would be so intimate, so perfectly one with God, that we would not *need* God."

The "need talk" comes from our *de facto* condition of *self-induced* dependency. Our self-caused *un*freedom constitutes the dependency itself that in nowise was given to us by God.

We *do* need God—critically so—granted our present condition. But the need is a condition that never had to *be*. An infinitely good and infinitely powerful God could never have originatively intended it.

Dependence is a drag on being-*with*. We cannot be *with* those we depend on in quite the same way that we can be *with* those we do not depend on and who do not depend on us.

Besides, even when we *must* depend on God and others, we do so independently or freely. Not even God can *make* us accept divine grace on which we so absolutely *now depend*.

We *independently* affirm our dependence and need for salvation—or *independently* reject it. Even if others can help us somewhat toward salvation by their prayer and counsel, we have to have at least minimal good will for their help to be effective.

In other words, we cannot be *dependently* dependent on God and others. We can then *only* be *independently* dependent. We defective *human persons* cannot be "unfreely unfree" like a tree; we can only be "*freely* unfree."

In this world of super inter-*dependence*, we can come to choose *independently*—in the independence of freedom—to exercise our myriad, *de facto* dependencies. The more we come to exercise these dependencies in a genuinely independent way the more we increase our functional freedom.

Chapter 13 What Happened to Friendship?

Or we can choose *independently* to exercise our dependencies in a dependent manner—to remain basically passive, unresponsive, and irresponsible. But the choice is ours, not God's. The freedom and independence is ours, not God's.

And so we are absolutely independent. We are either independent *with* God—thanks *both* to God *and* to us—or independent *of* (or *from*) God, "thanks" only to us.

The most notable atheist of the 20th century, Jean-Paul Sartre, quite famously put it: we humans are "condemned to be free." We cannot *not* choose. Not to choose is to choose not to choose. We are radically free beings.

But he really did not suspect how true that is—how essentially free *God created* us to be.

Created to Be Free

Theists can understand this essential or necessary freedom, but in a thoroughly positive way. We are *created*—not condemned—*to be free*. We are committed or covenanted by God to be free in receiving and exercising our act of being—the being we are called to be and *do*.

In wisdom and love, God cannot create us dependent and unfree. In the gift of creation, we *persons* cannot *not* be free; we cannot *not* be independent *as whole beings*. By exercising our gifted freedom badly, however, we can gradually make ourselves effectively unfree.

Even if we did create massive dependencies on God and on other creatures by originatively dropping out, we did so *independently* at the moment of creation "out of nothing." Through God gifting them with their own independent power, all created persons exercise their gift of being, whether they *will* to relinquish true freedom or not.

And we fallen ones—we drop outs—are now really destined to "re-receive" the gift eventually: either independently *with* God in heaven or independently *apart from* God in hell.

Only our still-servile minds prompt the question, "Do we not depend on God, even in heaven, for exercising our gift of being?"

The new perspective replies: if we think we *depend* on God for the gift of *being*, we are still absorbed by the world of *becoming*. We ought to begin consciously entering the world of *being*, wherein *all is gift*—*all* is giving and receiving, not just delivering and getting. All is more than becoming. All is *be*-ing, including becoming.

God creates beings to be and to be themselves and to do freely—yes, independently—the *whole* of their *own* beings. We are given the ability either to receive our being as independent *or to receive it as dependent*. In either case, ultimately the receiving act itself is an *independent* act.

To receive our own being as independent does not mean we have to think of ourselves as "self-created" or in any way "self-centered." Nor does it mean we are dependent on ourselves rather than God. Self-*dependence* is the surest way to hell.

Indeed, it is only because we are self-centered and self-dependent that we fancy ourselves as created originatively dependent on God. We are so impacted by our self-dependency that we lack gratitude for our *being as a gift*. We seem unable to know God as infinite Love who *gifts us to be us—to be finite*—without rendering us in any way *dependent as a condition in being*.

If we were to be given *being* as finite *and dependent*, that would mean that we were lacking something proper to us, on the basis of which the "dependency of finitude" would occur. There would seem to be something lacking about being finite. But what *else* could be *lacking*? Only infinity.

Such thinking reveals a latent pantheism and that might explain something about our spiritually unconscious desire to be God—to *be* infinite. We are inclined secretly to think we *ought* to be divine.

There is no dependency in being as such, because there is nothing of dependency in God. To be is to be-*with*, not to be "leaned on," nor to lean at all.

There is also, of course, no *finitude* in being as such. There is no *finitude* in God. God is the only *infinite and necessary* kind of being; and finite, created beings are not necessary beings.

But finite being (finitude)—unlike dependency and *un*freedom—is what created persons *are, if they are*. This kind of being is a free gift, given by activity of infinite freedom's giving. Created persons are essentially and necessarily limited—by ontological priority—to being *at first* absolute receivers, and not "dependers." *Purely active* receivers—passive not at all.

Chapter 13 What Happened to Friendship?

Malevolent creatures, like Lucifer and similar spirits, are limited beings who *entirely* refused to be and to be who they are gifted to be. They continue to exercise *independently* their gift of being—but *apart from* God. They are not at all independent-*with* God.

Their willed independence-*from* God has made them completely dependent on themselves, without being willing *or even able* to acknowledge that self-wrought condition and without being willing or even able to call out to God to save them. They are inexorably—*by their own independent will*—"stuck on themselves."

As much as they might *will* not to *be*, they cannot *not be*. The giving of being is an unconditional act of God's infinite love, which they freely and independently try in vain to thwart. Their exercised independence *from* God sets them totally adrift from the prospect of coming into any union *with* God. They are *so* self-centered that they cannot freely (independently) admit their self-*caused* dependence *on themselves*.

Absolute refusers of being try to rule their own being and that of others by tyranny. They even attempt to annihilate themselves and to torment others into non-being, which is impossible. Like all other created persons, they received from God an absolute, independent ("self-sustaining") be-ing. But they are the created persons who are *self*-seduced—fixated on themselves—and trapped into being self-frustrated forever.

Other self-frustrating created persons—like us—harbor within their hearts a partial *yes*. There is at least a flicker of real love, and maybe much more. The gift of being that every person receives from God includes within itself the independent power to be-*with*.

The divine Giver gives each person a unique being that *is* the active power-to-*be-with* of a friend. That power is still "within us." But it is lost and we are trying to find it, with the critically *needed* power of a Friend.

Chapter 14

What Happened to Freedom?

Where is God? Is God *hiding* from us? How can we be authentically free when we do not see God? Being seems dark.

In theistic traditions, many people get the idea that perhaps God has intentionally withdrawn from us, for whatever reason.

Some think God hides so that the divine glory does not overwhelm our freedom; others, that God keeps distant because our sinfulness is so repugnant; and others, that by the divine concealment we can appreciate more deeply our desperately dependent condition; still others, that God withdraws as part of our purgation.

In the midst of these *projections*, the thought does not seem to occur to us that *we* are the *only* ones who *can* withdraw. We might be unwilling to admit it, but God did not and *cannot* remove from us *the infinitely loving presence* of divine Being. *We* are the ones who have pulled back and continue to withdraw. We do so at a level that is profoundly unconscious. We unconsciously attribute to God our own undulations of presence and absence.

Our indecisive condition might even be punctuated by claims of how *God* has been "doing this" and "doing that" in our lives. Such expressions hold some truth, and they literally abound in the Hebrew and Christian Testaments. But we can be readily misled.

We might think falsely that God acts quite like we do. But does God *really* indulge, say, in pouting? In vengeance such as ours? Does God do role reversals? Play games?

When Jesus healed someone, he apparently was often heard to say, "Go your way, your faith has made you whole," or something quite similar. The divine power to heal and to create—to create *out of our sinful condition* as well as *out of nothing*—is infinitely *ever present*. No withdrawal there.

But the infinite love of God is still not "enough." The *faith* and *will* of the recipient is *also* decisive. We *must do* something crucial. We must believe and deeply receive both the covenant of creation and the totality of redemptive life. Waiting around for God to give us the grace is serious spiritual sloth.

God is *ever* faithful to us. We are the only question mark, the only *maybe*, the only persons doing the hiding. By wondering whether God has withdrawn from us, we are *unconsciously* shrouding, even from ourselves, *our hiding* from God.

Again, we are prompted to conclude that the first act of creation had to be *interpersonal*. At that timeless moment, God truly showed unlimited love and unlimited power to be intimate with us; and *we* must have somehow dis-graced ourselves.

According to Christian perspective, God said, in effect, "Be—and be *with* Us—the unique being We are giving you to be."

But we received with less than immediate and *full* gratitude God's offer of sharing: in being and in consummate friendship. We—not God—created thereby the dependency that massively abounds in all our relationships. We—not God—created the blame chain that binds us. We—not God—caused the very ground, into which the tree of the knowledge of good and evil was planted. We now live the life of this tree.

Despite our self-abased condition, God's infinite love has provided the potential for recovery. By the complex processes of earthly life, we can cultivate some of our response to the gift of redemption. We can begin to come up, out of hiding, and walk toward the Light.

Hiding Our Lost Independence

One thing ought to be clear to believers: when God says BE, *all is done*. All that can be *is*. The new being *is*—absolutely, entirely, and in freedom. Every bit of relativity and partiality, caused by freely created persons imperfectly receiving their own being, is included within this absolute act of God. Not as "part" of the act, but as the necessarily free response of the creature *to* the act, from *within* the act itself. (To be *within* the act of God is *not at all* to be *part* of it.)

The new outlook on creation emphasizes the difference between God's way of causing and our ways. God is not an insecure creator, who must continuously prop us up in being, lest we fail to *be* what

Chapter 14   What Happened to Freedom?

God *gave* us to be: a *being* of *our own*. While the *giving* act of God is infinite, the "*gift* act" that we *are* is not an "infinity" or "infinite being" of our own. But it is our own finite *be*-ing that we *do*, well or not so well, "for sure and forever."

Thanks to God, this be-ing that each one *is*, *once in being*, has no *need* of God *in order to do its being*. All power of being and of receptivity is gifted unconditionally.

If a given being does not receive completely the *gift* of being—its very own self—then this creature *is* in total need of God *in order to be saved from self-destruction*. Think of Adam and Eve. Hiding from God after their fall in Eden, they provide but a significant *symptom* of the concealment of *being*. All of us originative sinners are self-constrained to carry out this suppression.

Not so with God. God does not play games. How could infinite Being do any Self-concealment? God has "nowhere to hide." God is everywhere. We are the ones doing the hiding.

We can play games with ourselves and call it God. In one of these games, we obscure *from ourselves* the *difference* between the two creations: the absolute, intimately celebrational one and the relative, redemptively healing one.

A common way *to keep ourselves in the dark about our darkness* is to *think* that finite beings could *not* really *know* the infinite. But how can we *not* know the infinite, however confusedly?

We *inevitably* know the infinite source of finite being. We know the cause right within the effect. We know infinite being right within our finite being itself. What we find most difficult to distinguish is where the depth of our finite being differs from the actuality of the infinitely causing God.

We do not know merely "*that* God exists," as many theists seem to hold. We do not know merely *the fact that* God is. We know the living Divinity.

We do not know God, however, in any grasping sort of way. We know by a "touching" kind of intellection—a murky intuition of the living God. *That* is *true* knowledge, even if far from full.

This knowledge is largely unconscious and preconscious, resulting from our defective protoconscious knowing of God, at the moment of primal creation. Our signature act of freedom was *necessarily* done by our purely active intellect (agent intellect) and by our purely active will (agent will). Done *badly*.

Even now, after the crash while in the process of recovery, our intellect is a bit like a hand. A hand normally cannot get a hold on a wall; but it can touch the wall and be sensitized to the surface of the wall. Similarly, our intellect cannot give us any grasping knowledge of God, but it does allow us to "feel" (not grasp) the Being of God who is infinitely beyond any *grasp*.

Some of us acknowledge that, whenever we know *anything*, we are really touching and feeling God, however obscurely that may be. Others continue their denial. In varying degrees, we repress our *actual knowing* of infinite being and the *degree* to which we know.

Because of our prejudice about what constitutes true knowledge for us—namely, that it must be the quite graspable kind that we can examine and get a handle on—we overlook the obvious. We *know* God now. But we are blocking ourselves from recognizing that it is so, since we would then have to reckon with the depths of the *origin* of *our* sin—not only the sin of Adam and Eve.

We are called to acknowledge some deeper conditions within our relationship with God. God is the independent *infinite* Being who gives to created persons independent *finite* being. God's very act of creating stands infinitely free and freeing. God also gifts—without conditions—*being* to creatures of different kinds of personhood. *God is infinitely independent Being creating finitely independent persons.*

But *we earthly humans* are now not *only finite* persons; we are self-*defective* ones. When we create things, we necessarily render the effect, the "creature," dependent upon us, even though it goes on existing without our "support."

One reason that the effect is dependent on us is that we are *not* causing something to be "out of nothing," but out of something. As causes, we always have "something" we use in order to fashion our effects. In order to cause, we depend on that "something." And *our* "creatures" or effects also depend on that "something."

A writer of a letter depends on the instruments—the pen or pencil or computer—and on the material or stuff (the ink and paper) out of

Chapter 14   What Happened to Freedom?   153

which the letter is fashioned. But even the letter itself, the "creation" or effect of the writer, depends not simply on the writer as agent and on the matter or stuff. The letter depends also on the things used by the writer, such as the pen or pencil by means of which it is written, and so forth.

In the *defective* kind of finite causing that we do, both we (the agent causes) and all our effects are dependent on something *other*. We depend necessarily both on the matter or stuff, out of which the effects are made, and on the instruments by which we fashion them. We are preeminently *other*-dependent.

In contrast, as the infinite Cause of *being*, God is infinitely free of anything at all that would render God dependent. And the created person—the effect of God's creation—is also *not* dependent on anything. God is neither a "something" out of which we created persons come, nor an instrument of any kind. We do not depend on God as some "Being Stuff," nor as some "Being Instrument."

At the moment of their absolute origin, created persons are called to be faithful to the *independent* being that each receives. At that moment, they are *free* to be free and to exercise their independence perfectly by being faithful to their *independent* being. But they are also *able* to exercise their independence badly by being unfaithful—unfaithful to their independence-*with* God.

Even now, consequent upon sin—both originative and original—we fallen humans do *not* depend on God in order to be "held in being." But we *are* definitely dependent in order to recover and to return *effectively* to the independent being we were called to be originatively. *We are now both independent and dependent with respect to God. We are called to be no longer dependent at all, but simply independent-with God.*

If we had received fully our own being, we would not be, in any way, a part of God. We would be simply finite beings—fully *united* with God. We would be truly God-*like,* without in any way being God.

The idea of human beings as a part of God is deeply ingrained in millions of people, East and West. This intrinsic dependence is claimed by pantheism and by those theories that regard creation as a *necessary* emanation from God.

In general, common to virtually all believers, there is a conception of the created person as *essentially dependent* on God for being-at-all. The common confusion includes our thinking supinely that the necessary *relationship* of created persons to God is the same as a necessary *dependency*.

The notion of *essential dependence* on God, however, projects onto ultimate reality the obvious dependence we have on God for life in this world. But we should consider whether we might not be intuiting something about our originative creation. We could be unconsciously reacting to the *ecstatically intimate* relationship that creation "out of nothing" could have entailed.

Besides, we might be confusing complete *relationship* with the notion of complete *dependency. We* definitely caused the complete *dependency*, but God caused the *complete relationship*. And we ought to acknowledge it, consciously, if possible.

True intimacy has nothing to do with dependency and everything to do with relationship and union. Our self-alienation prompts us to obscure the difference.

Inasmuch as we are sinners in this sin-disruptive world, we are massively lacking in intimacy with God and we *thereby depend* on God's grace for our becoming (our be-*coming*) and our destiny. Even so, we *also* depend (*independently*) on ourselves, especially for our final destiny. God's grace cannot force us to be holy, just, and loving. We either *do* our own *yes*-saying independently or it does not get done—ever. The infinite power and grace of God *can be refused* by the *essentially free will* of the created person.

At the moment of creation *out of nothing*, we had the opportunity to know immediately all that we could possibly know—*and to love* all that we know. Our *powers* to know and love were purely active. We were face-to-face with God far more than Moses ever was on earth. We were beholding God in being and in truth, *though not in glory*. We had the opportunity to *love* God, ourselves, and all others to the fullness of our finite powers. By our own unique, God-gifted ways we could have *thereby* entered the *eternal glory of God*.

Since there could be neither a *subject matter* of creation nor any instrument involved, there was *no dependence whatsoever*. The idea of a free and perfect creature's dependency on God for *being* comes from failure to realize the difference between the reception of being

Chapter 14   What Happened to Freedom? 155

as done by perfectly sinless creatures, and the reception of being as done by sinning ones—sinning in that very reception itself.

We fail to recognize that our *initiating* sin has caused *all* of our dependency. And this same sin with all its consequences makes us think that the dependency is *natural, essential, and necessary*. We are self-duped.

We keep ourselves *distanced from God*—hiding—by thinking that God could not possibly give us beings that are *not* dependent on the divine Being. *That* is playing hide and seek *with ourselves*. We hide from who we are in the divine sight, and then we claim to be seeking God, who *could* not hide. What a game!

Projecting Our Dependency and Egocentricity

Moreover, our present manner of knowing involves premises and conclusions that naturally *depend* on one another. *This* dependency is the natural "business of logic." One item of knowledge depends on another within our minds and we reason to conclusions by steps of thinking that depend on one another. So, we inevitably project *unconsciously* onto "the way things are" this curious necessity of dependence (*logical* necessity) that is largely involved in our present *redemptively* human manner of knowing.

We readily substitute logical necessity for the *beingful*—strictly ontological—freedom of the God-creature relationship that we once knew. Method trumps content, because we are hanging on to our primordial sin against the freedom of being.

We suppose things *are,* or have to be, the way *we* have to *think* they are. But the dependencies inherent in logic result from the *fall* of knowing, not from the *all* of being.

Tragically, in the theist tradition, we are inclined to think like the following. God granted being *first*. Then eventually we use our gift-being that we "got from God" in order to *act*. Our *acts* are ours to do, but *our being is not ours to do*.

We think we do not "do" our being, but *acquire* it or *have* it *in order to* do or act, freely or unfreely.

But this way of thinking conveniently overlooks the *infinite* power of God to gift us with *our own* be-ing. This be-ing we *alone* can *do*, from the non-durational moment that we receive it.

At that non-temporal, beingful moment, there is not "first this, then that." There is simply "now this, *and also* that." Now there is this act of being, *and also its own response by itself to itself and to all others.*

Originatively, I *am* my act of being *which is my doing*—mine to do. You *are* your act of being *which is your doing*—yours to do. Not your doing as causing your being to be, but your doing as *receiving* and giving to yourself and all others, the "world of you."

God is infinitely able to create *pure acts of finite being*—created persons. These acts of being are acts of the *person-beings* so gifted. They are not somehow acts of God, but acts of the recipients alone. The receivers can finitely create right from within themselves either union or disunion with God—either heaven or hell—or they can effectively put themselves into the purgatory we are now suffering.

Only within empirical, material reality does the cause-and-effect relationship entail the priority of substance over activity. But our passivity-inclined mentality thinks instinctively like this: "You've got to *get* something before you can do anything with it or about it. That's only logical."

Yet, in trans-temporal realities, substances and their activities are "simultaneous." To *be* a certain created person is to *do* the whole being of that person. To think that God is even doing the least "part of it" is to be pantheistic.

There is, of course, what has been termed an "ontological priority" of being over doing. But that perspective stems largely from our knowing of temporal and functional being and our fixation on it.

With respect to the unique doing that is our *being*, that which is ontologically prior is the creation-act of *God* that gifts us to be. But *that* act—the creation act of *God*—is not at all some "part" of the creature. The gifting act of God (the creating act) is *not* the being-act that the created one *is*. The giving is not the gift, even though the giving itself (the creating act of God) is *also* a gift of a different (interpersonal) sort.

What is *of* the creature—indeed the whole of the creature—is the act of *created* being that the finite person *is and is gifted to be*. Each one *is* his or her act of be-ing. This act or actuality is wholly the reality of the created person himself or herself—and not at all an "act of God." We must get our own pantheistic hooks out of it, and stop trying to drag God into our own predicament of flawed being that has been caused by how we *received* and *are doing* the act of be-ing that we *are*.

The *act of God* is the creation-act that is responsible for *gifting* us with *being*. *Our* being, not any other being. God's act cannot do or be the act of the *gift* itself.

Of course, God is a gift to us, too. But God is not the gift that we are to ourselves, which God creates for us. God is the gift that we *unite with* by our own *willing* to be the "*gifted* one." We have not, however, been fully willing—originatively or otherwise.

The finite person did not create self at all…out of "nothing." The person is self-created out of *something*—specifically out of the free, finite, perfect gift of *being* that this person *is*. In receiving the gift of be-ing, this person creates self out of self—out of that wondrous gift of God known as his or her very *being*.

But our originative sin heavily tends to block us from conceiving any relationship that is truly free. Not free *for*, nor free *from*, nor free *of*, and so forth. Just free, or free-*with*. Among other things, sin is primarily a violation of true *beingful* freedom.

Failing to Love Freedom

God's prodigality in gifting all created persons with their full and perfect "inheritance" of finite goodness and freedom does beg better understanding. We have acted like alienated children: *both* prodigal children, squandering our inheritance, *and* self-righteous children, jealous of God's generosity in creation and redemption. We have *self*-centeredly indulged in our perfect freedom at creation and now we refuse to re-exercise fully that freedom in love toward God and one another.

We have failed the gift of freedom. And now our thinking seems to demand that we created persons are *either* independent of God *or* dependent on God.

Atheistic and agnostic people attempt to regard themselves as *independent of* (or *from*) God, either because they think that there is no God or that there might not be. Theists often reactively regard themselves as "possessions" of God who desires their complete dependence for being and doing. By ideas of conformity and divine possessiveness, these theists conceal from themselves the freedom of a *pure relationship of union with* God.

Moreover, theistic believers who do not even recognize their own radical complicity in the *origin* of evil are inclined "naturally" to think that their dependency on God for redemption is the *same* as their relationship to God in creation. Ignoring that their dependency must have been self-wrought, they contemplate this dependency and project it upon God. They then regard this depending as coming from a universal law of causality, not only in the redemptive world of creation *out of something*, but also in the absolute realm of creation *out of nothing*—if they were even to recognize such a world as distinct.

The truth is that, at the moment of originative creation, those free human creatures who attempted to establish some independence *from* God showed an unwillingness to be fully *independent-with* God. Paradoxically they caused a *real dependence on* God. This real dependency, then, set up a corresponding need for liberation from self-inflicted intransigence and confusion.

The dependence and the need for redemption were created by the sinning creatures right in the midst of receiving God's absolute gift of *independence* and freedom-to-be. The gift of independence can never be taken away; it can only be fulfilled or self-frustrated.

We remain independently finite *in essence*. But we are now, on account of partial denial, *also dependently* independent *by nature*. Our *nature* no longer flows coherently from our *essence*. As the disposition of our essence to act, this nature was twisted by our first free act.

Other created persons, however—the good angels, for instance—who fully (sinlessly) received their being from the absolutely loving Friend of Being are wholly like that Friend. They are *independent with* that Friend, *not independent from* that Friend. These creatures were gifted with their independent being; and they fully received the gift. God co-creates with them fully mutual intimacy.

Our reactionary concepts of our "independence from" and of our "dependence on" blind us from appreciating our own potential for this ecstatic union of shared independence.

Chapter 14   What Happened to Freedom?

One might wonder how we fallen creatures could have been so stupid. Why did we not "catch on straight away" that our original *hesitation to be* would necessarily inflict on us such pain, separation, desperation, and threat of everlasting damnation? In any case, at the moment of creation "out of nothing," we were *totally* free to be fully who we *cared* to be.

We were not, as we are now, so egocentric in our concern not to hurt *ourselves*—whatever else is done to others and "to God." But, with the perfect resources of creative finite freedom, we were quite able either to love immediately and fully forever or to cause the mess in which we are now self-immersed. We did sabotage our freedom and created the very *capacity* for the *repression of being*, at which we are now so adept.

We are self-skewed toward pragmatic self-centeredness. In space and time, we are so often motivated to choose God "for our sake"—for what we can "get out of it." But, at the first, non-spatiotemporal moment of creation, our *ability* to be motivated was quite pure and unspoiled. What this protoconscious moment "was" is, strictly speaking, unimaginable. But it *is* intelligible or understandable to knowers who are willing to drop their defenses for awhile.

We have to try to hold our present, jaundiced motivations in check while we surmise what it must have been to act freely in the moment of the divine love initiative. We ought to challenge the very attitude that prompts us even to ask the question about why we were so stupid—not to mention so uncaring. Asking that kind of question shows how far we are from our lost absolute freedom and is itself a symptom of our very first, free-act of *self-seeking* disposition toward being-at-all.

The Scene of the Lost Freedom and Friendship

In order to understand our predicament better, we might consider a scenario of divine creation. How might God, in the covenant of creation, see reality differently from the way we do?

As we are being created, in that strictly non-durational moment where all happens at once in perfect order and freedom, we can conceive of God (or each Person) saying:

"Be who and what you are. I give you to yourself to *be* yourself—to be the way I am creating you. You are given to be fully yourself, without reserve. By this very being I am giving you to *be*, say *yes*, fully and independently (on your own). Then you and I will be completely intimate friends forever. You will be you, and I will be I, sharing our being with each other.

"Once you *are* and are *you*, you are a free and independent being. I can never withdraw my gift of being, and you will not be able to not-be. What you *do* with your being is *fully* your own *will*.

"Your independence is naturally limited: you are not able to create other beings 'out of nothing,' as I can. But, even as you are, you can create *out of yourself* a complete and total response to the gift of being-yourself.

"It is true that, if I had not created you, you would not be. But this does not mean that you are necessarily dependent on me. I give you an independent being—like me in being independent, but finitely so. My giving is free and unqualified. My giving is my unlimited love.

"If, however, you do not say with gratitude, 'Yes, I will be *fully* my finite self,' you will cause yourself to be dependent on me: not my first intention for you. By faltering and stumbling, by saying *maybe*, you will gravely distort your likeness to my being. I am Who am. There is no shadow of *may*-be in me.

"So, if you hesitate and say any degree of *maybe*, that will be your own independent *will*. You will be dropping the gift. With all others who similarly fail, you will cause cosmic matter to exist, with its time and space, wherein you will fall, to be eventually conceived and rooted *there*.

"You will then have to struggle, suffer pain and anxiety, and inevitably die. You will have cast yourself out of your own being, right from within your being. You will find yourself in a condition of poverty—poor in who you are, as well as in your *awareness* of who you are.

"If you then hope for recovery and healing, you will definitely have to *depend* on me. My unlimited love will be there for your reception and healing. But you will then still have to *receive* the grace of my love, finally, with an independent *yes*, not a *maybe*.

"Only if you would repent and would receive my love, *freely and independently willing your dependence on me*, would you be able to

Chapter 14   What Happened to Freedom?

recover your fresh, natural and functional, independence. Only then could we be fully intimate friends as I intend us to be.

"See what you would lose in saying *maybe*. Those who say fully *yes* would be completely with me in communion of totally intimate freedom and love. We would share mutual independence in beingful bliss forever, just as we are—as I am infinitely and as these, your companion created persons, would be finitely and fully. This *shared* independence is possible *both* because of *my* infinite perfection *and* because of *their* full reception of the independent perfection with which I have *unconditionally* gifted them."

Friendship with God and with Others

Happiness transcends the polar opposition between independence-from God and dependence-on God. Perfect happiness is the union of *shared* independence-with God.

There are two main ways that we can shut ourselves out from full communion with God. Either we determine ourselves to become independent *from* God or we *insist* that we ourselves must be *forever dependent on* God. In contrast, shared independence *with* God—infinite Being sharing with finite being, and finite being sharing with infinite Being—is the supreme condition of genuine happiness for finite being.

The ultimate joy of finite persons is a state similar to what many Christians understand as God's Trinitarian joy. The Christian belief is that there is one God: one divine Nature of three Persons. These Persons are mutually *independent*, even though the second Person is infinitely begotten by the first, and even as the Spirit, the third Person, proceeds infinitely therefrom. Each Person is essentially divine, God of very God: independent *with*—not independent of or from—the Others. Each Person enjoys the Others through infinitely *shared* independence.

Created persons, of course, are not of a divine nature. Yet, they are like God in being persons. They are beings with the power to know *who* is and *what* is, and the power to love God, themselves, and all other beings. As knowers and lovers of all being, created persons are originally meant to be, in a finite way, mutually independent: the better to be *friends* of God and of one another.

But multitudes have lost both the freedom (independence) and the friendship. We who are *maybe*-sayers have *refused* to receive *fully* our being—thereby creating chaos within and around us, dropping ourselves into the dependencies of the crashed creation. Much of our functional power to share independently with one another and with God has been lost.

If we had not fallen, we would *be,* and *be ourselves,* without fixations of any kind. We would not be seduced by ourselves, and so would not be hung up on having God make us whole. We would be independent *with* God, without even knowing (*experiencing*) how it is to be independent *from* God or how it is to be dependent *on* God.

As it is now, who can readily conceive anything that is created independent and in freedom-with-God? We project onto God our own self-centric notions of how we would create if *we* were God.

We would, of course, create things dependent on ourselves. So, we would think this is the way God should give being: on condition that the being obey its nature, otherwise it should not be at all. We tend to think like tiny tyrants.

Who can conceive of creating anything *essentially inferior* to us that would have the *ability to defy us*? Our automobiles, books, TV sets, and other "creations" cannot do so, though they might not always work the way we would demand. (We do not, incidentally, *create* our offspring; nor are they *essentially inferior* to us—and indeed they *can* defy us. Plants and animals *are* essentially inferior to us, but we do not *create* them.)

Having originatively deformed our own freedom, we now find it difficult to see what real freedom is. If *we* were God, we would not let any creature "get out of hand." In so thinking, we "reveal" our own primordial wish that God be like us—or that we become like *our own idea* of God.

A total remedy is needed. We must admit to having committed a first, originating sin that is influencing us here and now *profoundly from within*. Otherwise, the prospect for our coming to be *like* God, as God *is*, will not be seen. Our blindness will make it impossible to see how God originally intended us to be and how we are still called to become like God in *shared independence* of being.

Chapter 14 What Happened to Freedom?

Somehow, we must come to acknowledge that *we independently* frustrated our *naturally* shareable independence in being, even while necessarily retaining our *essential* independence in being. We truly damaged our *nature*—the disposition of our essence toward activity. But our God-gifted *essence* remains: a unique and *perfect* ability to love and to share independently-*with* God.

Even if we do not know how to utter words about it or to form the words, we need to *repent profoundly* at the core level of our *being*—of our minds and hearts. Despite any confusion about the truth of "the details," we ought to be open to the fullest extent of our *be*-ing, here and now. Otherwise, that shareable independence and freedom of nature, and of our *consummate ability to love*—the basis of our friendship with God—could become permanently lost.

Part IV Hope for Final Intimacy

Chapter 15

Recovering

"Repent, repent." We hear the cry of the prophets.

But we might still wonder. Repent of what? Stealing a penny from a playmate at age six? Was that a *first personal* sin?

Our reflections so far would indicate a need for repenting of far more than that. Even children should be profoundly sorrowful over stealing—stealing from their *original* relationship with God. That originative theft from God is "ageless." It was not done in *any* time or space.

In fact, we were not tempted at all. Only goodness abounded. And no one else could have managed to cause our *originative* self-deprivation "for us"—not even our first parents. In the originative creation (ex nihilo), God was our *only* parent.

We are at present a self-stricken community of human beings. Our *basic common* recovery—our *redemption*—has entirely depended on God's gift of restoration. The recovery of individuals and peoples who are lost in sin has been already celebrated in Sacred Scripture and in communal religious practices.

But *personal* recovery, our *salvation*, not simply our redemption, depends on us, as well as on God's infinitely loving activity. This recovery includes our *willingness* to understand, *to the best of our ability*, what *really caused* our earthly condition, and to repent *as fully as we can*.

We are now reaching for our absolute origin. But how can we begin to understand God's creating us "out of nothing"? We cannot recall any "experience" of being created. Nor can we relate directly with God's act in itself. After all, who can create "out of nothing" even a speck of dust?

But we can at least *try* to know the act of God. And by examining the contents of both Faith and reason, we can actually participate—however generally—in *knowing* the act of *being created*, that is, our act of receiving creation. This act of receptivity at the moment of creation out of nothing is not at all the same as the creating act of God by which it *is*. But it is done by us in the same instant. We can know it spiritually, even though we cannot remember it.

We can endeavor to understand things of our common experience, including the workings of natural substances and the interactions of people. Also, in prayer as well as reflection, we can try to reach beyond our present limitations and deficiencies of mind and heart. We thereby begin to reach out to God our Savior.

But our attempts do not go strictly "beyond us." We are extending ourselves to a being who is within us, yet who is other-than-we. We try to unite with the being who is *unlimited*, and thus able to be *within* us, without being limited *by* us. We might be said to *unhide* ourselves from God by unhiding ourselves from ourselves.

Moreover, God is within us by our being totally within God—by the structure of our being.

Even so, we still seem to be "far distant" from our Creator and our creation "out of nothing." We are almost required to take creation-out-of-nothing for granted. It is so *immediate*.

But that should not be surprising. One of our major occupations in life seems to include taking people and good things for granted. Our practical minds tend to short-circuit the meaning of *be*-ing and to focus merely on the "what" of things.

What is this? *What* is that? As long as we can get it into a category (a *what*), we tend to think we know something—or *someone*.

But we systematically overlook the mystery of *why* this person or thing *is* and is *this way*. We miss out on seeing how differently anyone or anything can be understood when known *as more than* such-and-such a *kind* of being, say, a *human* being or a *vegetative* being—as an item in a category.

We also know that each *personal* being *is* quite dynamic in *be*-ing. Everyone comes with a history and destiny far greater than we can see clearly at this point in our development and recovery.

Trying to Know Our Being

What then does it mean to be, to be-at-all—to be, rather than *not* be? One practical way to think about being-at-all might be to take an imaginary trip. Try to think of yourself as *not being*. No thoughts. No feelings. No awareness. No potential. Nothing.

You can make enthusiastic attempts to imagine and to conceive this nothingness. But no matter how strenuously you try, you cannot really think yourself "out of being." After all, here you are.

Yet your *being* cannot be "experienced." Perhaps your heartbeat or your headache can. But your *being* is *known* with certainty, *despite* its not being strictly "experienced."

To *be* is radically other than *not* to be. The trip is finished almost before it begins. Being-at-all is your greatest gift, no matter *what kind* of human person you are—no matter how brilliant or generous or popular.

You might be good at walk-ing, talk-ing, breath-ing, and think-ing. But your most important activity is the activity of *be*-ing. *Be*-ing is an *act*—an *act*-ing.

How well are you *doing* your act of *be*-ing? *That* doing—that *loving*—is far more important than all your other acts combined. So, when someone comes up to you asking, "How are you doing?" they might be more caring than you suspect. They could be inquiring subconsciously about your *be*-ing.

Another way to see the impact of *being* is to notice how lacking in gratitude we are. I might wonder: Did I ever, directly and seriously, thank God for creating me? Not simply for redeeming me. If I have only half-heartedly thanked God for bringing me into *being*, then I have not fully *received* this supreme gift. In the midst of all my religious talk, I might be avoiding it.

Did I ever fully receive the *gift* of my being? If it is possible to do so in this life, purely and profoundly, surely it can happen only in the deepest forms of prayer.

And if I do not receive well my own *being*, how can I respond well to anyone else in this *receiving* way? How can I see another person as a *being*—as a miracle too great to comprehend?

That would bring us then to another imaginary trip. We can try to imagine, as *not being at all*, the person in this world whom we love most richly. When I try, I seek to imagine no smiles, no embraces, no sharing. No presence. Nothing.

But there she is. She *is*. And what a difference my *awareness* of her *being* could make in my relationship with her. If only I were much less dull, dense, and ungrateful by normal inclination, the difference would be more than astounding. Even her death could not take her *be*-ing away from me.

Perhaps, such imaginary trips should become regular occurrences. Everyone I meet ought to be fully received—loved in his or her unique activity of *be*-ing. What is the meaning of our existence in this world if it does not include efforts like these—efforts to know ourselves and one another as *being*? *Really* being.

To Receive or Not to Receive

Appreciating my being-at-all is not an ordinary occupation. Most of the time, I am doing things that require little contemplation. Day after day, I go along living out my subconscious *may*be.

I live rather tentatively, not giving my whole heart in any of my actions. I do my "have to do's" and "want to do's" in the branches of my life and never really get into my roots, where my response to *being* most effectively is occurring.

Despite my weak awareness of it, my root response to *be*-ing is empowering all that I am and do. Even though it is almost totally unconscious, lurking under my consciousness, this partial response to being is the activity of all my activities. My response to being is done by my *activity* of *be*-ing. I respond to my being by *be*-ing.

At the root level of my freedom, I am *be*-ing my *being*. I am *doing* my *being*. After all, there is no way that God can do it *for* me...and still be God. Or, at least, *I* would then not *be*.

Only *I* am doing my be-ing. And I am doing this most momentous of all my activities either well or poorly. How well or poorly is most difficult to discern. But observations can be made.

Chapter 15   Recovering

In my usual attitude of normal consciousness, I am largely passive, dependent, and dysfunctional as a *personal* creature of God. Even if my activities bring success and are applauded by others I can be doing my activity of *be-ing* rather badly.

My originative failure to receive fully the *gift* of being has created the basic passivity *within* my matter-and-form (my essence). This passive way of being is commonly called "body and soul."

Similarly, my present degree of passivity is warping my whole life and all my relationships. Recovering my original *gift* of being is impossible without much more active receiving of the *gift* and of the *Giver*. I need to take my being for *gifted*, not for granted.

Even now, whenever I stop and try to receive well the *gift* of being, everything shifts from the passive toward the active. I accept more responsibility for who I am, and for how I respond to whatever happens. I hold myself and others accountable for the good and bad things we do to affect one another. I do not blame others for the predicaments I find myself within, even when these others seem to have had a big hand in landing me there.

I hold myself especially accountable—personally responsible—for even *being in this world* where my own and others' actions and attitudes can help or hurt me. I recognize my basic cosmic condition as deriving from some kind of root-problem with myself.

And when I become tuned to my *be*-ing activity, I have more confidence in the bare truth that is revealed constantly. I believe more effectively that my present condition of confinement to the cosmos is entirely a matter of mercy, as well as of justice.

Here and now, I am into recovery from originatively bypassing complete union with God. I suffer cosmic and spiritual captivity, while I work on my problems. I try to make things better. Yet, in the midst of my difficulties and trials, one thing is critical: my *attitude* toward them.

Am I outraged about the way certain people relate to me or to other human persons? Am I resentful about how God seems to be absent or uncaring? And do I want change to occur in other people and in adverse conditions, rather than in myself?

My sluggish *unwillingness* to become fully receptive to *whatever* happens keeps my *be*-ing heavy and self-frustrating.

Only a receptive attitude can make authentic change possible. *My* receptive attitude. So, I have to admit that I am suffering from a self-affliction of profound proportions. I am challenged to acknowledge that I cannot heal myself without the care of the divine Healer.

What I have to do is not so much to give as to *receive*. While it is true that in giving we receive, it is also true that only in *actually receiving* are we really *able* to give.

Receiving is not at all the same as acquiring. And giving is not just producing, making, or responding. Like true giving, receiving is *other*-centered (Gifter-centered), not *self*-centered.

Authentic *be*-ing is executed by receiving in a giving way and by giving in a receiving way. The basic attitude with which I ought to do everything is both givingly receiving and receivingly giving.

A prime example is my listening and speaking as activities quite different from merely hearing and delivering the message. I do not simply hear—or "wait out"—the words of someone speaking to me. I actually receive them actively by giving myself, and by being present to the speaker.

And when it is my turn to speak, I speak listeningly, that is, I give or say words in a manner that is *receiving*: open to further dialogue, correction, and whatever way my partner might respond. I am, so to speak, my own best listener.

My attitude becomes authentic insofar as I am habitually givingly-receiving and receivingly-giving: givingly receiving the *being* of others and receivingly (respectfully) giving myself to them and their concerns. I speak listeningly; and I listen givingly.

Part of my *root*-problem is that I "act out" so often and "act in" rather sporadically. I tend to speak before I know or even think I know. I tend to give advice and try to solve problems—my own and others'—without taking sufficiently into account what is involved. I engage in impulse buying, impulse reading, impulse TV-viewing, impulse chatter.

This "acting out" seems to be active, but so much of it is just a *reaction* of my largely passive self to outside stimuli. It enables me to escape for awhile the incredible passivity and boredom that is mine, especially down deep.

Chapter 15   Recovering

Perhaps surprisingly, the reverse attitude, a kind of "acting in," can be compatible with diverse overt actions. But this "acting in" is a special inward activity, a pivotal attitude. More specifically, it is an "acting *with*-in."

I am most active when I *receive* who I am, as well as when I *receive* whatever is happening to me—both the good and the bad. Receiving means *actively, not passively, letting something be as it is*. I try *not* to make it other than it is before I am in touch with its *being* and its *kind* of being.

Even the reality of evil should be received as it is, before being counter-acted. If I suddenly feel sharp pain in my chest, I am called to declare, at least quickly, a fully receptive *yes* to the misery before taking remedies.

This "acting within" of receptivity is not introspective. It is not a withdrawal. It is really a heightened communion with the being of anything that is. The "acting within" of receptivity connects me—even reunites me—with the truth of myself and of all others. Then my outward actions can become genuinely *act*-ive. They can be gifts to my neighbors and to myself.

By saying to my Creator, "I receive"—instead of going passive and reactive—I can begin to recover from my root-reluctance about *be*-ing my *being*. I can begin to grow toward my original splendor as an image and likeness of *I am Who am Who is Love*. I can actively involve myself in the space-time process of *returning to the original creation through the redemptive creation*. I can live within the joy of being redeemed.

The Redemptive Paradox

Redemption, however, within the space-time world is a paradox, a mystery of blended meanings. Deeper meaning of what it is to be receptive in this world will come from acknowledging *both* the absolute, originative creation *and* the supplemental, redemptive creation. Then these creations can be seen as fully continuous, yet fundamentally different, endeavors of God.

Jesus once told a parable about a withered fig tree in a vineyard. The owner remarked how he had given the unproductive tree its opportunity and expressed his desire to cut it down, since it was fruitless. But his gardener bargained for one more year. He said that he would attend to it, and if no good results were forthcoming even then, that they could cut it down (*Luke* 13: 6-9).

While Jesus might not have meant it directly, this parable could apply to the two creations. We badly *received* our first creation—the one that is "out of nothing." As a result, we became barren, self-withered persons, not really giving perfect love to our infinitely perfect Creator. We were presented, however, with one extended opportunity "to bear fruit" here in the cosmic world—in creation *ex aliquo* (redemptive creation)—where "our case" could gain special attention and religious cultivation.

The deeper, preconscious meaning of this parable—the spiritually unconscious meaning—might include various dimensions. But one thing ought to be quite certain. According to the "new worldview for theists," God's primal creation involves beings who are *persons*—and *only* persons. These persons include *human* persons in a form that is immensely different from what we consciously know now. Originative creatures were perfect persons. No one was created who was even slightly imperfect, or even "temporarily" so.

The original creation did not begin with the cosmos, where every material creature is inherently imperfect. This temporal world where all creatures become involved with passive matter is a secondary, derivative, "second chance" world.

God causes the heavens and the earth, the fish and the birds, and so forth. And this activity can be seen as God creating a ministerial world. God creates the multitudinous particles, chemicals, plants, and animals out of the passive reactive energy, emanating from our originative *maybes*.

This world's coming into *being* was necessitated by the originative self-affliction done by innumerable human persons. But its purpose is to minister actively to the recovery of *maybe*-saying persons.

In other words, the space-time universe is part of a *maybe*-world—redemptive, salvific, but *not* original. We are all trying to "swim" here in the "backwaters" of the originative creation.

So, if we are going to be redeemed and effectively saved from "drowning" in our own *existence*, we will be involved in both a horizontal process and a vertical moment of decision.

Chapter 15   Recovering

On the one hand, the growth and development of *sub-personal* creatures in the space-time world, leading into and through the human, is the "horizontal" process. On the other hand, our *personal* decision to accept the Redeemer and receive the truth about who we are and who we are not—to acknowledge and to repent—is the "vertical" moment of decision.

The horizontal process was caused by the "crash." The calamity was far more than a "fall." Vast subhuman energy was emitted as a result of the originative, intrinsic self-collisions. This energy and its partial potential for aiding *human* recovery remained within the imperfect, developing, *subhuman* creation. Thereby the reactively developing cosmos served to prepare a place that would minister to the healing of suffering-recovering human persons—as they came individually to *ex-ist* at some point in space and time.

Within the immense ministerial process, these sufferers would have to decide. Person by person, they would determine whether their *yes-no* condition would become, in them, finally a *yes* or a *no*.

My life in this world, then, is my opportunity to repent of my *yes-no* condition. I am going through a redemptive and salvific process that calls for a decision to say either a final *yes* or a final *no* to the gift and to the Gifter.

But, even if I say a relatively decisive *yes* today, tomorrow is still coming. The testing continues. The depth of my sincerity today is tested by the challenges of tomorrow.

The process goes on. My *yes* today might not be there tomorrow. Other decisions can weaken and undo my *yes*. The process and the testing end only with my death. At that moment, my undercurrent choice about *be-ing* is finally decisive.

Of course, my previous choices influence critically that final choice. They include my originative (sin) choice as well as every morally significant choice that I have made after my conception many years ago.

On the one hand, where someone has constantly said *yes* in both ordinary and extraordinary moments of decision-making throughout many years, his or her final choice is most likely to be *yes*. But we are spiritually vulnerable persons, susceptible—because of our own originative sin—to the vicious attacks of malign spiritual forces. Under the personal pressure of Satan, someone could say *no* finally.

On the other hand, anyone who has led a life of vicious crime in this world and said thousands of *no's* would likely say *no* finally. Such a person could, of course, repent and say *yes*. But there is no "pressure" to do so. In aiding our freedom of will, God's unlimited love is a source; but it is never a force. The root of our being is an essential freedom *to receive fully, or not to receive, the presence of infinite Love.*

We are all facing the redemptive paradox of enduring, at once, both the temporal process and the decisive moment. The horizontal process and the vertical decision-making intersect each other. We dare not reduce this ongoing, crossing point to one or other of its components. That would be to reject the paradox, the cross.

And it can happen readily. We can say *no* quite effectively either by disparaging the (horizontal) world of the redemptive process or by denying ourselves free access to transcendent Being at every (vertical) moment. On the one hand, the self-righteous—whether 'spiritualists' of the 'old age' or the 'new age'—regard themselves as above, and exempt from, the ordinary practices of piety and of communal life. They disguise the horizontal dimension of religious life. On the other hand, the humanists of various kinds deny that they need anything other than the horizontal virtues of existence, free of any fancied transcendence.

Genuine wisdom, however, recognizes that carrying this cross of paradox is the main burden of our earthly *existence*. The mystery of opposites that is contained in both horizontal and vertical truths continuously beckons us right to the end of our lives.

The instant we become more passive and reactive than receptive, we drop the cross. But, even when we do, we can "take it up" again. As long as we live, we can become receptive anew.

And by *receiving* God's redeeming love, in our saying *yes* to the frustrating existence that we are carrying—especially to any conflict in our hearts—we *can* bear the redemptive paradox to the end.

No Recovery without Redemption

Redemption, like creation, is exclusively a *gift* of God. We were originally created *from nothing*. But now we must be brought out of

Chapter 15   Recovering

the slavery of *maybe*. And like creation, redemption is a gift to be fully *received*. In all our decisions and actions, we are responsible for receiving well or poorly *both* our being *and* our becoming—both our originative and our redemptive creations.

At the moment of originative creation, our semi-divorce from God was caused by a freely reticent response. But, along with our partial *no*, we did say a partial *yes*. Our hesitant *yes* gave us a *grounding for recovery*. The *yes* in our *maybe* ensured the *possibility* of our return to the gift of being as it was originally given.

Without the distinct activity of God our Redeemer, however, we could never even hope to attain the perfect gift we effectively, if partly, refused. The *no* in our *maybe* was suicidal. It thrust us into passivity—a condition "closer" to nothingness than to God.

Our present perception of even the greatest and holiest persons as being "highly active" in this temporal world can be misleading. The activity of these saintly ones on earth is minimal compared to the originative power to *act* or the *active potency* with which they and all of us were originally endowed. We are pitifully unaware of the extent of our present *self*-abasement. (We do not like to hear that. But, if God's first creative act caused an *immaculate creation*, it is an obvious implication.)

All of our egocentric withholdings from God's infinite Gifting Power and Love can be traced to the originative divorcement. By our *maybe*, we were self-ensconced in passive potency. Yet now we *refuse even to wonder whether* we were originatively gifted *solely* with the *active* potency to be and do—completely without any passive potency. We take it for granted that God created us with passive potencies—in a *maculate or stained-by-passivity* kind of creation. Theologians have sold short God's creation.

Moreover, we can hardly redeem ourselves from our passivity of being and from our opaque matter any more than we can create ourselves "out of nothing." We cannot repent and recover simply by saying *yes*. We require the redemptive action of the One whose *gift* of creative love our *maybe* had distrusted and tried to "re-structure."

As we are now, we may have good intentions. But we cannot get far. Our deep *yes-no* is influencing everything. This primal *maybe* causes contingencies to abound.

Maybe we will live long. Maybe we will die tomorrow. Maybe our friends will help us with this problem; maybe they won't. Maybe this is the right thing to say now; maybe it is not. We are in a *maybe* condition, no matter how aware and mature we become.

In the maelstrom of *maybe*-ism, however, we can still be in touch with the originative Power-Person(s) that gifted us to *be* and to *become*. Within our own continuing endeavors to *receive* the personal invitation from God who is Love, we can hope for recovery of being and of function.

Physical healers minister to our bodily wellbeing. Psychological counselors help to alleviate emotional and mental burdens. Spiritual ministers can offer direction and consolation. Various attempts to bring people into union with a common spiritual base can provide some progress toward wholeness.

Yet efforts of these kinds often presuppose the fiction of *ultimate* self-sufficiency. Thereby they compound the root problem of our not having received well our being "out of nothing"; and they can convey a false sense of spiritual and emotional growth.

Without our *doing* a *receiving* of the *divine* Redeemer, we remain fractured, fragmented, and alienated, despite our holistic talk and walk. Self-sufficient "recovery" is a grand illusion.

Also common, however, is a mistake opposite to that of the self-sufficient recoverers. Some traditional religious believers often dismiss pain and struggle simply as "God's will." They see the next world as a kind of spiritual security blanket. By their attitude they reveal an *efficiency notion* of repentance and recovery that makes God their "high class servant" who *gets* them to heaven without their own wholehearted participation in the horizontal and vertical processes.

But God is not a dispensable commodity. Nor a super-anaesthetic. Both the "self-sufficient recoverers" and those who are "expediently religious" require the same thing.

They need personal involvement in, and movement toward, the transcendent love of God. Both unrighteous and self-righteous must receive salvation by moving *out of self* and into the personhood of God, through the ministerial universe.

Chapter 15 Recovering

A Voice in the Wilderness

In book one of this trilogy, the story is told of Steven, a bright and promising college student, attending his 21st birthday party, given by friends. He found himself in jail the next morning trying to sober up.

As he was trying to come to his senses in jail, his friend appeared and told him why he was there. What she said was the last thing he wanted to hear: that drunkenly he had killed two people with his car the night before.

He could have said, "I didn't do it; someone else must have." Or he could have blamed the whole catastrophic incident on his friends who set up the drinking party.

But he did not protest. He tried to get further information about what really happened. He took the time to sober up; only then could he begin to understand adequately what he had freely done to get himself imprisoned.

He only vaguely recognized his friend, Maria, at the door of his cell. But he was open to the message: You messed up your first act of freedom as an adult human being.

Steven repented. He accepted full responsibility for what he had done and for its consequences. Profoundly sorry for the pain and suffering of the victims and their families, he did what he could, *for a lifetime*, to ease their suffering.

We can do like Steven. Even though we have a long history of selfishness and of failing in freedom, we can *convert*. We can even "act in" like the prodigal son, after having "acted out" for a long time. The prodigal one had become imprisoned by his own desires and willfulness. But he recalled how good it was to be in his father's house and how careless he had been. He then changed his attitude.

We can change and come to ourselves. Unlike the prodigal in the story, we might not be able to "recall" earlier conditions of life. We never actually lived within God-our-Father's beatitude. But we can surmise what we were called to be at the moment we were brought absolutely into being. We can begin, and continue, to "sober up."

We do not "call to mind" any first sin because, we might say, such a sin was too traumatic to our whole being to be "remembered." But we can still realize within our hearts that our own willfulness—now manifest in many desires—imprisons us. And we can eventually come to believe that God could not have allowed such a condition to be *forced* upon us, unless we brought it about—unless we somehow forced it upon ourselves.

God's infinite justice and goodness should not be mocked by our thinking that God creates pristinely any conditions that are less than perfect in freedom and design. We all need to stop overlooking—consciously or unconsciously—the *immaculate creation.*

Thanks to the grace of God gifting us into being, we are able to repent of our own ill reception of that grace. From our adverse willing, our present condition resulted. We are here in the pitfall of our own making—space and time—where every bit of conscious knowledge is increased in uneasy alliance with the depths of the unconscious mind. But where sin has taken hold, only grace can supersede.

Like Steven, we can ask forgiveness of our Creator and of our created companions in being. We can change our attitude toward those who have said fully *yes* to God (angels and saints in heaven) and also toward those who, like us, have so far said merely *maybe*.

Maria, Steven's friend at the jail cell door, was like a voice in the wilderness calling for repentance. From Moses and Isaiah within the Hebrew tradition, to John the Baptist within the Christian, and to Mohammed in the Islamic, prophets have been calling people to convert. All people must profoundly acknowledge their greedy, lustful, prideful choices and dispositions in the world of good and evil.

The voices crying in the barren wilderness of our withdrawal from the gift of being also imply that our ordinary choices stem from something in us that goes deeper than our most profound *awareness.*

When the Baptist cries out, "Repent, repent," he is including little children in his pleas. All who are *conceived* in this world are called to repentance in proportion to their ability consciously to recognize their sinfulness. The first sin of children is not simply squabbling in play with their siblings at age two or three. *Originative* sin is a given condition of our conception, of our coming-to-exist in the human family on earth.

Chapter 15   Recovering

Like Steven, beginning to attain sobriety in captivity, we, too, can become aware of our true situation here in the enclosures of space and time. We can acknowledge the barred windows of the cosmic prison. We can repent for more than we can *consciously* recognize. Saintly people have been doing it since the historical beginning of Revelation.

We can be wise enough to realize that effects have *proportionate* causes. Good effects have proportionately good causes; and bad effects, bad causes. The bad effects include living in this good and beautiful world of sin, sickness, anxiety, trauma, and death. These must have a cause *in another dimension of being.*

That originative cause warrants all the evil we might ever have to experience in this world and in any further purgatory. The *principal* cause can *only* be *ourselves* in freely refusing to respond *fully* to the incomparable *offer* of being intimately beloved creatures of God.

Our call is to recover, as best we can, from the crash in creation. Such really happened. Because of the spark of love in the *yes* of our originative *maybe*, we are *able* to repent and to *let in* God's healing ministry. Alternatively, because of the darkness of the *no,* we *can continue* to be closed to the infinitely intimate heart of God.

Chapter 16

A Call to the Three Traditions

We are grateful for the gifts of divine Revelation and supernatural vision. Nonetheless, *how deeply* are we *willing* to receive them?

We know how readily Revelation can be distorted by not being received well. In fact, between the three major traditions of theism disagreements about important matters abound.

The Jewish tradition continues to look for the promised Messiah, even as the Christian tradition claims he has come, and worships Jesus as God and Savior, while the Islamic tradition says Jesus was superseded by Mohammed as God's principal prophet. These are mightily different *ways of seeing*.

Yet, we should be mindful that all three configurations of belief and culture are rooted in the revelation of the God of Abraham, the God of infinite power and intimacy—the one and only God who saves. Jewish, Christian, and Islamic people turn their hearts to the same Being and to the promise of becoming free forever. Mightily common *ways of seeing*.

Concerning *how* redemption and salvation are to be interpreted, however, we must deepen our *willingness* to receive, to be changed and transformed, and to be renewed.

Theists believe God is the Supreme Being, who created with infinite power and perfection. Still, there would seem to be an enormous problem about the way the three traditions counsel us. They tell us to live a life of revelation, but they never really give us sufficient reason *to stop blaming God in our hearts* for the way the *original* creation turned out.

How do we explain the suffering of those who, for one reason or another, are functionally incapable of sinning in the world of space and time? We ought to confront *seriously* the broken lives of tiny children—before and after birth—and even of those adults whose lifelong mental impairments cause them to be functionally unable to commit even the slightest sin.

Millions of human beings have lived who were never functionally able to commit themselves, in this world, freely to the will of God. In light of this mega-reality, the traditional claims about the gravity and universality of our sinful condition in this empirical, space-time world would seem to lack sufficient credibility.

Although they participate together in this credibility gap on the origin and meaning of evil, the three traditions of theism do share profoundly the belief that God is the infinitely good Being and that we are profoundly sinful. Despite various incompatible teachings on the "details," large and small, wherein there are sharp conflicts about what is true and false, *all believe* that only the one Personal God can save us.

So, the fundamentals of the doctrines—at least those concerning the creation of the world and the origin of evil—are *not necessarily* matters of *false* teaching. What seems eminently desirable is that the whole of theistic belief be summoned to give a *deeper* accounting. The traditions may need to take a leap of development in the basic meaning of the doctrines concerning our origin. These teachings require a *deeper way for us to see what they are revealing*. Revealed *truth* needs better *theology*.

A Shift in the Theist Worldview

A new theist worldview would change the perspective on evil and suffering. There would be a revision in our understanding of how God could allow torture and devastation to afflict innocent children and others.

The perennial *mystery* of evil would shift from an attitude of "how could God condone such a thing" to the question of "how could we 'innocent children' have *done* anything to deserve such treatment."

The present book and the whole trilogy of which it is a part is not proposing a "new Faith," but a further deepening of traditional Faith and wisdom. The suppositions—that God's creation is *interpersonal* and that we ourselves responded *immediately* by freely failing—might be considered simply as tentative theories.

Chapter 16 A Call to the Three Traditions

But, even if taken only as hypotheses, they could prompt theists to examine the abiding paradigms or models of understanding—shared over many centuries—by which they have been taught and by which they are leading their lives.

The traditional paradigms were once themselves hypotheses and theories that served to interpret the main data of Revelation. They can be revised, even while foundational truths cannot.

The revelations that God is infinitely good, loving, and powerful and that we are all sinners—along with other claims—are neither hypotheses nor theories. These are truths.

But the manner in which these truths are *conceived* in relation to one another is open to grand supposition and revision. It is also the potential subject for authoritative religious teaching.

In any case, the longstanding frame of reference for most theists includes, at least, the following two general versions.

One segment of believers tends to think that, for the coming into *being* of human persons, God creates passive matter out of which gradually higher and more complex forms arise until the combined workings of God and nature yield the glory of physical creation: humankind. At a certain point, God creates each individual person by infusing a spiritual soul. This train of thought might be called *evolutional theism* or *theistic evolution.*

Another segment of believers tends to profess that God creates primary creatures of every type—especially animate ones—directly or immediately at various points of time. Each species is created all at once. God then allows these natures—including the human—to propagate offspring of their own species or kind. The species may develop, but only within themselves. This approach today is known as *creationism.*

In regard to sin, a general archetype is presupposed. The usual interpretative pattern states that the origin of human evil occurs *only after* Adam was created from the earth and after he and Eve were placed in the Garden of Eden. There they disobeyed God's explicit command and originated human evil.

This perspective implies that God can and does create creatures—even human ones—in an imperfect state, including Adam from the dust of the earth. But, even more critically, it says, in effect, that

God does *not* allow self-reflective human creatures—other than perhaps Adam and Eve—to exercise full, perfect, and decisive freedom *from the beginning of their being*. We *descendants* are forced to be created under *submission to the sin* of our sole prime progenitors *and/or to its consequences*.

These traditional paradigms or patterns for understanding serve the specific Revelation about our created, sinful condition and help us to receive it and believe it. But they are hardly the fullest *expression* of the *content* of the beliefs themselves concerning the creation of humans and the origin of human evil. There is much room—yet within significant doctrinal limits—to re-conceive and reinterpret what is really being believed.

The supposition of the present book offers another perspective. It requires a major shift in our consciousness of creation and of sin. Its sharp contrast with the traditional view allows us to wonder which of these different, yet continuous, ways of integrating vision seems more plausible.

Which viewpoint, in other words, is less inadequate to the mystery of being? No interpretation explains everything in detail. But which one affords us deeper, more heartfelt participation in the process of *understanding* what is true?

The Power of a Paradigm

Participation depends on our paradigms. A paradigm is an overarching model or pattern of conditions and assumptions by which we judge everything else. A working principle, akin to a worldview, the paradigm determines how the activities and natures studied are necessarily viewed, in order to live according to the most coherent, intelligible whole.

When we change paradigms, we do not change endeavors. We simply adjust the set of postulates and assumptions under which we study, and in that newer light we evaluate everything else.

For instance, when scientists changed, in great part, from the Newtonian world of physics to the Einsteinian world of relativity, science did not cease to exist. Nor did scientific experimentation and speculation become less important. Just the opposite occurred.

Scientific endeavor and its "natural revelations" received a grand charge of voltage in efforts to explain more phenomena. The new

Chapter 16 A Call to the Three Traditions

paradigm explained the phenomena more coherently than did the Newtonian set of assumptions.

Similarly, suppose theists relinquish the idea of the older view wherein "God creates *ex nihilo*, in serial fashion, multitudes of imperfect creatures, only some of whom are perfectly free." And they begin to entertain a newer one where "God creates perfectly *ex nihilo every person*, having the perfect freedom immediately to determine his or her destiny." Then with such a shift of viewpoint theology, philosophy, and religion would be either dealt a setback or advanced from within.

But, while theistic paradigms are quite similar to scientific ones, they are also different.

On the one hand, scientific paradigms are apt to come and go. No matter how effective older ones might have been, the newer ones *replace* the older—though not entirely. While Einstein performs, Newton leaves the stage—or plays a bit of background music.

On the other hand, theological and philosophical paradigms do not tend to replace one another. Rather, the newer ones deepen and enrich the older—not by substituting for them, but by throwing more light on the same subjects.

The common basic teachings are there. God, who is infinitely good and infinitely powerful, created us. God is an infinitely good Creator. And we are fallen creatures, totally in need of God as our Savior. Our sinful condition in this world would bring all of us to damnation without the saving power of God being granted *and being received.*

This is the way we *know* the Revelation to *be*. But the Creator's activity of creating should be more deeply received *by our minds* as well as by our hearts, the better to penetrate our hearts and our actions. And the truth of our own perfect finite freedom ought to be more deeply received, despite how personally painful that reception might have to be.

Obviously, this unique gift of perfect freedom has been somehow profoundly diminished. We can recognize this easily as we go about our lives in space and time. The prophets and the whole tradition explicitly call us to face the depth of our sinfulness and slavery to sin.

But, in addition to the consciously proclaimed revelation, there is perhaps an unconscious revelation about this sinfulness and its origin. The unconscious revelation is similar to the largest part of an island hidden below the line of ordinary vision. The Judeo-Christian covenants implicitly, gently—not explicitly, harshly—induce us to get in touch with our own *receptive* participation in creation "out of nothing" and in the origin of human evil.

While so much more could be said, this book and its trilogy are attempting to indicate the grounds for receiving more deeply, in our common hearts, what has always been revealed in theistic Scripture and tradition.

The Painful Change

Does it make any difference whether, as a member of the human community, I have a decisive part in determining the origins of good and evil? Does it matter whether I am really able to cooperate, or to refuse to cooperate, with the principal decision of the community's leaders, say, Adam and Eve? Does it make any difference whether I am personally involved with the very origin of evil or whether I am an innocent victim of it, passively bludgeoned by the sin of my first parents?

Obviously, there would seem to be an immense difference. The disparity is similar to that between active and passive predicaments. For instance, *either* being the president of a nation that is intensely negotiating with terrorists about the fate of the inhabitants who are under the threat of nuclear annihilation *or* being a couch potato watching on television the negotiations and the fate of oneself and one's family.

But which is truer? Is it truer to say, as the new way of conceiving holds, that I with others, including Adam and Eve, am an *originator* of the evil in this world? Or is it truer to say, as the traditional interpretation seems to claim, that I got bombed by ill-choosing first parents whose original sin deprived me of my "creation right" and effectively forced me into joining the "sin brigade"?

At first, I don't like either alternative. I prefer to think I am a good person having little to do with sin and evil—and certainly nothing to do with the *origins*. It is better for me and everyone else that I be positive rather than negative. Is the idea of the original sin of our first parents not negative enough?

Chapter 16   A Call to the Three Traditions

But being *totally* positive about the *original* condition of my being *in this world* is not being *real*. The obvious frustrations and painful tragedies of life are being excluded. If I assume that I am simply good, without personally active association with the *origin* of evil, I fail to respond adequately to the perennial human question, "Why *me?*"

We began Book One in this trilogy by noting a real life happening in the life of Alan. He and his wife, Stephanie, were the parents of a growing family. One day Alan seemed to be a bit late for work. He backed his car out of the driveway and *unknowingly* ran over and killed his own toddler son. The tragedy had a rippling effect on all of his family and friends. And on us, once we learned of it.

Under similar circumstances, however, such could have been done by any of us. More importantly, Alan stands as a vibrant symbol for how we *could have* "run over" our original freedom with its opening to a free, *immediate*, and ecstatic life forever. If we had accepted that originative opportunity fully to affirm the gift of our own being and the Being of the Gifter, we would have excluded the experience of pain and willingly entered rapturous joy—then and forever.

Bitter realities force me to think again and again about why I am *here*. I am essentially good, but then I am immersed in considerable evil—socially, individually, and environmentally. To live is to suffer and to risk assault from the forces of physical nature and from the moral misdeeds of strangers, friends, and family—not to mention threats from vastly superior forces of evil.

My body gets sick, my mind fumbles at times, my feelings are mixed, my spirit reveals some dispositions that are less than fully virtuous, and I am headed for the colossal destruction of death—at least, physical and emotional death. While I am basically good, I have inclinations toward evil. And, especially, evil has inclinations toward me. I become prey even when I pray.

Could this inherent connection with evil have come through the design of a Creator who is *infinitely* good and powerful? Could this connection with evil have come to me through the "permission," if not the design, of this Creator without my freely-given permission, too? The major message of this book has been that a "yes" to either or both of these questions is a great miss "take."

The idea that we are fundamentally *victims* of the transgression of Adam and Eve represents a false "take" on the holiness of God and the freedom of created persons. God is infinitely perfect Freedom, who creates—directly from nothing—only *perfect* finite freedom.

God can and does create an imperfect world, but always *out of something*—out of the spiritual and material remnants of an original crash. God "cannot" *create out of nothing* an even slightly imperfect world, and still be "God."

So, I can no longer regard you and me as *essentially* victims of someone else, including God. As painful as it is to receive, the truth must be that you and I are personally involved with the *roots* of good and evil. This is the truth, unless, of course, *you* are some kind of most rare exception, having agreed freely and fully to live here as a finite redeeming co-operator with the infinite activity of God.

Holy Ones Lead toward the Light

If this new view is true, why have we not heard more about the idea throughout history? And where is the scholarly documentation? Why should I or anyone else take it seriously?

Souls have been saved without it. Great heroes and saints never thought they were *personally* responsible for an originative, even if partial, denial of being. What difference would such a consideration have made for them?

These thoughts are almost inevitable. They have to do, however, with the *conscious* acknowledgement of personal responsibility for the origin of human evil. But we can know and act on the truth of something without ever bringing that truth into consciousness.

Toddlers, for instance, know and act on the truth that they cannot walk sprightly as do others around them, but they do not bring it out as a proposition in their consciousness. Even when we are adults, our every practical learning endeavor is usually undertaken with the unstated, subconscious truth that the practical knowledge is sought from an instructor who knows more than the one being instructed.

So, there is a big difference between how people closest to God would become aware of personal responsibility for the origin of evil and how the rest of us might hesitate to do so. When confronted by this idea consciously, would not the holiest be some of the first to acknowledge it?

Chapter 16   A Call to the Three Traditions

The saints' awareness of their own sinfulness and of their acts of human alienation from God, *through their own fault*, is ardently developed already. They could hardly be surprised to be advised—if done by properly recognized religious authority—that every human being in the cosmos (past, present, and future), with the rarest of exceptions, is a co-originator of the evil that afflicts us all.

Saints within the Christian Church, for instance, have profoundly identified themselves with the incarnate God's sufferings on behalf of each one of us, including themselves. To be instructed further in the mystery of God's painful world would be much easier for them than for us. They have a developed capacity for *receiving* the things of God and for knowing how deeply we deform our own human freedom by even the slightest offenses against the Beloved.

Because of their sensitivity to the *heart* of God, people ardently devoted to *believing* deeply, and to *doing* faithfully, also have a more profound sense of causality than we do. They do not deal with things merely on a practical, yet superficial level.

Saints experience everything as *being-within* the heart of creation where everything is super-related to everything else. These holy ones feel intimate to the least little good thing or action. They are repulsed by the slightest offenses against God and fellow creatures.

They *know* that God offers them infinitely intimate love at every moment. They are pained as the infinite tenderness of God is being constantly rebuffed by *their own* hardness and ignorance—as well as by the heartless attitudes of others.

Intimate lovers of God realize that the *sources* of sin are *entirely* in the hearts of those who *do* the sinning. They are supremely sensitive to our free failure to love God with whole hearts and souls. So they are particularly positioned to see that the normal episodes of guilt that we experience over past or present sins in *this* life could be considered as *symptoms*.

Our temporal spasms of guilt would seem to radiate from our core guilt for the origin of sin—the supremely causal sin—now largely repressed or denied. "Out of the depths I have cried to thee, O Lord: Lord, hear my voice. Let thy ears be attentive to the voice of my supplication. If thou, O Lord, wilt mark iniquities: Lord, who shall stand it" (*Psalms* 129:1-2).

There would seem to be no limit to the depth of the need we have for God to rescue us from our self-wrought predicament; and the saints are the first to recognize it. Many are known to seek out, or to ask for, increased occasions to suffer for the sake of their own and others' salvation: sheerly out of a burning love for God. The idea of an originative sin would be more than just an idea; it would be the holy ones' natural platform for acknowledging our total need for redemption and salvation.

People of demonstrably heroic virtue live intimately with the causes of their aspirations and actions. They do not merely teach or preach the way of profound justice; they practice it with uncommon courage. We who act in pale imitation of such holy ones are inclined to teach and preach and behave while living largely out of touch with the sources of the ultimate truths that we proclaim.

We are often locked into the pragmatic policies and practices that might serve today, but blow away tomorrow. Religious leaders and teachers—even those of exceptionally good will—can be clouded by their own practical responsibilities when exercising their ministries. They are inured in the standard patterns of interpretation that have served so well.

Nevertheless, deeper soundings on truth concerning creation and the origin of evil can develop only through *contemplative* hearts, and even then with difficulty. The vast theistic tradition of mystical theology and spirituality testifies to the dark night of the soul and to God as a truly *inaccessible light*.

We approach God only through the dark cloud of unknowing, relinquishing all egocentric attention to consolations of the senses, of the mind, and of the spirit. For the mystics, the necessary way to *see* God is through self-abandoned, ego-less love.

As we journey toward death and to the wrenching away from our fixations on earthly concerns we are called to live in the *dark light* of knowing God's welcoming love. Could it be that this knowing is commensurate with a knowing to which we are also called: knowing our *originative*, self-blighted, missed union with God, out of which all creation groans and is in travail for the daylight of salvation?

This book on the new viewpoint for creation and sin supports the notion that we do not and cannot *remember* an originative sin. The claim is that we *do know* it, even if we do not *know* that we know it.

Chapter 16 A Call to the Three Traditions

Such a view faults no one for overlooking the prospect of personal responsibility in the heart of creation—at least as far as our practical activities and insights from this world are concerned. Just as good physicians are inveterately inclined to treat symptoms and overlook the systemic causes of physical disease, religious leaders can, by their training, consistently overlook the common, universal cause of *all particular guilt—an originatively repressed act of freedom.*

Moreover, simply to make the painful acknowledgement that we are each personally the cause of our own plight in this world would not indicate sainthood. The only test of a saint is a life lived in true abandonment to God and to spiritual purposes at every moment. It would seem, however, that if presented with this new perspective, the saints—especially the deeply repentant ones—would be those most willing to give it serious consideration.

At any rate, the new viewpoint on personal responsibility—if it were to be accepted—would require a painful conversion in our self-concept. We would have to stop watching the world largely through the remoteness of mental television and begin to live-a-vision—a vision based on a deepened spiritual intuition and knowledge of the heart. We would have to become people who know who they are, and who they are not, basking darkly in the brilliant light of God's mystical marriage—offered to us, but self-deflected, *at the moment of creation out of nothing.*

In ages past, the saints might not have been ready to articulate rationally or conceptually what they *knew*. But perhaps they quietly attained something of the new understanding far more vitally than we who might now talk about it will ever surmise in this life. Holy people lead us to the light, not so much by their rationally objective sight as by the intuitions in their hearts and by the luminosity of their lives.

The Sole *Origin* of Evil

"We have met the enemy, and it is us." Whatever the context, that catch phrase from a Walt Kelly comic strip has a profound meaning. We do not have to be saints the better to appreciate it. Every sin, every effect of sin, and every inclination to sin within us—in all its *reality*—can be traced to...*us*, first as individual persons, and second as a "community of disunity."

Sin is from within. The defects and sins of every imperfect human being *originate entirely* from within. The activity of Satan and the original sin of Adam and Eve are conditioners for our sins and for self-destructive intentions and behaviors. But they cannot be called causes or agents of *our* sins.

Every human being in (finite) likeness to God is *self*-determining. Each one determines the *kind* of human person he or she will be—whether fully *yes*, fully *no*, or *indecisively so* for "a time."

All of our sins and vices, as well as our virtues—*all of our moral and spiritual activities*—are matters of original freedom and not of necessity. They stem from the same capacity within each of us: our personal human *will*. We are originatively endowed with an *agent will*, a *finitely pure act* of volitional *power* to cooperate with the infinite presence (grace) of God.

There must be a supreme, ultimate willing *activity* of this perfect personal power that is protoconsciously the *prime* cause of every one of our acts—virtuous or not. All of our multitudinous acts of good and bad choice made at the specifically moral level are mainly symptoms of this specific, *primary* causal act: our supreme act of freedom at the level of *be*-ing.

The *sole* origin *of our present personal destiny* is not the will itself as a power. *We are.* We *do* the willing by *acts* of willing. By the *primal willing activity,* we have received our being with willful deficiency. The partial failure was *of* the agent *in* the act—not at all in the perfect *power* to will, gifted by God.

God, moreover, does not determine our *final* personal destiny. *We* do. God affords us the gift of *being*: of being-at-all, of being who and what we are, and of being *able* to affirm the goodness of it all. But only we can determine whether ultimately we accept *willingly* these incomparable gifts.

We have to consider carefully our first, supreme, pristine *activity of knowing and willing*. Therein we can characterize ourselves as *being* both the preconscious and the protoconscious *source* of our conscious daily acts. These acts are the flowing results of a whole concatenation of levels of conscious and unconscious life for which they are a kind of culmination.

Chapter 16   A Call to the Three Traditions

We can infer as much. After all, our everyday acts are wounded ones—especially those having some degree or kind of freedom. And all the rest may be characterized as wounded, if less obviously so. Or maybe more obviously so.

This deepest (*protoconscious*) *activity of willing*, therefore, must be the specific determiner whereby we are the *only cause* of our *maybe* kind of originative being—including our existence in this passively material world. Nothing or no one caused *this particular act* of freedom to be, except the sinning person himself or herself. God is the cause of our freedom as a perfect *power* to do and be, but cannot be the cause of *any* of our free *acts*—whether of virtue or vice—nor of our *maybe*-saying response to *being*.

Some might say that only God is the cause of our freedom. So, they would assert that only God can be the ultimate cause of the evil as well as the good that we *will* with that freedom.

However, that is to miss the *gift* of being, and of freedom *as a gift*, absolutely and infinitely given to *us*. We *exercise* our *own* freedom, not God's. We have dishonored, however, that *perfect* power to be free by its first free *act*, of which we are the *sole* agent.

Our originative *act* of freedom is a singular cause in respect to its effecting personal good and evil. (We cannot "blame God" for this one.) If, through our *agent (doer) will and its respective agent intellect*, we had acted perfectly well in receiving be-ing *ex nihilo*, none of these lesser imperfect acts could *be*.

Our originative, supreme activity of willing is caused not by the gift of freedom itself, but by us, the *doers* of this perfect freedom. From the moment of actively receiving our creation, we were the only agents capable of the *yes*-and-*no* that resulted in the present ambivalent disposition of our soul. We said neither *yes* nor *no*, but both *yes* and *no*.

This "unhappy fault" (*our* unhappy fault) within the purely free *willing* on our part is the ultimate reason why we are still yearning for life and love, but doing it often in such inept ways.

We are blaming much of our situation on others and making a supreme effort to conceal from ourselves this ultimate responsibility for how we are *be*-ing. If only we had a better way of conceiving this supremacy of each person's *agent* will, we could increase the occasions for our understanding, and for cooperating with, God's purposes. Perhaps we could say that each one of us is an *agent being*. We *will* our own be-ing, for better or for worse. We do not will our being *into* being. But we do will our being in *doing* this being-gift.

The new paradigm of personal responsibility for our every activity and experience is *another way of seeing* this primal willingness. It can serve as another window through which to see the light of God's truth. The vision afforded might be cloudy at first, then increasingly translucent, eventually to become transparent for many.

In regard to evil, each human person, by the originative sin, is the primal—not immediate or proximate—*cause* of all the evil he or she perpetrates and for which he or she suffers, willingly or unwillingly. This originative sin is really the only reason we are in this world of *maybe*—of disruption and corruption—as well as of promising truth, goodness, and beauty. This primal sin is the supreme cause of our structural defects of being. From this sin has emanated all the major and minor weakness, dullness, confusion, and transgression in our present life.

Many of us acknowledge the massive role of Satan and other evil forces in the institution and protraction of Adam's original sin in space and time. Nonetheless, we are called reasonably to admit *also* the primacy of a supremely *personal* cause of self-affliction. Were we to do so, we would let the infinite immensity of God's grace and mercy radiate all the more in our lives. We would be allowing the light and warmth of this mercy to heal us more readily.

Despite being critically self-wounded, we are *essentially* free. The infinite presence of God ever invites us to confirm God's infinite covenant of intimacy with us. Our response is free. God says, "I am redeeming you with my unlimited mercy." We can say, "Thank you, with *all* my heart and mind."

Part V Replies to Questions and Difficulties

Chapter 17

Critical Questions: Challenging the View

My intention has been to stimulate readers into seeing more deeply the truths of creation and sin. I also hope that this final chapter of specialized focus on the ideas will be an occasion for increasing our faith, hope, and love.

Readers who are inclined philosophically and theologically might wish to ask some critical questions about the new view, as presented in the first two books of the trilogy. (Another section of questions will be provided in the third book.) Here are samples of questions, with my basic responses.

The Three Theistic Faiths

Question. There are points of major disagreement between and among Jews, Christians, and Muslims. How can you write for all three of these theistic faiths?

Response. I am writing primarily *within* these theistic faiths, not necessarily *for* them. In comparison to the various other traditions of ultimate meaning, both East and West, the points of *agreement* between Jews, Christians, and Muslims are momentous. So, I have little trouble writing in relation to these three beloved traditions, without expecting any measure of agreement or disagreement. I am willing to learn from all others, both within and outside my own tradition of Christianity.

I try to express the way I see things in the light of my particular religious tradition and conviction. Then individual readers can sort out the meaning for themselves. My prime purpose is to educate, not advocate.

Q. Many believe in the original sin as traditionally taught and defended. How can you credibly challenge this teaching when the Scriptures, traditions, and authoritative doctrines of none of the theistic religions seem to indicate what you do?

R. For centuries, the monotheistic traditions have not significantly deepened their roots in the being-based (ontological) meaning of reality. They do relatively little reflection on God's *act* of creating "out of nothing," on what it must have entailed, *and on what it could not have entailed.*

Wittingly or unwittingly, they stay close to a model of creation as something done by a grandiose maker or fashioner of things. Modest attention is given to the Creator as originally creating by the infinite heart of Love.

Moreover, in the development of their doctrines, none of them systematically considers the moment of creation *out of nothing* as it relates to the spiritual dimension of our once fully super-conscious, now largely unconscious, mind. Who even asks why we *have* an *unconscious* mind? Why does every idea, every memory, every image—no matter how brilliant—seem to emerge, albeit quickly, from within the unconscious life of the mind? Why does every light seem to come to us from out of darkness? Why not light from finite light?

Furthermore, the creation of angelic persons is hardly mentioned. The Scriptural accounts of *Genesis* do not begin at the absolute beginning. These accounts leave us with an inestimable gap between the creation of angelic persons and the creation of human persons.

Created persons, however, are not *that* different from one another. I have indicated creation's "missing link": our originative personal responsibility for the way we *are*. This "missing factor" more than suggests an imperative need for renewed efforts to strengthen our understanding of the Scriptural and traditional views of the main theistic religions.

Chapter 17   Critical Questions: Challenging the View

Adam and Eve

Q. But millions believe that Adam and Eve were created before any other humans—that they are our first parents, and that we inherited *their* rebellion.

R. I believe that, too, with respect to *this* world. But let me respond with another question. How does the blame chain, involved in our belief, help anyone to *grow* in the spiritual life? Does it really help people to let them believe they have *no responsibility for incurring* the guilt and/or the consequences that accompany original sin?

It is true that many folks become holy *in spite of* their conscious assumption that we are not personally responsible for the *origin* of evil that affects us. After all, the key is to realize the *depth of our sinfulness and to repent*, whatever the "details" of origin. But by insisting on a sense of personal identification with both the good and bad that "happen" to us—including the transmission of original sin and/or its consequences—we might provide an unprecedented boost to personal integrity and growth in the Spirit.

Q. I do not think we have to *blame* Adam and Eve. All that we have to do is to put ourselves in their place and wonder whether we would have acted any differently. This thought could break the blame chain.

R. That thought might soften the blow. But the chain is still there; it is not really broken. Not until you and I are willing to admit that we actually did what they did, and that we must have been *originatively* co-defectors with Adam and Eve, prior to creation out of dust, will the blame consciously be on us and no longer on them alone. Then, also, the ultimate blame will no longer be *unconsciously* on God.

We do not represent Adam and Eve as much as they represent us. Through them, God conveys the message of our faulty willfulness in common with them. We are surely called to *receive* the message with greater heartfelt intent.

Q. I thought Adam and Eve were our first *parents*, not our first representatives.

R. They are both. Parenting and representing are not exclusive. As our first parents, Adam and Eve made it "apparent" to us that we are off-center and cast out.

Q. According to your version of creation, all of us were created "out of nothing," at once and together, with Adam and Eve. As a result, we might say that we are their brothers and sisters. But how can they be our first parents and also our "siblings"?

R. It is a matter of both-and, not either-or. Like husband and wife even now, once two people marry they become spouses, but they remain as brother and sister under Adam and Eve. So, once we were conceived in the line of our prime parents, we remained their brother or sister under God.

I am saying, then, that our first parents represented all of us who were destined to be conceived *through* them. We were *conceived through them because we had done what they did.*

Not in the Garden, but in the *heart of God*. If you do not think so, are you not *unconsciously* blaming God for an original injustice?

Q. But some believe Adam and Eve are merely symbolic.

R. Others believe that they are literally real, and still others believe they are partly both. I think Adam and Eve are a real couple, with great symbolic meaning. Whatever point of view is valid, if we are willing to magnify our reflection on what it all means, we can see that our own personal freedom is involved.

The story of Eden, for instance, can give us some indications of how our own signature sin could have happened—*within each of us*. The symbolic side of the story might reveal a personal meaning that is much deeper than the historical events.

For example, we could consider the Adam and Eve *within*. They could be said to represent two reciprocal parts of each one of us in our be-ing. Adam would be the part of ourselves that is designed so that we can *give* in a receiving, respectful manner. Eve would be the part of ourselves that is designed so that we can *receive* in a giving, active way.

Chapter 17   Critical Questions: Challenging the View   199

Just as we are coming to know how the left and right hemispheres of the human brain emphasize different kinds of activity, we can similarly realize two "hemispheres" to the human person's spiritual life. Everyone is *both* Adam *and* Eve within. Men are both Adam and Eve within. Women are as well. But the way "Adam and Eve" relate in a man is correlatively different from the way they relate in a woman.

At the moment of creation "out of nothing"—when we said, with all the power of our God-given be-ing, *yes-no* (*maybe*) to that gift itself—these inner powers (*Adam* and *Eve*) must have done their part.

Eve, symbolizing the naturally gifted ability within each one of us to *receive-oneself-in-being*, must have freely turned, at least slightly, away from the gift of be-ing. Our capacity to "be at home" with God and one another was willfully distorted. Right within this free act of giving less-than-full-thanksgiving for the gift of being, the receiving power of our being would have been thereby freely self-distorted.

We must have willed to be choice-abusers, rather than to be full affirmers of be-ing. We had perfect freedom to *receive* ourselves *fully* in being, but we did not *will* to do so.

Instead of genuinely *receiving* our being, we placed ourselves in a condition that *rejected* it—at least partly. With this disaffirmation of our own unique being, we have been doomed to live in the passive (non-receptive and opaque) world of space and time, and destined eventually to die. Indeed, such a *maybe*-saying, right at the heart of who and what we are, would have helped to *cause*—along with the similar denials of other perfectly free human beings—the world of *passivity "par excellence"*: matter *as we now know it*.

By this *being*-abuse—deforming our God-gifted and purely active potency to love—we would have created for ourselves our own *passive* potencies, those abilities to "be done to" and to "be done in" as found in the classical philosophical tradition. Pure *active* potency (sheer ability to *do, to receive*) would become passive-reactive. As we initially treated ourselves, so also others would necessarily be able to treat us: to *act upon* us, not simply to be *with* us.

Passive potencies (specific abilities to *be done to*) would abound as a kind of massive residual condition following our inner Eve's semi-betrayal of our purely active potency to receive, in a giving way, God and others. As a result, eventual death would be necessary as an effect of this original, if partial, *no*-saying.

Also, the inner Adam of our be-ing, the capacity within each of us to *give-oneself-in-being*, would have failed to give self fully to the Eve, the receiving capacity *of* our being.

If we were to put it in terms of the *Genesis* account, it would be as though Adam *could* have said in the Garden, "No, Eve, I will not eat of this fruit. I will continue to be a giving-self-in-being: giving to and with God." Instead, Adam had said, "Yes, Eve, I will eat of this fruit. I will not give to God and to you the self that we *are*, but will try to give a self that, in some ways, we *are not*."

Eve, in effect, said to God, "I will not receive *fully* this being that I am. I want to receive the kind of being you, the Giver, are. I do not want a sheer gift-being; I *will to be* rather a Giver-being, like you."

On the one hand, Eve, the receiving power of being that we *are* and that we *do*—*be*-ing is chiefly an *act*, not just an "actuality"—said, "I will to *be not* a purely active receiving power of being. I am *willing* to be a somewhat passively receiving power of being: give me a being I am *not*, or else I will *take* it."

Eve, like Adam, is a power within us *to give in a receiving way and also to receive in a giving way*. But Eve, the feminine-within, emphasizes the power to receive our *be*-ing in a giving way—to receive givingly, not just to "receive," to be passive. But she freely said *partly no* to self-being. By that very saying, through our inner Eve, we freely created a cataclysmic *outsideness* for ourselves—the very "shell" that makes us impervious to our own originative sin. Our beings were turned inside out, individually and communally. They would remain that way forever, if supernatural regeneration had not been offered by the *Word* of God.

On the other hand, Adam, the masculine-within, emphasizes the receivingly giving power of being that we are and do. In effect, he said to God, "I intend *not to give fully* this being that I am. I *will* to give to self a kind of being somewhat as *you* are, a Creator-being. I am unwilling to give a strictly gift-being; I want to *be* more like a Creator-being."

In other words, the giving power of *be*-ing that we *are* and that we *do*, our inner Adam, declared, "I intend to *be not* a purely receptive

Chapter 17 Critical Questions: Challenging the View 201

giving power of being. I am *willing* to be an aggressively giving power of being. I will give myself and others what I *choose*, not necessarily what I *am*."

By failing in the first act of his *quite essentially* free will, Adam became *pro-choice on be-ing*. Adam, the power to give our being in a receiving way—that is, to give receivingly, and not just to "give" performatively—freely assented to the *no* of Eve, the receiving side.

And by that very articulation *we* freely created the hyper-kinetic frenzy of fitting forms onto experience, in which we are even now engaged. We always see the form of anything as dominating the matter that is seen as passive. In this condition—of the form lording it over the matter in both human and subhuman realities—we would exist necessarily and forever, unless we were offered supernatural healing by God's infinite power to love.

Q. You apparently think that we changed the structure of our beings by this primal, originative "choice" about being. How can mere creatures alter their own beings that were, as you say, perfect gifts of God?

R. We "changed" the structure of our beings by *adding distortions* to the way we were given to be. We twisted and partially blocked our own beings from themselves within themselves—not entirely, but definitely. We are now consequently *both* perfect *and* imperfect beings, rather than being simply perfect *human* beings in response to God, as we were infinitely invited to be. We are, one might say, "disvalue added" beings.

If the Adam and Eve within our being had said fully *yes* to the gift of being, then we would *be* differently. We would not be suffering imprisonment by our minds and hearts, nor enduring disease and death—for once *or* forever. We would be enjoying freely the beauty and goodness of our own gift-being and that of all others, and especially enjoying the being of the divinely gifting Creator.

Since we have somehow partly denied the absolute goodness of both creation and the Creator, we have somehow changed our own being-structure. Not entirely, but radically. For us to effect an entire change would be ontologically impossible. But to change radically is the possibility of *personal freedom*.

Because of our ontologically torqued condition, we can be sure of our *inability* to judge *with ontological certainty* the moral character of our actions and those of others. Nor can we really estimate, based on what happens to us in this world, the degree of one's positive and negative aspects of originative *maybe*. Saints can be devastated. The hellish can lead charmed lives. With normal conscious knowledge, we cannot know certainly the ultimate value of anyone's actions.

What would have happened if we had said fully *yes* at the moment of creation? We would have fulfilled our power of being: to be a unique, powerful, free act of being. Our *purely active finite freedom* would have been fulfilled, and not tragically impeded.

We would have engaged in the sheer activity of *be*-ing whom God gifted us to *be* forever. We would have been pure *act*, sheer *do*-ing, *without defect* in manner of doing or in capacity to do *the finite being that we are*. We would each be a sheer act of praising God. Not angelically, but humanly and personally.

We would be living in complete intimacy with the infinitely loving God and with all the friends in creation who also said fully *yes*. The infinitely intimate, personal God would be the essential, radiant personal presence in our lives.

In short, we would be what we now hope to be after death. We would be "at home" with God, living fully united with God's will, in supreme joy, peace, and love forever. We would be God-centered in mind and heart, and not even partly centered in our own wills.

By contrast, in this limited *and defective* world of space and time, of passive matter and reactivity (motion), we are self-*centered*, not merely self-concerned. We are still far from becoming God-centered in thought, word, deed, and attitude.

Although called to the supreme condition of everlasting joy and happiness that we could have received from the moment of creation, we are now in danger of losing life entirely. If we refuse *truly* to repent and be saved, we will commit ourselves to frustration and despair. Forever. *That* is pure *finite power*, the sheer ability for *self-determination*.

Of ourselves *alone*, we can effect nothing worthwhile, much less attain the original joy and happiness for which God created us. Now we *absolutely depend on God's gifts of redemption and salvation* in order to return to our originally gifted self—independent *with* God, without any of the "dependency drags" on intimacy.

At this very moment, we are *not only* limited beings; we are *also* deeply *defective*, both in our being and in our doing. Besides, we are understandably confused about what it is to be free yet limited—to be free, functionally and naturally, as well as essentially.

Freedom, Potency, and Guilt

Q. Natural and functional freedom? What is the chief difference between these two kinds of freedom?

R. Let me illustrate by noting something less exalted than the heart of our freedom.

Right now I am responding in writing to your question. Even as a human being in the womb, I had the natural ability to write. At that time I was naturally, if not functionally, able to learn how to write and to write eventually with increasing degrees of functional ability. As a human embryo—even then—I had the *natural* potential to read and write.

This quite natural—not functional—capacity does not constitute the embryo of a rabbit or a dog. Such are *naturally unable* to read and write. So, too, the *functional* ability is impossible for them.

As human at any age or stage, I have the natural capacity (the nature) to be able to choose reflectively—something that plants and animals do not have. (Plants and animals have their own natural capacities—even at their earliest stages—that I do not have, such as natural abilities to yield peaches or pine needles, or to bark or purr, and so forth.) No plant or animal has either the *functional* or even the *natural* ability to write creatively intelligible communications—ever.

Chimpanzees might do "look alikes" at human communication, but such represent really one of the more human-*like* activities and abilities that chimps and other animals exhibit. These likenesses, however, serve as neither identities nor equivalences. My "barking" like a dog or "purring" like a kitten is neither real barking nor real purring. My substance does not allow it. Moreover, the substances of a dog and a chimpanzee do not allow genuinely *reflective choice*, even when they hesitate *instinctively* between alternative courses of action.

Turning to the reflective human freedom of self-determination, we can say something like this.

My *natural* abilities to exercise deliberation and free choice, as well as my abilities to read and to write, were ever-present at the beginning of my existence in my mother's body, even though I was not *functionally* able to do these activities at that point. I lacked the functional potency. Plants and animals never have either the natural or the functional ability to do these things.

The *functional* potential to do anything can come and go. But the *natural* potential is there at all times as a *disposition* of the essence. Natural potential is simply the power to be *what* one *is, and to act accordingly*. It cannot be gained or lost, as can functional potential. Nevertheless, it can be damaged, even gravely, by bad functioning.

Even the surgical removal of the eyes of an animal or of a human would result in the loss of the functional, not the natural, power to see. Not even permanent impairment can destroy nature and natural potentials that flow immediately from the essence (the *whatness*) of the creature.

Both the essence and the nature remain even when there is total impairment of the nature by loss of the functional capacity. Essence and nature remain. Function is gone.

Natural potential, therefore—not *functional* potential—serves as the telling feature of the essence of anything. Confusing these two radically different, but highly related, kinds of potency-for-action—the natural and the functional—impedes our thinking and demeans our self-concept.

Q. How are these two kinds of potency, natural and functional, involved within our response at the moment of creation *out of nothing*?

R. If we can recognize the difference between the natural and the functional, we can see that, even at the moment of creation, we must have been gifted with something more foundational: an *essence-freedom*, deeper than both natural and functional freedom. Essence-freedom includes, but is not the same as, the *natural* and *functional* dimensions.

We need to recognize also the difference between the essence and the nature, between the essential and natural freedom. Although the terms are often intended synonymously, the *essence* and the *nature* mean something quite different, yet highly related.

Essence is fundamentally *what* something *is*. *Nature* is *how* this something is *disposed* to act. *Nature is the essence as ordered to (structured for) activity* (including "function"). The nature of peach tree, for example, is peach-treeity (essence) *as ordered to* producing peaches—and not pears, apples, or kittens.

When we consider the powers of freedom, we can see something similar. By immediately saying our originative *maybe*—by that *functional* act—we severely and directly damaged our perfect, gifted *functional* freedom. As a result, both our functional freedom *and the natural freedom it expresses* became quite imperfect, distorted, and incapable of recovery or of rehabilitation *on their own*.

But our *essence-freedom*—the core of our freedom, coincident with the *fundamental kind* of being we are and always will be (our essence as persons)—was not specifically damaged. This inherent freedom to be—as the likeness of God that we *are*—was deeply *dishonored* by the crash of our nature, even as God was dishonored. But as the structure of our unique being—gifted by God's word, "Be"—it is inviolable at once and forever: in heaven or in hell.

So, now, as we awaken to our plight in being, we find ourselves with *both* imperfect natural freedom *and* imperfect functional freedom. The natural freedom is imperfect in that our essence is still intact (still perfect), while the *power to act according to this essence* (natural freedom) is impaired. Through miss-exercise of *functional* freedom, at the moment of being-created, we have damaged *both* our functional *and* natural freedom.

Natural freedom is a *disposition* to love. We are called to *be* love and *do* love. We are lovers by nature. So, both our functional and natural powers of freedom are now involved in the process of being "reconstituted"—toward final good or final evil.

Our original perfect freedom of essence might *not be known in our present life by us at first*, since we are overwhelmed by our fallen condition of imperfect natural and functional freedom. Our perfect *essence-freedom*, however, is foremost in God's giving, receiving, and providential love.

Our essence-freedom is first in being, but it is the last depth of freedom we come to acknowledge redemptively. This core freedom is the basis *in us* and *of us* for final repentance and reception of God's gift of redeeming grace. We are merely touching upon it by our reflections in this book.

This perfect freedom of essence constitutes the standard for all of our activity. It is really impossible, for instance, that a being *have* imperfect freedom without also *being* a perfect freedom gone awry. The perfect freedom of the essence—freedom as a person—*cannot* come and go; it is the God-gifted heart of any free activity. But its *disposition* to act wholesomely (its nature) can become slightly or grossly imperfect.

We were gifted with *perfect* functional freedom (potential) to act, at least at one point—the point of our *creation within the heart of God*. Otherwise we could not *be im*perfect. We could not exist as an impaired perfect being.

It is critical to realize that our spiritual power to act freely is not like the case with merely physical things. Physical things, like trees and beetles, are part-beings, not whole beings. They lose all their physical "perfection" when smashed or damaged. Spiritual realities, however, are always, *at their core (essence),* perfectly the way God gave them to be.

Yet spiritual realities, such as human persons, can "become"—by their own failure of will at the moment of being created—*somewhat or even fully dysfunctional in their ability to act well*. In their nature they thereby are rendered imperfect, while ever remaining in *essence* perfectly free, as God willed them to be.

The travesty of *being* that we call hell means that persons who are essentially free—with a perfect essence of freedom—have exercised their functional and natural freedom so badly that not even God can save them: they have completely disqualified themselves.

Their *natural* freedom is totally self-perverted, such that they are both functionally and naturally *unable to receive* any love at all. They have effectively abandoned themselves to satanic influences.

Receiving infinite love then becomes especially intolerable. (God's saving power never overwhelms our freedom, but ever cooperates lovingly with the natural and functional freedom of created persons to whatever extent they *will allow*.)

In contrast, what we call the ecstatic life of heaven means that persons, who are essentially free, have exercised that freedom fully. They "functioned" perfectly. So, either God does not act to "save" them ("*originative* saints") because they immediately said fully *yes* or else they are those who, having said *maybe*, have *come* to re-exercise their freedom by repentant activity in space and time, such that God *could and did* save them ("*ordinary* saints").

These latter persons—*maybe*-sayers—cooperate directly with God and variously with the benign influences of angels and saints in the providence of God. Their freedom is not only perfect *essentially*, but is made also perfect *naturally* and *functionally* through the process of their cooperation—by their *receiving* justification and by being sanctified.

Any being that has imperfect freedom is imperfectly in freedom decisively because of some *self*-damage, and *not principally* from any "outside" causes—including both demonic and human forces. The *im*perfection of freedom is definitely an "inside job."

In fact, all good and evil in the spiritual world is self-caused. Such is not the case in the physical world, where everything happens, as it were, "from the outside." In the passively material world, one thing can smash another without itself being significantly damaged. But in the spiritual world, whatever you do *toward* others, you do *to* yourself. And whatever you do *to* yourself, you do *toward all* others.

For created persons, then, love is universal; so is hate. We love others to the degree we truly love God and ourselves. We love God and ourselves to the degree that we love our neighbors. Love and the freedom to love are equal opportunity powers. Hate and the ability to hate are the underside of freedom.

Q. But would not our spirits be crushed with guilt were we to realize the truth of our *personal* share of responsibility for the *origin* of evil in the world?

R. No, because we would finally have a credible response to the constant question, *Why me*? Why is this confinement of soul and body and all its attendant pain—actual and potential—*happening* to me? Why am I *subject to* so much "chance evil"?

A big problem is that we are not only rooted, but fixated, in this world of good-*and*-evil. Consequently, we can hardly conceive of ourselves ever *having had the opportunity* of immediately entering a world of *goodness alone*.

True theists really believe in the *infinitely* good God who "reaches out infinitely powerful arms." God saves us from ourselves and from our calamities: but only to the extent that *we* are *willing*. God loves us unconditionally and can forgive us of the most appalling crimes, *if* we repent—*freely* turning our lives around—*and meaning it with our whole being*.

One big problem has been that we do not realize how awesome is our sin and how awe-inspiring is God's love-response to our self-debased, originative freedom.

God redeems us from the being-based (the ontological)—not only the moral and psychological—guilt of co-producing, and falling into, this world of good-*and*-evil. We have only to receive with gratitude the gift of knowing who we are and who we are not, and to determine to change our hardened hearts by prayer and action.

Even within the traditional frame of reference, our off-centered condition is seen as so deep that it affects the structure of the kind of being we are, at the level of *nature*. For example, many believe that original sin makes us naturally vulnerable to disease and death: physically, psychologically, morally, and spiritually. The traditional view simply requires development in order that it acknowledge the originative *sin in being* that *causes* every weakness in the *levels* of our being.

Plato, Aristotle, and Origen

Q. But isn't your "ontological way" of developing the theistic tradition really Platonic and dualistic?

R. Definitely not. However, I do identify partly with Plato's kind of understanding. For instance, this prominent philosopher from the

Chapter 17   Critical Questions: Challenging the View

headwaters of Western civilization understood that *something* was *essentially* wrong with this world of passive matter and motion. But he did not really seem to know *why*; nor did he associate the *origin* critically with *personal freedom*. He tended to think that evil was largely a matter of ignorance, and not of anything truly malicious.

Accordingly, the realm of pure Forms, as he viewed it, lacked a *personal* connection with the cosmic world of corruption, into which he thought we had somehow fallen. And his meaning for freedom was mainly moral and political, not beingful—at least not explicitly.

Yet Plato knew, at least, that we needed liberation from space and time, and that we were related dynamically to another world, of which the present world *reminded* us. This is one reason why he has been, for many theists, inherently more attractive than Aristotle.

Plato recognized that there is a world of structure transcending the cosmos. He regarded all solid knowledge as based on a mysterious reminiscence of this *other* world, where our total satisfaction might be found.

His self-limiting frame of reference, however, generally regards being as split into the separate categories of mind and matter, or soul and body. At least, most of the philosophical streams that can be called Platonic have seen it that way.

So, we hunger for a worldview that is even more ontological than Plato's. One that is not relatively static like his. But also not one that is "dynamically static" in the passively processive way of so many contemporary thinkers. The "dynamics" of evolution and process merely represent an opposite way of concealing the heart of our *being*.

We yearn for a perspective that deepens understanding of our roots in being, that profoundly celebrates the (original) *essential freedom* of our being, and that remedies the dualistic manner in which Plato's worldview functions.

Dualistic worldviews regard this present world as an inexplicable prison. They may or may not have an explanation for how we got here. But they are weak on explaining the very origin of the world (the prison) itself. Moreover, they hardly attend to both sides of the paradox: that *this same world is both confining and partly salvific*.

I am claiming, however, that *both* the world itself *and* all of us—with perhaps the most unique exceptions—are here by *our own irresponsible doing*. Everything, both the good and the bad in our lives—including this whole world *itself*—is decisively the result of a *merely partial* exercise of *complete* responsibility in our originative decision about *being*.

Platonists and the other dualists, such as today's reincarnationists, have their own versions of responsibility. But it is a kind of *partial* responsibility.

Reincarnationists, for instance, are prone to believe that we are present in this world and suffer what we do because of how we lived in previous *temporal* lives. They are as passively fixated on the spatiotemporal world as are their opposites, the traditionalists.

The worldview that I am proposing, however, does not imply any *previous* life that was at all *functional in this world*. But it does claim a life of *being*—a non-durational *relationship* with eternity at the moment of creation "out of nothing." Ontologically prior to the *bodily* temporal life that we *have* and are now *experiencing*, this originative life was not *given* duration. It *caused* its own duration.

Because of the present limits and defectiveness of our nature, we have to use temporal terms, of course, for both temporal and non-temporal realities. But whenever we begin to think of eternity as being either "before" or "after" time, we ought to make a mental correction and say, "That is not a *temporal* before or after, since all of time is itself a real, but skewed, mode of *relating with* eternity."

Unfortunately, we then might be inclined to think that we are really co-eternal with God, as Aristotle held to be the case with the passive matter of the cosmic world. But even as we do so we are, subconsciously at least, still thinking of eternity as an indefinitely long duration, rather than being *not at all* durational.

In thinking of God, many philosophers perennially have confused ontological or real infinity with the pseudo-infinity involved in quantity and mathematics. The latter "infinity" entails an "absolute indefiniteness," and is not at all a real infinity.

In contrast, real infinity is an absolute unlimitedness: *no limits at all*, rather than being some kind of limit after limit, number after number, "as far as the eye can see" or as far as the mind can discern.

Chapter 17 Critical Questions: Challenging the View

The pseudo-infinity of quantity is not at all any unlimitedness. Its "unlimitedness" is effectively caused by greedy, grasping minds' frustration in conceiving it. In our frustration, we call its inherent indefiniteness "infinite." The sphere of quantity and mathematics, however, as well as the whole cosmic world, is one massive-passive *finitude*. This particular kind of finitude constitutes a defective and compensatory, as well as limited, *kind* of being.

Nevertheless, God's non-temporal being is infinite—eternal, and truly without beginning or end. In contrast, our non-temporal being is finite and had a "pre-temporal" *beginning* within eternity.

Hence our being is not specifically eternal. Yet, as the result of immediate (originative) sin, we had another beginning: a beginning of *time and of space*. And there is neither time nor space between the two beginnings. They are both "instantaneous." But within that "instant" of being gifted with being, our pre-temporal response, *maybe*, "happened" and caused the temporal to be.

In one sense, Platonists show better vision than Aristotelians and many rationalists of the Western tradition. The latter see no basic fault with the natural world as we find it, whereas the former know there is something radically defective about it, even if it is at base originally, though remedially, good.

Of course, there are versions of dualism that seem to regard matter itself and even time as basically evil. Relative to those egregiously antagonistic dualisms, both the Platonic and Aristotelian approaches offer much truer notions of the world, and of soul and body.

Q. Since you think that Aristotle's philosophy is basically short sighted, how can you accept any of his views as true?

R. Let me respond with an example. If I were a kind of "specialist" who was studying your feet, I could learn much truth about them. But if I did not see well how your feet are connected with *you*, then I would be shortsighted.

The Aristotelian worldview really misses out on the relationship between the natural world—the world of *passivity* in matter and motion—and the *undistorted,* active world. The latter includes both the supernatural (God's nature) and the undistorted "natural world" of God's pristine creation *ex nihilo*.

Aristotle thought that the spatiotemporal world was *the* world: ultimately co-eternal with God. He did not acknowledge a primal *creation*. Insofar as he simply "studied feet"—the natural world as it exists—his views contained much truth. But he seemed to have little idea of either an original sin or an originative one and how this physical universe is inherently flawed because of such. So he did not see well, as it were, the "connection of feet" with these more basic truths. His principles of nature and of being are remarkable, but beg development.

Q. How then is your view different from that of Origen, the early Christian theologian? He seemed to accept a kind of pre-existence. He thought we had a life of learning in the spiritual realm at first, and then some personal beings became distracted and were punished for it by being consigned to the present world of space and time. That was presumably *our* fate.

R. Origen wrote in powerful allegories and figures of speech. And, after his death, there were controversies surrounding "Origenism."

Moreover, centuries later, theological interpretations that were based on the scholastic tradition found it difficult to deal with what he says. Scholasticism made special efforts to be engaged in non-metaphorical conceptualization.

Long after the time of Origen, theology and philosophy developed a highly cultivated trail of rationalist discourse. This development was good, but it became overdrawn and rigidly categorical in certain ways.

Regrettably, we find that most intellectual traditions, including parts of scholasticism, tend to begin or, at least, end in *univocal thinking*. This univocal mentality of "one and the same meaning for a given term every time it is used" cuts off insight into beings in their *be-ing*. Thinkers then fail to be sufficiently *analogical* in the meanings they develop. They fail to allow the richness of various—simply different, though related—meanings for the same term, especially for the term *being*.

A truer perspective on the meaning of *being* would accept poetic and metaphoric meaning, but temper it with careful analysis. Great

Chapter 17   Critical Questions: Challenging the View

strides in developing the meaning of analogy were made by Thomas Aquinas and other medieval philosophers. That endeavor is ongoing.

Analytically analogical thought is not necessarily antipathetic to figurative and allegorical thinking. Respect for both a proportional analysis and poetry is crucial. Healthy meanings can be regarded as both cerebrational and celebrational.

Origen had an insight into *being*, but he did not have access to its development in the science of being-as-being. A systematic address to being was really discovered by Aristotle, whose most important texts became known in the West much later than the time of Origen. Moreover, Origen may have been misunderstood by Augustine, as well as by subsequent theologians of lesser insight.

The "distraction" from being to which Origen is thought to have referred can be figuratively interpreted. It need not be taken literally. Obviously, there was no initiatory life of learning in the spiritual world, literally speaking. Creation is the gift of unique and perfect *being* to every recipient.

No *learning* would be necessary or even possible at the moment of creation "out of nothing" (*ex nihilo*). All requisites for a perfect, immediate, and consummate act of freedom-fulfillment would be gifted.

At this (finite) beginning of our being "before" time, we engaged in the super-dynamic *act* of full responsibility for our being. This beginning was not temporal; it was perfectly beingful or ontological, and therefore can only be said to be "before" space and time in a non-literal way.

Rather than occurring "sometime" after creation itself, as Origen would have it, the decisive act (or signature act) of our being was an *immediate* response to the gift of being "out of nothing." I claim that this first act "was" or "is" a being-to-Being (creature-to-God) act of full freedom and self-determination on our part. Among many other things, we can say that our willful defection co-caused, with fellow failing humans, the ontologically skewed conditions we call space and time.

In contrast to Origen's scenario, there was no "distraction"—nor a temptation to be distracted—involved in our supremely free act of response to creation. Distractability—the ability to *be* distracted by being a self-looking-at-self—comes only with the consequences of this first *untempted* sin in be-ing.

Origen, along with Augustine and Aquinas, failed to realize the *un*tempted nature of our first free act of be-ing. It was an act of a *necessarily perfect power*. With that perfect finite *power* fully to affirm God, self, and others, *we* failed to *act* perfectly.

The imperfect—such as this first *exercise* of our freedom—can come from the perfect that is finite; but the perfect finite can never come from the imperfect. Not even God can "make" something perfect *out of the imperfection itself,* once the imperfection is *freely* constituted by sin.

God is, however, the infinite power (called grace) by which the imperfectly self-rendered creature is able to repent—to *turn freely* from ontological paralysis. By the infinite mercy, the self-inflicted person is able to come back freely to an originally gifted mode of being—now to be repaired. But even then the repentance can occur within the creature only because this created person said initially at least a partial *yes* to *be-ing*.

Origen had insight into our beginnings, but he did not have a background in the meaning of being as such. Nor was he cognizant of the systematic study of psychodynamics and of repression that has fruitful implications for understanding at least the rudiments of an incredibly more profound kind of repression: *spiritual* repression. Today attention to such considerations makes it possible to give a more analytic exposition of our "first encounter" with God and with ourselves.

Origen seemed to miss the freedom-gift that is *being*. He is said to hold, or to speculate seriously, that everyone will be saved—even Lucifer—granted an immense duration. God's *infinite* love will apparently convert the most hardened willfulness.

But this is to miss the *gift* that finite freedom really is. Origen and many others fail to see how this freedom belongs entirely to the *receiver* of that gift, and not at all to God, the Gifter. The *being* of our freedom is an originative *gift* of God: thoroughly *ours,* with no attachments.

Through their fully-gifted finite power to will, Lucifer and his minions can everlastingly resist even infinite love. God's infinite

Chapter 17   Critical Questions: Challenging the View   215

freedom in love necessarily, perfectly, and unlimitedly *lets created persons be themselves and be their own freedom*. These creatures are *able* to distort their gifted freedom to the maximum in hatred.

Both Origen and his critics do not seem to realize the power of the first act of freedom exercised by every person—whether angelic or human—at the originative, interpersonal moment of creation *ex nihilo*. Therein, with their completely *qualitative* power to exercise self-determination of being, Lucifer and others willed to hate. Both their functional and natural freedoms were *thoroughly* corrupted "on the spot" and they could not be recovered. Not because of anything "lacking" in God's infinite love, but because of everything lacking in *their* own *willingness* to love.

Their hopeless condition is permanent; but it is not because God's infinitely giving power of love and forgiveness is defective. Rather, it is because these created persons totally perverted their own ability to *receive at all*. They flouted their power to receive *both* the finite being that they are *and* God's infinite goodness and power *by which* they were gifted to be.

We are normally blinded by our propensities to project, onto other kinds of freedom, our present semi-functional exercise of freedom in this world of "maybe-itis." As a result, we can hardly come to know what a sheer act of free and total *yes* or *no* is really like.

Many seem to think of God's "infinite freedom" as some kind of "infinite permissiveness." God is, however, infinite mercy without being "permissive" at all. Our calls for mercy are only as good as our sincerity: realizing the certainty of our sin and of everlasting unworthiness in the face of unlimited love. If we call out for *mercy* and really mean *permissiveness*, we are deceived. We harbor deceit. Such a mind cannot enter the kingdom of heaven.

We can open to mercy only as we open to love, willing the truest and best for everyone, including ourselves, no matter what we must endure. Not to be willing is not to do love, nor to be repentant. It is there that God says, "I know you not" (*Matt.* 25:12). We determine ourselves to fail in the gift of freedom.

Q. Some have claimed that there seems to be an ontological gap in Origen's account of the origin of sin. They ask, "How can an already perfect, God-given freedom—that is presumably fully

realized in every respect—determine itself to anything less than a state of perfection?" Is not your viewpoint subject to the same objection?

R. No. This objection assumes that the gift of freedom is coming as "already exercised." We can notice the misunderstanding embodied in the expression "presumably fully realized in every respect."

Actually, if *this* freedom were fully *realized*, it would have to be the *creature's doing*, not God's. As gifted by God, the freedom of the creature is perfectly what an absolutely free and infinite Giver would give: *freedom*—to be exercised fully and immediately *by the recipient*, and not at all by God, whose freedom it is not.

In fact, it would not be "perfect *freedom*" if it were even partially exercised *as being given, rather than as being received*. So, this objection would seem to evidence the slavery that we implicitly impose on God, presuming apparently that God has to "do things for us."

But God does "God's things" for us, not "our things" for us.

We must be careful to realize that God does not give us *God's freedom* to act—not even a "portion" thereof. God gives us *our own* freedom to act: notably the *ability* or *power* or *potential* to *receive* perfectly the perfect freedom that is ours. This ability is a perfectly active potency, not even a partially passive one. And we necessarily *do* the receiving *by that freedom itself*.

If God offers a gift of *freedom* to the created person, God surely does *not exercise* that freedom-gift *for* the creature. God gives to every *created person* the freedom-*power*—not the freedom-*act*. The created person is not able or "free" to refuse the *gift* of freedom *as being given*. But the person is *totally able to exercise*—fully or not fully—his or her own perfect (gift of) freedom *as being received*.

The creature is unable effectively to say, "I do not want to be a *free* creature; I want to be unfree (an "automaton") and to have God 'honor' this request." But the creature is able to determine how well or how poorly the gift of being-free is actually *received*—from fully acceptive reception even unto totally rejective reception.

God originatively gives us the *purely active potency* to say fully *yes* to being and to being-*with* God. But God cannot possibly give

Chapter 17 Critical Questions: Challenging the View 217

the activity of *doing* the self-determination. *That* is ours to do *on our own*.

We have the *power* to act by the grace of God, but we have to *do* the *act* on our own. *Help* from God *cannot* occur in the execution of this *first* supreme *act* of *freedom* to *be* who we are.

Help from God is necessary, however, once we damage our power of freedom originatively, and as we start acting against it within the redemptive world. God's grace is then more than mere "help." It is life-saving.

We do not want to admit what was definitively the case at our absolute moment of origins. We defend our primal repression of protoconscious freedom by whatever rationalization springs to mind. So shameful would be its admission.

Objections like this one about "already perfect freedom" reveal our fixation on the spatiotemporal, cosmological framework under which almost all theology and philosophy is worked out. I call it the *cosmolock*. Within our theological perspectives, we unwittingly do cosmological metaphysics, rather than ontological metaphysics,.

Because of our obsession, we think that the *gift* is some kind of a "product" that has to exist quasi-physically *before* we can act *with* it and *by* it. We regard the gift as an "instrument," rather than our very *being*. We are quite numb to the reality of the gift-giving (God's act, grace) and the gift-receiving (our act) as being mutually immediate.

We are sure, rightly, that gifts cannot be received *before* they are given—whether temporally or simply ontologically. But we do not realize how these *originative* gifts—as distinct from post-creational gifts—are received, *not before* they are given, and *not after*, but *in the same non-durational moment in which* they are given.

We try to *imagine* how it could be that we could receive a gift without first taking some time, however momentary—as we do in this world—to recognize it as such, *before* saying "thank you" or "no, thank you." We definitely project our relatively passive manner of receiving—that is quite indigenous to us now—onto our pristine, purely active (not at all passive) opportunity to receive the gift of being-at-all.

A special problem with Origen's notion is that it does not go to the metaphysical roots. It does not acknowledge the *interpersonal* act of creation itself. Yet it is within *this* act that God gifts to each created person the unique, perfect power of self-determination. *Immediately and in perfect freedom,* the finite person *does* the gifted *be-ing* in his or her own way—within the "constraints" of the *kind* (or *essence*) of perfect person that he or she *is*.

Whatever imperfection there is within our freedom comes entirely from us—from our first *act* of freedom—and not, even a little, from God. God confers only perfection; and we *receive* this freedom-perfection-power by an *act* of *that power itself,* perfectly or not so perfectly (imperfectly). *We,* not the power, do the receiving. We receive *by* the power, but we do so—we *will*—with the power's *act* that *we* cause.

The power does not act; only *we* do. The receiving is done *by us, through* our exercise of the perfect power. The *power* is God's gift to us. The *act* is ours alone. *Our gift to God.*

Because theologians do not recognize creation out of nothing as necessarily involving us and our freedom, they discuss our acts of freedom as they happen in this world only, where every act needs support by the grace of God. They overlook the conditions for the *originative* act of our freedom wherein God's grace was *not in question*. Including ourselves and our power to act—to love—God's grace was all there was. *All* was grace, including the pure grace of freedom. Our *being* was simply a grace of God.

But the act of *response* was ours, done fully *within* (not *by*) the infinite life of God. The question of grace or of God's help did not arise. We needed no "help": thanks to God. Thanks to the perfect power with which God gifted us.

Blinded by our present self-passivized condition, we seem unable to recognize our gifted *primal* ability *to receive purely*, and without any passivity or hesitation. We are unseeing now because we do not have a sufficiently *functional* ability *to receive*. We *tried* to "ditch" receptivity at the originative moment of *be*-ing. And we habitually reinforce this primordial dodge.

The distinction between freedom-power given (God's doing) and freedom-power received (our doing) should be easy to understand. We only have to reflect on human acts of intelligence and will, even as they occur in *this* world.

Chapter 17 Critical Questions: Challenging the View 219

We can realize, for example, that for all the preparatory sensation, external and internal, that precedes and inherently feeds cognitive-volitional acts, the acts themselves do not "take time" any more than they "take up space." They are instantaneous. They are immaterial or spiritual acts, not material and temporal ones.

These immaterial or spiritual acts of knowing and willing can be associated with certain moments of time. Ultimately, they may even be acts that establish conditions for these temporal moments. But they are not *of themselves* constituents of time and space. Spiritual knowing and loving cannot be correlated with temporality *one-to-one*, even as intellect and will cannot be correlated with spatiality *one-to-one*.

We can, however, only represent the relations of intellect and will with time and space by pointing to their correlation as real, yet less than "one to one." The analogy is one of proportionality.

When we read someone's handwriting, for instance, we know that the "ink scratches" are just configurations of ink totally confined to space and time. But we also know that the particular contours are not caused by *merely* spatiotemporal elements, such as temperature, humidity, and smoothness of paper.

The intellect and will of an agent are involved in the causation of the particular physical squiggles of clearly identifiable wording. The "scratches" are *both* utterly physical *and* profoundly *un*physical. They are both material and immaterial in being and in signification. The immaterial communication transpires *in and through* space and time, without being itself essentially confined by these physical dimensions.

We must break with our propensity to temporalize and spatialize *everything* we think and do in our daily lives. Otherwise we will not be able to understand how there could ever be a non-durational *moment* in which we made a "momentous" self-determination—before God and all creation—that landed us *here*. We will continue to be hooked by a spatiotemporal perspective and insist on framing every meaningful reality as having a particular time and place, no matter how figuratively we might express it. We would seem to have our "spatiotemporal mitts" on everything.

Origen was caught in that preoccupation and so were those who tried to critique his thought. They do not realize that to think of a literally perfect time and space is equivalent to thinking of a square circle. The *perfect* time and the *perfect* space, like a square circle are impossibilities or contradictions.

A flawless space can only be postulated in mathematics, not in non-mathematical reality. And all mathematical calculation itself is a compensational manner of thinking for those who are inured in space and time: in order to function there practically. Space and time in themselves are antithetical to every *perfect* being—being that is completely self-active.

Even today theologians might insist that God must have created originally a perfect time and space, from which we have fallen. They unconsciously project something as essentially imperfect as time and space onto the result of God's originative act of creation.

But time and space are intrinsic to material *passivity*. They are not simply attributes of matter, but of passivized, *unreceptive* matter. Time itself measures motion, a kind of activity that intrinsically involves passive potency. And space itself measures extended or distended matter—the kind of matter that represents alienation and reaction to being purely receptive.

Only in the "next world," wherein time and space, matter and motion, can find "fulfillment" will there be a kind of "perfect time and space." Time and space are co-dimensions *both* of distorted receptivity *and* of sacramentive healing. These magnificent metrics could become "perfected" by a *de*-passivization of matter.

Glorified time and space, once enwombed in eternity, will be part of our final recovery. Time and space, along with our physical matter, will be as "perfected as possible."

From the Christian perspective, the spatiotemporal and all the other wounds of human passivity will be sanctified by the healed wounds of the Body of Christ—healed, but forever visible in the glory of redemptive love.

Some Challenges from Thomistic Thought

Q. Your hypothesis is astonishing. Nowhere in Holy Scripture is it recorded that our original creation constituted us as perfect finite spirits with a primordial, fully conscious, and totally free response to God.

Chapter 17   Critical Questions: Challenging the View

R. My hypothesis does *not* say or mean that we were originally created as perfect finite *spirits*. Rather, we were created as perfect finite *beings*. The meaning of "finite beings" includes originatively human beings, of form and *unpassivized* matter, as well as beings of pure form without matter, known as angels. This means that there is an important difference between perfect *human* persons and "pure spirits" or angels, as traditionally conceived.

In line with Thomas Aquinas, I hold that an angel is the unity of an act of being (*esse*) and an essence only, and not, as with a human person, also a unity of substantial form and prime matter. But I do not mean quite the "same thing" as Aquinas.

To the contrary, *originatively* speaking, God creates both angels and humans as pure finite acts of *being*. Every person *as a person* is a *perfect kind* of being. There is no *passive* potency.

An angelic person is a simple unity of an act of be-ing (*esse*) and an essence—the intrinsic receptivity to this act of be-ing. In that essence or receptivity there is *no* passivity. Each angel *is* its own act of *finite* being, even as God *is* God's pure *infinite* act of being. Each angel *is* likewise its own receptivity (essence) to its be-ing (*esse*)—as well as being its own "species."

As created *ex nihilo*, the human person, too, *is* its act of being. But the *kind* of being of each human is not that of a simple essence, as it is with angels. The human kind of *originative* personhood (human essence) entails a unity of form and matter.

The form is pure "givity" (power to give) even as matter is pure "receivity" or receptivity (power to receive). Humans are, then, a double receptivity: a receptivity of essence with respect to be-ing (*esse*) and—within the essence—a receptivity of matter with respect to form.

In contrast to the traditional ontology, there is a great difference of meaning here. We ought not to take matter and form as found in cosmic, recovering being and then blithely assume that it is (or was) *effectively the same* as matter and form in *originative* being.

Aristotle, Aquinas, and the whole scholastic tradition seem to have overlooked something. They have failed to notice the "free dive" or "free defiance" of multitudes of human beings that caused their own breakdown of monumental ontological proportions.

Ex nihilo, the *natures* of all unique human persons are dispositions of their individual (or personal) essences and constitute originative unities of perfect "givity" and perfect receptivity. But, by their originative *acts* of partial unwillingness, those human persons, who thereby definitely distorted themselves, caused their natural "givity" and "receptivity" to be, as it were, twisted.

The givity and the receptivity, constituting the originatively gifted structure of any human person as a person, were impaired in their flow from the essence. The originative sinful activity did cause the "additional" counterparts of essence that might be called *formativity* and *passivity* ("form" and "passive matter").

These latter effective principles could be detected by the mind working cosmologically. But, ontologically, the originative structure "behind" them—the structure of the very essence—was hardly accessible without explicit recognition of *each* being as being. Such transcends cosmic parameters.

By the first (flawed) act of human freedom, the substantial forms of these "plunging humans" were thereby conditioned to act not as intrinsically *giftive* with their matter, but as solely *formative of* their matter—matter that, by the "plunge, was transmuted into being reactively passive.

Angelic persons, however, are different. Within the "*inter*personal creation" hypothesis, angels directly said either *fully yes* or *fully no*. They *could not* "hesitate" or be "unsure about their essence" as human persons *could*. Being of simple essence, angels could not be indecisive about their essence.

There was "nothing"—there was no receptivity or "parts" (called traditionally *form and matter*)—to be indecisive about. Hence, they could not be indecisive about their *esse*—their being-at-all. They *are* directly and simply their (*finite*) acts of being—even as God is directly the *infinite* act of being. Everything the angelic person said about its essence necessarily referred to its being.

But human essence and human being are not as simple. Being of complex—yet totally active—essence (the power of being what they are), human beings could be either decisive or indecisive about their essence. Hence they could be decisive or indecisive about their being. They *are* quite really their (*finite*) act of being, but *less simply than angels*.

Chapter 17 Critical Questions: Challenging the View

By their first, signature act of freedom—an act that was truly a freedom of *esse*, of be-ing—multitudes of human persons acted imperfectly. They thereby caused or created *substantive* passivities known in the tradition as "form and matter." These two principles of *nature*, along with various *secondary* passivities, are first discerned in the philosophy of nature and in "cosmological metaphysics."

Perhaps many, perhaps a few, human persons said *fully yes* or *fully no* and would not have been subject to redemption and the headship of Adam. In our egocentric fixation, we are not inclined to realize this prospect. What we call "creation" is centered on "redemptive creation"—the kind in which we are now most critically involved.

As mentioned earlier in this book, philosophers and theologians have contemplated "being-finite" and have mistaken it for "being-imperfect." They thereby imply or declare that only God is perfect being, when they should say that *only God* is *infinitely* perfect being. Moreover, they have failed to recognize practically that God cannot create anything other than perfect finite beings with perfect finite freedom—*purely active* potencies to receive and to give.

To say less is to *demean the power and glory of the Creator*. By saying or implying that God can or does create "out of nothing" *anything passive* we exhibit the prime *symptom* of our originative *maybe* and its *repression* that *caused* the unconscious—spiritual, psychic, and physical unconscious—to *exist at all*.

The root of our being's passivity includes letting us be affected adversely by others. If we were *not at all* passive, we would simply *interact with* others—as do all those in perfect beatitude—without being adversely affected by them.

Concerning our "primordial, fully conscious, and free response to God," I do say that we must have been created perfect in being and freedom. And I also insist that we immediately responded as full *human* persons to the gift of being: we were *able to receive* our being, consciously in perfect being and freedom. Yet we did not.

That the being with which we were gifted was fully free, I affirm. I also affirm that it was fully conscious. But I do not mean—as the objector assumes—that it was the *same kind* of consciousness found in this empirical world. The essential term is not "conscious," but "immediately free and responsible."

We cannot assume, as a model for that originative consciousness, the kind of partial, dim, and broken consciousness that we know now.

This *first* act of personal freedom is nowhere recorded in Holy Scripture. But that is not surprising. How could it be understood or even conceived without the readers and hearers having access to the resources of consciousness afforded historically only much later than when the Sacred books were written?

As Jesus seemed to indicate, the Holy Spirit had much to teach in depth that "the present generation" could not tolerate. And future generations, including ours, have perennial work to do in preparing our own minds and hearts for meditating on the *ever more profound implications* of Scripture.

Many theologians and philosophers of Faith today are subscribing to the idea that, at the point of human origins, there must have been a kind of human evolution from animal awareness to human self-consciousness. But that evolution is likewise not recorded in Sacred Scripture—and for quite obvious reasons. Besides, as the present book would indicate, the *usual* interpretations of evolution and of its possible application in theology and religion are, at best, weak.

We try to differentiate the data of Revelation from *what we take to be* the implications. We then use the resources we have gradually developed to attend to an ever more integrated vision of the whole.

The power and efficacy of the unconscious mind is just one of those resources. The increasing progress in the physical sciences is another. These and further resources can contribute to a genuine development in our understanding of the original Revelation. But they must be examined in the supernatural light of Faith and of sound *ontological*—not simply cosmological—reflection.

Q. You think we respond to the act of creation, immediately from the first moment, in full consciousness and freedom. But if that were so, we would have to be pure spirits. We would not yet be at all human: embodied spirits in which our minds would require our bodies to carry on our conscious functions. Only later would we "pure spirits" be *infused into* a body. But such a radical change in nature and species would mean that it could not be the same *person*.

Chapter 17 Critical Questions: Challenging the View 225

R. Why would we have to be "pure spirits"? What we would have to be is pure *beings*—perfect *beings*—with the power to know and to will-to-receive our being. The questioner seems to assume we *know* that human beings are *necessarily* bodily and passive in being, with functionalistic powers called organs, as well as emotions, intellect, and will. But such is an example of taking our first perspective on ourselves—the manner in which we come to know ourselves at first—and assuming it to be ultimately the way we are and were created to be. The new perspective challenges that assumption and also affirms the ontological difference between perfect *human* persons and perfect *angelic* persons.

The age-old perspective presumes that God has created humans originatively with inherently imperfect parts, such as the functional organs, tissues, drives, and acquisitive attitudes. In the new view we claim that these features of being human are developments within multitudes of human persons like us. We immediately negated the greatness of human being, fell from originatively-gifted perfection, and produced *thereby* the *need* for a functional, redemptive creation.

An important part of this redemptive creation is our organismic bodily being. This recuperative creation included the development of *functionalistic faculties* in the processes of coming to a potential repentance within our *being*. By our partly self-negating, originative exercise of freedom, even our celebrational intellect and will were passivized and functionalized.

The expression "pure spirits" seems to indicate that the questioner is overriding the prospect of there being *pure human beings*: human beings whose relationship of form and matter is not necessarily a divisible or conflictive one.

In *originatively unfallen* humans, the matter—as the receptive principle of essence, in contrast to form as the "giftive" principle—is *not at all passive*, but is *as highly active as* the form. In order to see this reality, we must carefully re-conceive our *meaning for receptivity*—gradually being done in our own time. Receptivity is not at all passive. Rather, passivity is truncated receptivity.

I distinguish human beings from angelic beings. Every angel *is* a finite act of being (*esse*) of a simple unique essence that is a sheer receptivity to this act of being. The angel's essence comprises a pure receptivity *within and of* the act of being.

But *within* the angelic essence itself there is *neither receptivity nor passivity*. That is, there is no "composition" of form and matter constituting the essence itself, as is the case with human beings.

And I am claiming *not* that humans are pure spirits—if that is equivalent to being angels—but that human persons are pure *beings.* We are *like* angels—"a little less than the angels," as the Psalmist proclaims it (8:6). We were created as *pure (finite) beings—perfect human beings—not as pure (or perfect) spirit beings*.

Unlike an angel, a human *is* a finite act of being with a *complex*, uniquely-receptive essence—one that is both form and matter. Form means that it is giving-dispositive as to *what* it *wills* to be. Matter means that it is receiving-dispositive as to *what* it wills to be. Angels are immediately dispositive in those ways by virtue of their very being, not by virtue of their essence as well.

Within the essence of human personhood we find the reciprocal relation of actuality and potentiality—although these will be defined in the new perspective quite differently, and accorded terms such as *givity* and *receptivity*.

In the creation of our *human* being—together with the angels—our pre-physical (not "spiritual") receptive self and giftive self are metaphysically harmonious and inseparable. But by our own will we freely failed to receive fully our self and to give fully our self to God and to all others. We failed in our receptivity and givity.

Thereby, together with our essence—and within God's love—our act of being causes our redemptive physicalization in space and time. The physically observable *expression* of being (misleadingly called our "body") is what is separable from us—at physical death. The originatively-gifted givity and receptivity of essence are *not*.

I thoroughly reject the phrase that we humans are—even now— "embodied spirits." That wording, at times, is employed even by remarkably astute Christian thinkers. But it bespeaks an implicit, yet actual, *separability* of the spirit and the matter that is counter to the *ontological* integrity of human personhood.

Where is this idea of "embodiment" coming from? Embodiment sounds like an implicit, externally imposed imprisonment, or at least a packaging, as if something confining merely *had happened to* these "spirits"—rather than *had been caused by* their own agency.

Chapter 17   Critical Questions: Challenging the View

Moreover, the questioner thinks that, according to my hypothesis, there would have to be a later infusion into a body. That might be because he is working from the idea of separability about body and soul found in most Christian philosophy.

In my theory, our *conception,* via sperm and ovum at a particular place and time, is not our *creation* at all. It is a dramatic and timely *point of awakening* for our ontologically comatose being. Thereby we begin a *functional* existence in space and time, for the sake of actualizing, together with divine grace, our potential return to the *integrity* of our originatively perfect being.

The human person is definitely the same whole *self* throughout—from the originative creation. Persons as persons can be self-estranged, but never "intrinsically separated by way of *self.*" That is, essential parts (such as originative matter and form) cannot become removed from their reciprocal inter-activity within essence, however dysfunctional the entity that they constitute may become.

Our originative sin, in effect, *added imperfection* to the finite perfect being we were created to be. We were rendered imperfect beings by adding imperfection to perfection—not by *destroying* the originatively gifted perfection, nor by *replacing* the perfection with a creation of imperfection.

The originative perfection *could not* be damaged. But the whole being that we are, including what *we* caused ourselves to be, was immediately self-inflicted with our own passivity toward God.

The ontological estrangement right within us toward all creation and toward our Creator is what must be healed. The process is one of redemption and *sanctification.*

In this way of understanding it, personal human identity is given special affirmation. The integrity of human *being* would seem to be acknowledged far more by affirming the perfect, abiding character of personal being as gifted than by the interpretation of mainstream theistic thinkers.

The Thomistic idea, for instance, is that at death the soul and body *separate.* For this latter view, after death and until the resurrection, we are only "incomplete substances": souls without bodies—and *not whole persons.* This tradition too readily identifies soul and body with form and matter.

The new view reveals much greater integrity. Death is neither a separation of form from matter nor soul from body. At death, *both* the form *and* the matter—including the soul and body—together *separate from* spatiotemporal *conditions*, leaving a residue of dead, placenta-like matter (the corpse).

The traditional idea is too attached to sensory vision, assuming that if *I* do not *see* a living organic body any more, then it no longer *exists*. My physical vision is accorded superiority over intellective and spiritual discernment.

In a simple example, we might note that when a sailboat goes out of sight beyond the horizon we do not think that it goes out of existence. Nor do we think that the sun ceases to be when it "sets."

Similarly, we have no grounds for saying that the *living body* of Joe, who died yesterday, does today no longer exist. In a deeper dimension of being, soul and body are called to fulfillment—not to a separation dictated by the eyes of physical observers and their lazy intellects. We have witnessed Joe's "soulset" along with his body recession, but we do not have to assume the posture of ego-centrism so readily presumed in other things: "me no see, it no be."

Something similar also can be said about the onset or "soul-rise" of Joe at his conception within his mother. Just because we had not ever before observed his living bodily being, we cannot assume that the whole being of Joe—form and matter—did not exist in some kind of latency before his conception.

Generations yet unconceived must also be awaiting "their time." Time, however, is not the framework of their *being*. Rather, their *being* and their prime determination at creation is the "architect" of their time—of when they *come*-to-be (existing functionally) in *this* world, and of whatever parents in whatever culture.

We would do well finally to admit that, for the human person, there is no such thing as "incomplete substance"—just an inherently damaged relationship. The change at death and many other facets of ontological structure require rethinking and better explanation. (My analysis of this dramatic change at death includes and also develops the Aristotelian-Thomistic one, but such detailed attention could not be included in the present book.)

Chapter 17 Critical Questions: Challenging the View

The resurrection of the body, as it has been construed by many Christian theologians, seems to be based on a notion of nature that takes into consideration an *original* sin, but *not* an *originative* one. According to such perspective, we children of Adam have never had a perfect human nature, but we hope to acquire it in glory by a final "reuniting" of the soul and body.

By contrast, within the new view soul and body are regarded as severely wounded—before and after death—but not separated. The notion of *separation* comes from putting too much weight on the physical and sensory dimensions of our being, such that the "dead body" is construed as the *same* "entity" or "principle" as the "living body" before death.

The new view stands for ontological integrity in God's created persons *as originatively given by God*. What created persons like us did to themselves could not possibly effect a separation of form and matter or of the soul and the body. What God has "joined together" ontologically surely no one *can* tear asunder. We can only damage severely, even fatally, our relationship to our God-gifted nature.

As an immediate result of originative sin, much of the energy emitted by our *maybe* did apparently separate into what might be called *excidents*. These emissions were not *immediately* essential to our existence. They were not the basis of our personal bodies; but they were the basis for our environment. Such errant human energy God worked on to create (*ex aliquo*) the eventually supportive forms of energy such as electro-magnetic, chemical, and biological, along with other subhuman elements, particles, and parts of the cosmos.

The development of these partial (non-personal) substances helped to form the matrix and basis for our redemptive grounding (at conception) and for our life in this world. At death, we lose our connection with, and sustenance from, these elements. But we do not lose our bodies as physical human energy.

Our resurrection from the dead is promised. All creation "groans" for it. Passive cosmic matter—even that of the stars and galaxies—was redemptively created by God, on our behalf, out of (*ex*) the energy emitted by our originatively sin-committing selves. This particular form of *maybe*-energy is or was "separated" or "scattered" (exploded-freedom) energy, as opposed to the (imploded-freedom) energy out of which our personal bodies were redemptively created.

In the resurrection of the body, we will be gloriously *reconciled* with this alienated receptivity (both the exploded and the imploded) by everlasting lives of love in God, our Savior.

We are the same person, before, during, and after sin; so we are the same throughout the whole process of redemption and salvation. There is no disruption of basic ontological integrity, as is the case with the traditional concepts that are locked into their unconscious fixation on the originatively faulty frameworks of space and time.

Q. A pure being could not have an unconscious or any totally repressed subconscious, because this being would then have no memory. There would be really no way of retrieving experience. Essentially, a pure being would be complete and permanent self-consciousness. Repression into unconsciousness would seem to require a body. In that way, part of one's being is not conscious, and there exists a shadowy area between the conscious and the unconscious. How could such a condition exist in a pure being that is sheer consciousness?

R. This characterization of the new perspective begs the question of how our repressed consciousness—an unconscious life—came to us originally.

If we had said immediately and fully *yes* to our *being*, we would be without an unconscious mind, and we would be blissfully united with God forever—*as human persons, not as angelic persons*. But having said, in effect, *maybe*, we created, *by that saying*, the split of mind—of the intellective self—into conscious and unconscious. The spiritual unconscious wherein our primordial sin must now be buried is not proper to us as human persons, but to us (intellective selves) *as defectively willing* human persons, along with Adam and Eve.

Repression of our *first* act of freedom did not "require a body" (i.e., a *physical* body). This incipient repression of being was specifically caused, along with the unconscious mind itself, by the power of semi-ill *willing* that we freely issued at the moment of receiving our personal *being ex nihilo*.

This act of simultaneously *creating* unconsciousness and burying the deed by which we created it might be somewhat portrayed in an image. We might recall the burial of people caused by the terrorist

Chapter 17 Critical Questions: Challenging the View 231

act on the World Trade Center in September of 2001. Before the collapse, we might say that there was neither burial nor burial ground. The badly willed act caused both. No pre-existing burial ground was needed, so to say. The collapse produced both burial and burial ground.

Similarly, our originative act of saying *maybe to God* caused the spiritual "black hole" of unconscious life (the burial ground) within us and also caused the interment of the act itself. That effectively negative act—the *maybe*-saying—was repressed.

As it is now, this originative sin is barely accessible to the tiny portion of conscious life that has been salvaged so far. This modest recovery-consciousness is what we are using even as we attempt in this life to know and to love right now—as well as to understand and to articulate this very statement about our condition.

Along with our prototypical repression, we caused the *need for* a functionally redemptive mode of being. This redemptive creation included, among other things, what we now know as wondrously fashioned physical bodies. These bodies are really spatiotemporal expressions of our pre-physical receptive selves. They serve also as expressions of our ontological need for redemption.

Our bodies are the result of God's creativity. They make it possible for us to begin coping with our self-caused, unstable condition, as well as with its ambivalent world (the cosmos).

In this book, I offer the basic grounds for knowing *that* we did commit and repressed an *originative* sin. God's infinite goodness and infinite power entail that God's very act of creation *ex nihilo* be perfect and that by this act we are gifted with perfect freedom to receive.

The only source of the resultant *imperfection* is the gifted creature, who was meant to do a purely active receiving and confirming of the gift. ("Perfect" in these discussions does not refer to process or development *necessarily*. The word etymologically suggests that. The words *perfect* and *perfection*, however, are constantly used by philosophers and theologians for attributes of God and angels, as well as of human persons.)

The questioner asserts that we fallen beings do not "take on" permanent bodies. That is true; we human persons do *not* "take them on." We *cause* them—within the redemptively creative power of God.

The *passivity* of matter-configurations—that eventually come to constitute our physical bodies, including our bodily organs—is *effected* by our originatively ambivalent disposition. This resultant passivity, however, remains thoroughly sustained by God's infinitely loving, redemptive activity—from the first moment of our imperfect reception of creation *ex nihilo*.

The creation *ex aliquo* (out of *something*) includes the whole of redemptive activity. God works with our immediately caused, initial infirmity of being. That infirmity includes our passivity of matter (of essence-receptivity)—expressed eventually by the existence of our developing physical bodies and our repressive-unconscious minds.

As originally failing creatures, why did we become passive and bodily, while ill-willing angels definitely did not? Because we have a relationship within our essence that angels do not. By the simple unity of being and essence that they are, angels can and do *say* freely only *yes* or *no*, both to being-at-all and to being who they are.

But unlike the angels, who are *simply* who they *are*, we human persons *are* complexly who we are. Our structure is a unity between being-at-all *and* our essence (who we *are*) and, as well, between form and matter (together constituting *what* we are: what *kind* of *who* we are—human persons, not angelic ones).

Because of the *latter* relationship we are able to say—to the gift of creation—*maybe*. The ability to say *maybe* is the underside of the freedom-potential to say fully *yes*. The latter is the purely active freedom-potential of our matter, that is, of the receptivity in our essence. The *ability* to declare *maybe* is included in the ability to confirm (or to deny outright) the kind of human (form-matter) person we are gifted to be.

We could have said fully *yes* or fully *no*. By saying *maybe*, we partially passivized our nature (our essence as ordered to activity) in respect to *what* we are, and we became eventually children of Adam. What we now know as our functional matter (our spatialized body) is the practical result of this partial passivizing of our nature at the moment of God's word *BE*.

Chapter 17 Critical Questions: Challenging the View 233

Our immediate, freely knowing response to *receiving being* could be said to have been this: "I *might* (not) serve." And by that *act* of indecisive "saying" we have constituted ourselves into our freedom-cramped mode of *being*—the partially passivized essence that we call "human *nature.*"

The *essences* of persons—angelic and human—remain perfect. However, in the human, if a passivization occurs with respect to the essence—a passivization *within* essence, though *not of* it—what we call the *nature* is affected.

The *nature* is the disposition of the essence to *act* in certain ways. Since the passiviz-*ing* is an *act*, the nature is effectively crippled. In the case of full affirmers—angelic and human—nature's ways are totally good. In the case of us fallen humans, these ways are partly good and partly bad. And in the case of full refusers, these ways are only bad.

Q. What evidence do you offer for saying that an infinitely perfect cause could produce *only* a perfect effect? Why not say simply that it could produce a *good* effect, not necessarily a perfect one? Why could God not produce beings that evolve upwards slowly from imperfection to increasing perfection?

R. If the result of the creation act *ex nihilo* is not perfect finite being (person-being with no defects in being and freedom), then the *doer* of that creating act is not a perfect cause, much less an infinitely perfect cause. The initial imperfection must come from somewhere or someone, and in the case of *originative* creation *there would be no source other than the Creator*.

The *created* one does not *do* anything by way of bringing self to be "out of nothing." Nor can this person, in the act of *being* created, *do* anything to anyone else.

The act of *being* created is the same as God's act of *creating*. Only God is *acting*. But the created person acts *immediately in response* to the act of being created; and in doing so, by this responsive act, can create passivity and start *doing* things *to* self and others, rather than doing everything *with* them.

Nor can the created one, in the act of *being* created, be "done to" by any other creature—by a "third party," so to say—since the act of creating is the act of God alone.

Besides, God is not "doing to" this created person "anything." Originative creation is not *ex aliquo*, out of something "to be done to," but *ex nihilo*, "out of nothing," toward which there is literally *nothing* to "be done *to*."

As gifted by God—not necessarily as received by self—a created person really *is*, and is *able* to *do* and to *do-with* others, including God. Such is not, however, an ability to be "done to." Do-ing *with* others—acting independently-*with* others—has no passive potency about it.

God gives created persons *only* perfect power. God creates directly only beings "to be done *with*"—and none "to be done *to*."

An infinitely perfect cause is infinitely *perfect*, never *arbitrary* (doing possibly this, possibly that). Where could the imperfection come from?

According to a scholastic axiom, *nemo dat quod non habet—no one gives what he does not have*. But if "no one gives what he does not have" then obviously God must be said to have no imperfection and so could not possibly "give"—in the very act of creating—any imperfection to the creature.

Moreover, the "nothing," "out of which" the creature is caused, cannot be an imperfection, any more than it can be perfect. *Nothing* is neither perfect nor imperfect.

Creation, of course, is wholly a matter of *being*, and *not* of *having*. So there is much more reason to say that no imperfection is possible. God does not "have" anything to give (in the "handover" sense). God *is*, and infinitely *gives* by being infinite.

Some might wonder about God not "having" finitude (limitedness) to "give" to the creature. But finitude is what the creature *is*, not what the creature "has." Only because God *is* infinite is the creature, the finite, able to *be* and to be its finite self. The created person could not be infinite without *being* God.

Besides, when we speak of God, we are talking about an *infinitely* perfect being. Does infinity confer special "privileges" such that

Chapter 17   Critical Questions: Challenging the View   235

God can make a right into a wrong, create an uncreated person, or let an unrepentant sinner into heaven? Hardly. Then neither can God be specifically *responsible* for an effect that is less than perfect.

Creation has been perennially recognized within significant parts of theism as a *freely gifted emanatio totius esse*—a *freely gifted* emanation of the whole (created) being. So the effect of creation can only be a perfect effect, a perfect creature. Such an effect could only be the *best* that it could *possibly* be, including the power to know perfectly and to will with perfect freedom. But it is *in the creature's exercise* of that freedom-gift that the *possibility* of imperfection arises.

If we think otherwise, as I say earlier in this book, God's Being is being dishonored—albeit unintentionally. Process—whether it be from imperfect to less imperfect or vice versa—is a prime mode of *imperfection* in being. The evolution that the questioner suggests might be his speculation concerning a *part* of God's *redemptive* creation, but it is quite foreign to *originative* creation.

We have a sad history in philosophy and theology of confusing God's infinity with some kind of "divine arbitrarity." We conceive freedom in the way *we* are able to create—ever *ex aliquo*, out of something—exercising a kind of arbitrary freedom among myriad options. And then unconsciously we project *that way* onto God's free act of creating "out of nothing."

Questions about whether the cosmos is the "best possible world" or whether God could make a world better than this one are common among theists. The history of philosophy in the West is punctuated by speculations of this sort; and such problematics are found even amidst contemporary controversies.

We make these projections of how we would create if we were God. But we do so only by blocking out our own insight. We know implicitly that God's act is infinitely free and non-arbitrary: *loving* us into being.

Creation *out of nothing* is an act of *God as God*. Its direct "effects" (sheer gifts) can only be perfect in every way—including being perfectly *able* to self-determine their destiny.

In recent decades, Darwinian evolution has been showing itself to be a colossal scientific misadventure. Confusion about the difference between variance and evolution reigns. Everyone admits myriad changes and mutations within species. But no one has proven that mutation has ever gone from a simple to a more complex species.

In addition, theistic evolution suffers from close association with Darwinism. Nevertheless, on less than strictly empirical grounds, perhaps some form of evolution, along the lines of the empirical side of consciousness development, could be seen as *part* of redemptive creation. As a processive causality, *ex aliquo*, evolution could be involved in the divine rescue operation. God could be viewed as working with immensely resistant, spoiled, created freedom to bring it back out of the mess (void) made by the originatively disruptive acts of freedom.

In any event, the activities of *becoming* cannot be the activities of *originative* being, but of *remedial* being.

Even theorists who are called "creationists" still labor under the pall of thinking that God could create *ex nihilo* by way of a *process*. They often insist on a process of six days, wherein God goes from creating lower kinds of creatures to higher kinds—from a void to plants, to animals, and more. And they assume they are dealing with creation *ex nihilo*.

This manner of viewing creation makes it into a bizarre process: creating *ex nihilo* the various parts of the whole process leading up to the human person. Such an interpretation amounts to a kind of 'dump theory' of the creation, whereby different species of physical creatures are "plopped" *out of nothing* into the process leading to man and woman.

God's infinite act of creating is envisioned as having to fit into our space-time framework. It amounts to thinking of God's act as a creation *ex aliquo* (a process) interspersed with acts "*ex nihilo*." God's originative act of *infinitely* loving intent is overlooked by creationism as well as by theistic evolutionism.

Whether the creationists or the evolutionists are right, their issue is not really about creation "out of nothing," but creation "out of something"—something that involved the void. When God created "the heavens and the earth," perfect created persons had to have already failed in freedom. They desperately needed to come back to full freedom *through the ministry of the whole cosmos as well as of ministry in the depths of the spirit.*

Chapter 17 Critical Questions: Challenging the View

God cannot *create* (*ex nihilo*) an effect that is simply "good" and not "perfect," since only God's Being and Activity are involved. The effect must be an *effect*—not another divine Person. But it must be a *perfectly* good effect, without even a slight mixture of imperfection and thus of process, including, e.g., space and time. The process world is the world of both good-and-evil and cannot come directly by the activity of God *alone*.

Q. This new perspective seems much too close to the classic Gnostic theme of a fall from spirit into matter. Some forms of Gnosticism seem to arise periodically throughout history in the Western world.
In these Gnostic challenges, the primordial choice seems to be done by some perfect spirit that remains totally obscure. Then a mythical *story* fills in the void.
But many enlightened theologians today are finding it much more plausible that the human story is not one of *falling* from a higher state, from spirit into matter. They see the story as an *emergence* from lower to higher. Creation is then regarded as including a special transition for us humans over the threshold of animal, self-centered consciousness to human consciousness. These theologians envision the human vocation as a special self-sacrificial love and care for all others. This condition, of course, is difficult and fraught with peril. It requires the critical help of God.

R. The new perspective does not involve a "fall from spirit *into* matter." In the new hypothesis, the "fall" is the effect of the originative sin that *causes* the passivization and physicalization of ourselves; it is the betrayal of our originatively pure matter. This matter was gifted by God and is our sheer *receptivity of essence*—a fully positive ability to receive—and not a passivity at all.

As mentioned earlier, our *originative* sin might be better called a plunge than a fall, since it was fully free. And the matter—insofar as it was *passivized*—was not "fallen into." It was *caused* to be that way by our free failure to exercise fully our perfect receptivity. This receptive capacity was gifted within the essence of our human personhood, at the non-durational moment of creation. We failed to *be* that gift and thereby co-caused, with multitudes of other human persons, an ontological explosion—a partial defiance of God.

Actually, it is the traditional "story" that talks about a "fall" in the passive way, as though Adam's sin was something with which we simply got clunked. In trying to follow this story, we project the passivity of our present, functional power to know onto something that could not have been passive at all—our first acts of freedom at the supreme origin of *our* being *and* of Adam's.

Yet, we have both theoretical and practical powers to acknowledge something awesome. We can admit that, right from the moment of originative creation, we could have exercised perfectly our *active potency to unite fully with God*.

But we obviously failed in that pristine response to being. So, we are now inveterately inclined to think that God created *ex nihilo* our *passive* potencies. God is thought, especially, to create prime matter *as passive*, rather than as solely active and as a pure *receptivity* of essence.

There is an inside *story* of creation that is quite compatible with the *Genesis* account, but not nearly as figurative. *Genesis* includes many figures of speech. God did not literally, for instance, "breathe" a soul into Adam's body. God has no lungs.

While maintaining harmony with the *Genesis* accounts, the "inside story" includes an *ontological* (being-based) description. It depicts something of who we are and what we did to our relationships by partly negating, from the start, our perfect God-gifted freedom in being. *Genesis* presupposes a background condition.

So, there is no mythical story in the new perspective. Even as is the case *with all traditional theological accounts*, this inside story works within Scriptural discourse and the documents of Tradition, including whatever of their content might be stated figuratively.

Moreover, Gnosticism claims to be a "privileged knowledge." The new perspective does not. The appeal is directly to reason in the light of Faith. And some absurdities in the traditional metaphysical accounts of our origins are likewise indicated. Notably, the new view challenges the ideas that God can create *directly* realities other than persons and that God creates directly prime matter and other passive potencies.

To the contrary, God is acknowledged to be flawless in creating human persons. All are gifted with purely active matter (essence

Chapter 17 Critical Questions: Challenging the View

receptivity). Each human person is seen as an unique freedom or *power to receive perfectly* the *kind* (*essence*) of being that one *is*. And God is seen to be *originatively* the Creator of perfect persons *only*—both angelic and human beings—with purely active essences.

Each created person is essentially constituted by the receptivity or freedom-to-receive perfectly within self the *being* that each one *is*. God's secondary, redemptive creation (*ex aliquo*) has included the immediate presence and the infinite power of God, working within the self-passivized matter and form of fallen human persons.

A truly ontological metaphysics can work within, and on behalf of, theology and is not at all esoteric knowledge. It might be, for most thinkers, new and challenging, but it is not in any way secret or privileged. Ontology is teachable to all functionally rational beings.

The challenge of the ontology of creation—telling it like it *is*—would seem to be the very opposite of Gnosticism. The ontological "story" cannot be stipulated effectively by evading—as traditional accounts do—the perennial question of Job about *why* good people suffer evil. The new perspective offered in the book tries to indicate that some traditional axioms and assumptions require revision so that we can give a truer answer to the question of evil *and to the Faith that is within us*.

The new theistic perspective might support some aspects of the questioner's suggestion of evolution. Evolution might be plausibly recognized as *part* of God's way of effecting our *recovery* from the "crash site" that resulted from our originative sin. But we must be awakened to how we have allowed this creation of *becoming* to be conflated with the creation of *being*.

Evolution could be in no way a creation "out of nothing." At best, it would be a creation out of something. The world of be-coming ("being coming back") ought not to be telescoped into the world of be-ing—a world that includes, but transcends, any and all becoming.

Finally, there may be good reasons why Gnostic thought recurs in every age. One of them could be that traditional theorists are not adequately addressing the deeper intuitions of the human mind and heart. And *that* will be the "privileged place" for the most decisive "evolution" of all: development in our ways of knowing and of living out our origin, identity, and destiny.

Q. What do you mean when you say that we should think more ontologically? And how is your ontological way different from that of Thomas Aquinas?

R. I mean that being is *essentially* interpersonal—totally relational. Only persons can say *yes* to being, and they say it *as* persons *to* persons. Christians even believe that this is the *only* way that God *is and relates* within divine Being.

In any case, being is basically interpersonal because only persons can relate with being and acknowledge it to *be*. The idea comports with Aquinas' recognition that only persons are being "in the full sense."

But this interpersonal meaning for being goes beyond Aquinas, for instance, by stating explicitly that God's originative act of creating (*ex nihilo*) could *only* cause *perfect persons*. Every human person is understood then to be fully interfaced with God. Each one is both responsive and responsible from the moment of creation (*ex nihilo*). And the claim also implies that the *Book of Genesis* is not concerned *directly* about the originative creation, but about the beginnings of the redemptive, recuperative creation.

I am now trying to foster *development* of the ontological insights of Aquinas that came emphatically from his Faith, as well as from his reason. My purpose is to bring the light of being *as being* more directly into religious thought. I likewise hope to let our thoughts in Faith facilitate liberation from the almost inevitable, but critically inadequate, cosmological *mindset*. Aristotle may have discovered the science of being *as being* (metaphysics or *prime philosophy*), but even Aquinas became stuck, in significant ways, by this biology-based, cosmological metaphysics.

We must become conscious that *as human persons* we are *not necessarily* determined by space and by time—either in our *being* or in our *knowledge* of being. We can truly know spatial and temporal things without any *necessarily* spatial and temporal considerations in our knowing activities themselves—particularly in our religious knowing.

Moreover, physical entities, such as trees and water molecules, are nonetheless *beings* and can be assessed and evaluated not only as spatial and temporal, but *as beings*, even if *partial beings*. Nothing

Chapter 17   Critical Questions: Challenging the View

could have been originatively created by God as *necessarily and essentially* a being of passivity. So, we must challenge the ordinary, passive meaning for physical nature.

The ontological (beingful) perspective subsumes the cosmological perspective, and it is not tied down to it. Although the cosmological is not essential to the ontological, it can be cautiously helpful from a pedagogical standpoint.

At least part of what I mean by ontological knowing is to begin knowing now in somewhat the manner we would have *known* if we had said *fully yes* to God and to *be*-ing. We can try to surmise what we would have been like had we not committed *originative* sin.

Without our committing originative sin, there would have been no real "thinking"—only purely active knowing, loving, and wondering in joyful awe. The *content* of what we would be knowing and loving under such pristinely effective conditions is *present* to us still. Yet this content is now obscure because our condition of knowing is so self-twisted that we can only *begin* to untangle ourselves.

Many people do not even care about thinking in the *light* of being and in a manner that transcends the usual categories of logic. They do not realize that there *is* a light of *being*, not to mention the ability to *see* with it. They just want to know "how to get to heaven," and so therefore how to "please" God. And they tend to confuse pleasing with loving.

Many evince little interest with respect to the truth as a good in itself. There is little sense of "let" and a macho sense of "get." Our failure to respond openly to *being* at our origins has hidden from us the *light* of the *be-ing* of beings. And this condition comes from our distortion of freedom.

Thomas Aquinas thought ontologically, but he was simultaneously inured in the biological perspective of Aristotle. Virtually all basic terms used in Aristotelian-Thomistic metaphysics or ontology were initially formed in the context of studying holistically the cosmic world of space and time. With such a start, trying to free these terms from their unnecessary limitations of meaning is something like pulling taffy. The cosmogenic meanings persist unwittingly, despite all attempts at a "judgment of separation."

Additionally, however, we desperately need the linear, practical kind of logic that suits cosmological analysis. We need it, at least in part, in order to work out our salvation. Here in our finite, defective, remedial creation, there is demanded a true exercise of logic that ensures profoundly thoughtful, prudential behavior.

As we now exist, our logic can be regarded as serving the self-impaired knower. So often, however, the knower begins to exist for the sake of logic, as can readily happen to scholars, seasoned and unseasoned alike.

In reality, logic should exist to *serve* both knower and what is being known. Logic should be exercised for the sake of *onto*logic—serving the structure of *being*, and not simply serving the finite, defective mind itself.

We can realize that there are the two basic kinds of real being—finite and infinite. But we do not have to regard real being as in any way entrapped by logical propensities and reflexes. Pure, unlogical being is either infinite or finite. There is no other kind of real being. Being is *not a logical genus*.

So, being can be determined to be both infinite and finite such that wherever being "is found" it is either infinite or finite being. And, for Christians, in the incarnate Word of God, being is found to be *both* infinite *and* finite.

Traditionally, thinkers have shown an inability or unwillingness to realize that they do not just know abstractions coming from knowing unique, particular beings. They directly know those unique, *singular beings*. At all times, the knowledge they attain *through their natural intellective intuitions* comes prior to the various logical concepts and compensations that occur for the purposes of inference and speech. *This* (particular being) that is being known—not any compensative abstraction, such as thisness or "haecceitas"—is and is *what* it is *ontologically*, independent-*with* any abstractions that the mind might spontaneously include.

Besides, all deeply religious truths can only be *consciously* known and appreciated with a paradoxical kind of logic. The usual *either-or* logics of ancient and modern times are not adequate.

Chapter 17 Critical Questions: Challenging the View

The needed paradoxical logic will include, but go deeper than, the practical logic of the West; and it will be far superior to the semi-paradoxical logic found in the East, such as the logic of *yin-yang*.

The latter logic amounts to an exercise attuned to interdependence and compensation—hot compensates for cold and *vice versa*, male for female and *vice versa*, and so forth. Even as happens in the logic of the West, the logic of interdependence fails to account for the *unique singular beings* that are being known.

True paradox requires a *both-and* logic. Therein the natural mind can allow us to see opposites that are not merely interdependent, but mutually *independent*. We can see, for instance, the truth of God being *both* infinitely *other than* (transcendent to) *and* infinitely *within* (immanent to) created (necessarily finite) persons, *without any identity* of the created and the Creator.

Genuine theism is not a really subtle pantheism. Only through true paradox—one that transcends the logics of "identity and separation" and of "mutual identity"—can truths such as that of our creation, redemption, salvation, and sanctification be authentically known.

Over centuries, under the massive constraints formed by the logics of passivity, theists within the three classical traditions have made remarkable developments in explicating these primal truths. Despite his excessive devotion to the simple logic and pedagogy of Aristotle, Aquinas set forth a personalism—if not interpersonalism—delving into the differentiation of reason within Faith. He made brilliant attempts with the scope of reason to appreciate the glory of being as afforded by the light of Faith. He was somewhat fettered, however, by a linear logic that was proportionate to space and time, but quite disproportionate to the main content of his probings.

Q. You agree with many philosophers that passivity in finite beings signifies lack of fulfillment or, at least, an imperfection. Where you disagree with them is in their idea that being finite and being fully receptive *necessarily* means having some kind of *passivity*, as well as receptivity.

You think of receptivity *without any passivity* as an ontological dimension of pure act—whether it is infinite or finite—and that every *direct* creature of God is a *finite, pure act of being*. This is really where you part company with other theists, including

Christian thinkers. Do you think that some could be brought now to agree with you?

R. Yes, but only by means of a better than usual understanding of *receptivity*. Crucial to the message is the realization that *receptivity is necessarily a dimension of pure act*. Pure act necessarily entails receiving as well as giving. I do think that Thomas Aquinas would agree, *if* he were to have the occasion to develop his metaphysics further. In fact, prominent contemporary Christian theologians and philosophers, including Hans Urs von Balthasar and, following him, David Schindler, Norris Clarke, as well as others, have written about receptivity—not passivity—in the Trinity.

But Christians have much more to do. Receptivity in *each one* of the divine Persons should be given recognition. And the procession of persons within the Godhead must include *receptivity in God, the Father—infinitely receiving himself* by knowing and loving himself in the eternal gifting to the Person of the Wisdom-Word. There is nothing passive or distancing in any true receptivity, particularly in infinite receptivity.

Judaic and Islamic traditions have a similar task in understanding God as supremely *receptive*, even though they do not believe in a trinity of persons.

A whole new development of classical metaphysics is implied. I am planning to express this new meaning in a subsequent book.

But agreement—however desirable—is never the main issue. We can be complacently in agreement with others and be in error. Truth, as best each of us can know and understand it, is the most deeply desired outcome. And, in this resistant world, truth (not necessarily agreement) is the perpetual desire of those who love wisdom.

Q. What can you say about the torture and murder of a child? Does such monstrous evil mean that originatively the child, as an immaculately-gifted person, freely had said *maybe* to God with a particularly negative emphasis, and thereby is receiving proper payback? You seem to be claiming that there is no such thing as injustice, if we go back far enough: to an *originative* sin. But *that* surely seems like an impossible stretch.

Chapter 17 Critical Questions: Challenging the View

R. That "stretch" is just as possible as another apparent extension: making the special effort to know God as *infinitely* good, loving, and powerful, and not just as the "most loving" Being of all. We can know God's unlimitedness (infinity) as *not limited*, and thereby as different from finitude. And we can do so without stretch or strain.

Moreover, neither case requires an impossible reach. No historical perspective is necessarily involved. Both the infinite love of God and our failure originatively to receive it are as close as the depths of our hearts, wherein both truths can be immediately, if confusedly, known. (And for *that* knowing, no "stretch" is called for, only a profound reception of what *is*.)

In the world of space and time, the torture and murder of anyone is a grave injustice. Heaven itself cries for due remedy.

But the enormity of each person's originative, untempted act of sinning is monumentally greater. Any injustice done in this world pales by comparison to our originative personal sin—however slight it might have been on the negative side of the *maybe*. Each one's originative sin was done within the brilliant light of God's infinite goodness and truth, and within the reciprocal light of our God-gifted finite freedom, goodness, and truth.

Our present precarious condition results from our originative *yes-no*. We find it *virtually impossible to face our signature sin*. But we know ourselves now to be in *this* world, a *maybe* world. And there is nothing *maybe* about *that*.

Maybe the child did commit a particularly egregious originative sin, at least relative to many others. And maybe not. For us, it is largely *maybe*. We are hardly in a position to make such a judgment about an individual, even in the midst of affirming the general lines of the good and evil, justice and injustice, found in cosmic creation itself.

No one can be judged as better or worse than any other simply based on present physical, mental, or moral appearances.

On the one hand, those who live seemingly saintly lives may abide hidden crevices of spiritual weakness, unsuspected by themselves as well as by others. On the other hand, some folks who manifest ugly features of attitude and behavior could possibly harbor avenues of undetected access to grace and glory.

We can be sure that a particular force of *yes*-and-*no* was effected right at the originative moment of someone's being and yet be sure likewise that *we do not know*, in *any* case, how forceful it had been relative to that of any other *maybe*-person. While entirely related to our cosmic existence now, our originative activity transpired in a *protoconscious* dimension of being that is different from our present condition.

Although it is often misused, the famous injunction, "Judge not, lest you yourselves be judged," would seem to apply. To judge can mean to evaluate and assess or it can mean to commend or condemn.

We must evaluate ourselves and others under many circumstances. But, ultimately, we *cannot be our own* judge of commendation or condemnation, much less the judge of others. We cannot honestly give a definitive approval or dismissal of the *being* of ourselves or of others. We are in the muddle of "*maybe*." We cry out to receive infinite Mercy.

Many individuals might undergo most of their due suffering right here in this world. Many others might have to wait for an immensely lengthy purgatory after death. Anyone *judging the character* of a particular person's *originative* sin and then basing the judgment on observed *temporal* affliction might be one who will suffer much more agony later in this life or in the world to come.

Normally, none of us can definitively say concerning individuals, *who* sinned *when*; much less, how badly. Nevertheless, we must try to discern our own condition of soul and attempt to help others do likewise, if we are called upon.

Besides, we must judge and we do judge about the meaning of life, who we are, and why we are here. We are even now living in both a *maybe* and a non-*maybe* world.

Not to judge about prime conditions for the destiny of all *is* to judge *negatively* about the importance of our present participation in life. We must judge, as best we can, what is good and what is bad. "Thou shalt not do that which is unjust, nor judge unjustly. Respect not the person of the poor, nor honour the countenance of the mighty. But judge thy neighbour according to justice" (*Leviticus* 19:15). And God will be judging us eventually on how sincerely we made efforts to find and to live the truth.

Moreover, we must be *open to God's way* of relating to what is good and bad. The infinite power, infinite goodness, and infinite justice of God are present—both at the moment of creation *ex nihilo* and at this very moment in space and time. God allows an evil because it comes due, granted the particular confluence of struggling human freedoms. God is the Creator of *real freedom*. So, it is good and just that divine Providence include the allowance of evil.

God cannot *do* any activity that is *even slightly, yet truly* unjust, nor for so-called good purposes. God can hardly be a manipulator or a "utilitarian in the sky" arranging the greatest good for the greatest number of people.

Christians, for instance, ought to believe that even the suffering of Christ was ultimately an act of justice. Not that Jesus was guilty, but that he *freely received* the commission of suffering unjustly for our sins—*because we could never do it adequately for ourselves*. By his infinitely loving response to us in our sin, his truly unjust suffering in space and time is eternally an activity of perfect justice. By his wounds, we are healed (1 *Peter* 2:24).

Blessedly, God's infinite justice is *not* our defectively finite justice. These are two radically different kinds of justice. By his suffering injustice, we are justified—if we contritely *receive* it. The justice or justification is not brought out of the injustice (of the sin), but out of the *yes* in our *maybe* and *through the activity* of God's *unlimited* love.

Christians could even reassess part of the meaning of baptism. The sacrament can be understood as removing the stain of sin caused by Adam and Eve here in the world of *be-coming*. But it could also be acknowledged, additionally, as releasing the *lockout of being* caused by the baptized person's originative deformation of freedom in the world of being. This critical sacramental release, hitherto known implicitly, would become known and lived out explicitly.

Many holy persons among us may be suffering in union with Jesus both on account of their own sins and willingly for the sake of the healing of many others. They are suffering justly.

Their suffering is just and due to them for their own originative transgression. But it is also just, if not due to them, because they are *freely* suffering injustice in union with Christ, on behalf of extending divine salvation to *other* persons under purgation. Their suffering serves to aid in "the final choices" of those for whom they suffer. They are receiving on behalf of these other sinners the grace of final conversion—if these choosers themselves ultimately cooperate.

We are all equal in dignity as human persons. But we are not equal in the *exercise* of our personhood.

Nonetheless, our approach to our neighbor must ever be based on who he or she is as *this* unique human person, gifted by God with an originative dignity. The person's originally immaculate essence still stands despite his or her activities of past willfulness that obscure it.

Q. You say it many times in this book: God originally creates only perfect beings. But there has been theological and religious discourse that, in effect, denies such a claim. So, it *sounds* like you are saying God creates God. Is not God the only perfect being that could be? Is not a creature necessarily, *in some sense*, an imperfect being, otherwise the creature would be God?

R. No, indeed. A perfect being created by God would not be God, because God is not only perfect, but *infinitely* perfect. (There could be, of course, no imperfect *infinite* being.)

Every creature that is *immediately created* by God is *perfect* finite being, capable of fully responding to God with knowledge and love. Such is a person.

Imperfect finite being, such as ours, is caused by those free finite persons who degrade their own perfect freedom in their very first act of *be*-ing who they are.

This means that the whole spatiotemporal material universe was not brought directly "out of nothing." But God created it out of "something" caused by us: out of our *may-be* response to our *be*-ing. Every element of the cosmos comes, through the redemptive efforts of God, out of the void in *our* self-frustrated human natures.

The infinite Being of God can only *create* (bring "out of nothing") *finite* beings. Yet, these perfectly finite beings (finitely pure acts, without any passivity) *cannot bring out of nothing* anything at all.

However, by perfect, God-gifted freedom, and in the infinite grace of God, a finite being can and does bring into being *out of itself* its freely chosen destiny within the covenant of God's creation.

Chapter 17   Critical Questions: Challenging the View

We are originatively God-*like*, but are not God at all. We are not like God in being finite, but *in being perfect*. We are like God in a finite way—that is, limitedly and perfectly—but God is infinitely *other than* we, in being and ability. Moreover, God's infinite ability is in no way arbitrary, as our defective, projective understanding so readily takes it to be. Christians, for instance, are often awed at Jesus saying, "Be you therefore perfect, as also your heavenly Father is perfect." (*Matt.* 5:48). They wonder how they can be "equal" to God in goodness.

But when a finite being acts perfectly in accord with his or her *finite* nature, this being is "just as *perfect*" as is God acting in accord with *infinite* nature. Both created and uncreated Persons can *be* perfect relationally and proportionately—finite to infinite.

All theists need an awakening to reality: God's originative act of creating caused an *immaculate creation*. The originative creation could not have resulted in any imperfect persons. If there were the slightest imperfection in the original freedom of the created persons to respond perfectly and immediately by knowing and loving, then there would be no hope for *ever* attaining *full* intimacy with God.

From the imperfect, only the imperfect can come. An imperfect ability to love, as an original gift of God, would be an absurdity.

Unless they have perfect natures from the very start of their being, sinful creatures have no perfection to "return to." Not even God could *restore* what is not there originally to *be restored*.

God is not a "value-added" creator and redeemer. God does not add perfection on top of what is already imperfect. Redemption restores the ability of each fallen human person to unite perfectly with God as originatively called to do. God creates only perfection from the beginning. There can be nothing *for God* to "add," ever.

In the act of *salvation*, God then restores perfect gifts to their original relationship, but only *if* these gifts offer their consent, fully and perfectly, by virtue of the God-given power of that original relationship.

Theologians and philosophers from the beginning have tended to subvert theology itself by treating God merely as a perfect Being and created persons as somehow not only limited, but imperfect, even as coming immediately from the heart of God. Until the admission is made that God creates originatively only perfect finite persons, theology will be self-hampered even in its most critical contributions to Faith, and it will limp along many fruitless byways of ultimate meaning.

One is reminded of a predicament not dissimilar in the world of science. In the last several centuries, the interpretation and valuation of empirical science has largely *undermined itself* by means of its own presuppositions. Short-circuiting has occurred, especially by the idea that only atomistic materialism is worthy of consideration as an ultimate base for scientific explanations. That very assumption is unverifiable by its own scientific, methodological, and procedural determinations. It undercuts the nature of science itself as a free-ranging inquiry into the meaning and dynamics of the physical universe. Science turns into *scientism*.

Similarly, theists constantly undermine themselves by the blatant, or often latent, avowal that created persons are necessarily imperfect and that "only God is perfect." All the promises of life with God in unending bliss are undercut by thinking that God's *infinite* love could not or would not create every person as quite perfect. Theists suppose blindly that *created* persons would not be perfect in being, freedom, and responsibility to love fully from the first moment of *being*.

Despite the rhetoric about "infinite love" and "miracles of grace" and so much more, believers are *unconsciously* wrestling with, and rebelling against, the supposed imperfection of God's act of creation. God's creation is taken to be *maculate, stained*.

Theology then becomes *latently* the studies of a finite God. And many somehow know it, even if not consciously. God is practically regarded as a grandiose mega-creature. Theology transforms itself into creaturism—where only creatures need "apply" as candidates for study. A cryptic *theologism* undermines further development.

Even as scientists can take their own methodologies too seriously, theologians can miss-function similarly. *Scientism* is the arrogance of disregarding physical nature as redemptively gifted by God. It overlooks material substance as being susceptible to study by *both* empirical *and* theological means. Similarly, *theologism* is the hubris of thinking that we would surely be God if we were perfect being,

Chapter 17 Critical Questions: Challenging the View

and failing to see that God is *truly infinite* in goodness and power—susceptible to study by *both* ontological *and* theological means.

Q. But this approach seems incredible. You think that only persons can be perfect creatures. Are other creatures not only imperfect *de facto*, but *necessarily* so?

R. Yes. Creation *out of nothing* is necessarily an *interpersonal* act.

Sub-personal creatures are *naturally incapable* of really receiving *actively* the gift of being *as a gift*. So, they are necessarily imperfect. Plants and animals are so passive that they cannot actively and self-consciously *receive*. They cannot receive at all; they can only be "done *to*"—never "done *with*," interacted *with*.

Some are much more passive than others. Animals and plants exist along a continuum of "holistic" passivity—from the greatest to the least—as *part* of the *redemptive or remedial* universe.

There could never be a perfect tree. *Treeness* itself (the essence of *tree*) *necessarily* includes passive matter and quantitative features like length, height, and weight, of which there is no possibility for absolute perfection—for perfect union with God. There is, in itself, no "perfect length," "perfect height," and so forth.

Besides, there can be no perfect tree because to be a tree is to be part passivity as well as part activity. Speaking of a "perfect tree" or a "perfect cloud" is similar to speaking of a "square circle." Such "entities" are impossibilities "even" for God and represent, at best, figments of our egocentric preferences.

Sub-personal entities are incomplete or partial beings, *essentially incapable* of the activity of receiving and giving themselves. Some, like chimpanzees, show beautifully and emphatically—through their imitative physical and emotive behavior—a peculiar likeness to the spiritual intentions of specifically human behavior. But they *cannot* know themselves *as selves*. They cannot know in a reflective way, as knowers intrinsically independent of all matter and motion.

Philosophers and theologians of Aristotelian character, however, realized that, among humans, there is a kind of *qualified perfection* that is possible. Such a condition, they thought, obtains only when passive matter and its intrinsic qualities are not *essentially* a part of the activity. And so, they recognized that the *idea* of even the most mundane physical substance—*as idea or concept*—is not physical at all.

They could see that when we cause an idea as such, the effect, the idea—as well as the activity strictly causative of it—is not itself time-bound or space-bound, even though it is cooperative with a particular temporal sequence. They have distinguished the intellect's obvious, but *extrinsic*, dependence upon some sense activity from its *intrinsic independence* with respect to the sense activity with which it *de facto* cooperates.

This realization also means that knowing your favorite tree in its *treeness* is knowing something of space *spacelessly*. Unlike that of even the highest kinds of animals, human knowing is *intrinsically* independent of matter and motion, even while *extrinsically* quite dependent. Human senses are necessary, yet extrinsically so, relative to the specific acts of *knowing* the *essences* of things in this world.

Many classical philosophers have recognized that the non-sentient knowledge and love—found only in persons, including humans—are essentially free of matter and motion in themselves, even when their objects are material things. Knowledge and love can be perfect, specifically as powers and acts of *personhood*, not of animality.

A big problem, however, comes with the traditional notion that *essential perfection* can include passivity. Spiritual creatures such as angels—and humans with respect to their own spiritual souls—are regarded as passive within the essence of their being. Even the good and sinless angels are said to be constituted by essences that are passive relative to their actuality of being. And so, in the common understanding, only God is perfect and known as Pure Act: actuality *without any passivity*.

This is a monumental mistake. It confuses *purity* of actuality with *infinity*. God is not just pure act, but *infinitely* pure act. By contrast, the prime intention of God in gifting persons with being had to be to create *finitely pure acts*. We were originally intended by God to be pure actualities—limited, specific, perfect (personal) creatures. God cannot *create* "out of nothing" any passivity at all.

Each created person—whether angelic or human—is "more or less" a likeness of God. Some angelic beings are much more "God-like" in their essence than others, but each one is a *perfect* likeness *at its own finite level*. We, however, as (specifically human) persons,

Chapter 17   Critical Questions: Challenging the View   253

were created to be not only perfect likenesses of God, but *perfect images*—perfect *complex* essences. We became *imperfect* images by our own defective act of first freedom. The word "image" here must be taken figuratively and symbolically.

Strictly speaking, finite persons cannot be "more or less" like God, since God is ever infinite in perfection. While the finite is supremely *related* to the infinite, it cannot be *comparably* related. There is no formal basis for comparison between the finite and the infinite.

Nonetheless, the whole of the finite world might be said to be related *comparably* within itself. Although some finite beings are *not* "more perfect than others" originatively—since they are all created *absolutely* perfect at their own level—some might be considered superior in *kind* of finite essence (perfection) relative to others. One finite essence can be higher in *kind* than another, while both are *perfect* in their own way—in their own unique likeness to God.

When the finite is considered in relation to the *infinite*, however, there is no basis for *comparison*. Yet there is *unlimited* basis for *relationship*. God is infinitely related to us, even as we are finitely related to God. As persons, we are *capax Dei*, that is, we are able to relate directly with God.

The relative or comparative character in respect to *being* applies strictly among ourselves as finite persons. We are more or less like each other in the finite essences with which God gifted us. And we are originatively related to God—not as imperfect to Perfect—but as perfect finite (unique individual and communal) ones to the infinite One.

Because philosophers and theologians scarcely distinguish finite being from imperfect being, they have often held that while we are related to (read: *dependent on*) God, God is not related to (read: *dependent on*) us. They have confused being related with being dependent. And they have not adequately discerned the difference between saying God is perfect and saying God is infinite.

There might be some excuse for thinking in moral terms that a perfect being cannot relate to (that is, "depend on") an imperfect one, even as the imperfect desperately needs (depends on) the perfect. But this thinking misses the distinction between perfection and infinite perfection. God's perfection is not finite perfection, but infinite perfection—*relating* to all being in an *infinite* way.

Q. I seem to hear you saying that plant and animal life are somehow effects of what you call our primal sin and, at the same time, are effects of God's *redemptive* creation. Do you really mean that *we* are partly causes of the existence of plants and animals? Frankly, this seems preposterous.

R. Bacteria, viruses, fungi, parasites, mosquitoes, snakes—in fact, all plants and animals—would not exist, I think, if we had *all* said *yes* to God instead of *maybe*. In that sense, we are originatively conditional causes of their existence.

Our sin occasioned their existence. But even so they would not exist at all without God's redemptive response. They are created by God *ex aliquo*: out of the breakup and fallout of *our* originative nature. They are thus *excidents* of our fallen human personhood.

In the redemptive creation, God forms these non-human creatures out of the primordial chaos that *we caused* within the originative, exclusively personal, creation *ex nihilo*. All subhuman creatures—including simple molecules—are human-*like* in *various* degrees; and they do anticipate, somewhat supportively, the decisively spiritual likeness to God found *specifically* only in humans.

All sub-personal creation "groans and gropes" toward a resolution of the massive energy that was originated and disseminated by the fractuality—the fractured actuality—of the crashed human persons in the originative miss-reception of their be-ing. Fractured humanity tries to be healed.

Q. You said that Origen, in the early Christian Church, did not have access to the systematic concept of the unconscious and of repression. But, even if thinkers in and beyond the 20th century do gain leverage, how can anyone then reasonably take the idea of repression that comes from within the psychological realm and project it onto the vastly different spiritual realm?

R. The psychological expresses the spiritual, not vice versa, even as the physical expresses both. We can take our first awareness and early study of something, such as the phenomenon of repression,

Chapter 17   Critical Questions: Challenging the View

and try to see whether it has analogous—not univocal—application to other areas of human life. Such is the way the human mind seems intended to work.

For instance, before we can know about divine creativity, we first know something about human makers of products and art pieces. And then we must be careful to notice that the order of *knowing* is the reverse of the order of *being*. So, even though *our* fumbly ways of making are a bit like God's ways, God's ways are *not* like our ways.

Similarly, there is a reversal in meaning when we study levels of activity within ourselves as doers of *be*-ing. We know about human *psychic* repression first; but we can come, at least later, to surmise human *spiritual* repression, which is prior in being.

In other words, psychic repression is known first, but is far less important in being and in truth than the spiritual repression that is part of the *originative cause* of our spiritual, psychic, and physical defects. And we must acknowledge that, while psychic repression is *somewhat* like spiritual repression, the latter is *not* at all the *same* as the better-known, psychic repression. Yet it is vastly *more real* in itself. (In addition, it is immensely more difficult to admit.)

Correlative to the psychic and spiritual unconscious, we ought to note the *physical unconscious*: that massive physical structure of our being that underlies our bodily anatomy. What we call our physical *body* is the consciously accessible structure of our physical *being*.

This overtly sensible part of our physical life is what is susceptible to death. But its underpinning counterpart, our *unconscious body*, along with the depths of the emotional and spiritual unconscious, does not die, but dislodges from empirically detectable space and time at the moment of what we know as physical death.

Our whole unconscious life longs for redemptive transformation upon the release of our hold on cosmic existence. As it is, *we are not so much conscious beings with an unconscious life as we happen to be unconscious beings with a conscious life.*

Once we can appreciate this reality, we will have effected a critical transformation of vision. And we will have acted according to what I would call the Aristotelian reverse principle: our way of conscious knowing *is* the reverse of the way of being.

Creation and Evolution

Q. You definitely differentiate between two kinds of creation: originative and redemptive. Within the latter creation, however, you do not seem to take a position on the controversy between theistic evolution and creationism. Why not?

R. Did the human community *in space and time* originate through a direct and complete act of God's *making* (creationism)? Or did we evolve from lower forms of life—through mediated activity of God (theistic evolution)? This issue is important. But, at this point in the history of reflective consciousness, it is probably not resolvable.

On one side of the issue, the side of creationism, God could have "miraculously inserted" into this material world a fully developed Adam and Eve at a particular point, with or without a preparatory "evolution" of lower forms and conditions. But such a couple could not have been a creation "out of nothing." Their origin in this world would have to be a "making endeavor" of God, fashioning them out of the "remnants" of a crash in freedom.

Even the creation known according to the theory of creationism is a *process*—albeit a "quick" one. Energy can be emitted in bursts of creativity. But the creation of such energy is out of something (*ex aliquo*), not out of nothing. Energy is necessarily an imperfect form of being.

God *creates directly*, however, only perfect creatures. Only the perfect can come immediately by virtue of *the* perfect. That is, the perfect finite can come only through the activity of the infinitely perfect.

We must begin to admit that the story of the Garden, as such, is not of a perfect couple, even though the conditions are described as approximating perfection—or seem to hint at *a state of perfection underlying the story*. Nevertheless, not even God can create a *perfect* being *out of dust or passivity*—the passivity would be a constitutive imperfection of the whole result. God is the *infinitely* perfect Creator who creates *out of nothing*.

Chapter 17 Critical Questions: Challenging the View

God is not a magician producing fantasy. The perfect comes "out of nothing." That which is originally *not*-perfect cannot be a *base* for the coming of the perfect.

On the other side of this issue, the side of evolutionism, the human community could not have come through merely "natural causes"—without divine power and activity. So, evolution *without God* is impossible.

And while the process of evolution *through God's power* is possible theoretically—despite the present lack of truly "empirical evidence"—it could not be the *same* as the original creation (*ex nihilo*). Its whole meaning is *existence*: a manner of being-out-of something lower.

Thinking that evolution could have been God's original way of creating (*ex nihilo*) was one of the immense mistakes made in the 20th century by the scientist-philosopher Teilhard de Chardin. His dynamic worldview has inspired a massive evolutionary perspective and discussion. It might contain merit, but only by way of partly explaining *redemptive* creation.

Evolution, taken fully into account, is an inherently flawed activity and could *not* have come *directly and solely* from God's activity, nor from creatures who were perfectly responsive to God's will. An evolution of consciousness could perhaps be part of the dynamic "natural cooperation" between God and *maybe*-saying creatures, who are in the *process* of actual redemption and potential salvation.

Contemporary theology is laced with attempts to explain origins through evolution. Many religious scholars have been prompted to re-think the nature of God in some respects. The burst of thinking known as process theology represents a systematic account of God and cosmic creation that tends to conflate the divine and created worlds, while trying to make God more dynamically relevant. The Creator-creature relationship is truncated in an over-reaction to the deistic and creationistic postures of the past.

Theology confronts profound challenges. Some evolution-inclined theologians in the Christian tradition recently have made important reflections concerning the proposal that God expresses vulnerability and is engaged in a self-kenosis or self-emptying toward all creation. They claim that the divine omnipotence is compatible with genuine humility and with a divine activity of love that is defenseless (not powerless) and vulnerable.

Christians, of course, believe that the Son of God endured an excruciating torture and death by crucifixion. So, from that point of view, the claim of God's susceptibility to being violently resisted seems unassailable.

Redeeming a self-corruptive people with incarnate love is a "task" even for infinite power. Infinite love is faced with the absolutely gifted freedom of created persons. These fallen persons are actively resisting God *through the dynamics of the subhuman world*, as well as through their own consciously contemplated determinations and the stubbornness of their unconscious lives.

But there is no vulnerability involved in creating perfect persons with perfect freedom to respond. Only the awesomely imperfect response of those created persons who freely demur would be able to "make God vulnerable."

The notion of an *immaculate creation ex nihilo* is far from being acknowledged by theistic evolutionists. And so, by an inner logic, many of them regard God as acting after the manner of a *mega-creature* or *mega-maker* who is self-abandoning, under the chaotic moves of matter in motion.

Actually, self-abandonment is not anything that God *does*. But it is something that we *think* God might be doing because we continue to deny that *we* are the one's who have radically abandoned *God*.

We are inveterately inclined to make it appear that God must do something extraordinary "even for God" so that we can be redeemed and saved. Projection onto God remains the hobgoblin of personal irresponsibility.

While they fancy themselves as rejecting the "metaphysics of the past," process thinkers often fall into the trap of championing a "metaphysics of the future." But the change of focus from past to future serves as escape. Theological "Darwinists" continue to work from the unconscious framework of necessarily spatial and temporal perspectives, even as their creationist opponents do. Both sides are *locked into* the framework of space and time.

Theistic evolutionists, moreover, are rather inclined to subscribe not simply to the data of biology and anthropology, but also to the

Chapter 17   Critical Questions: Challenging the View   259

dynamics of evolutionary *biologism*. They tend to find support therein for the grand idea that everything in the past and present is "explained" by whatever might *turn out to be*.

Biological determinism makes it impossible to escape some kind of metaphysical "teleologism" (subverted teleology). Because of the contemporary climate, both theological and scientific minds are inclined to deal with *purposes* that are *inherently natural* and then to reduce them merely to "outcomes."

The idea of "natural selection" is highly selective. Process thinkers almost inevitably transfer to the future the *meaning* of existence and the ultimate sense of responsibility for who they are, both *now and forever*. Going from being hobbled by the past to being held hostage to the future is hardly an improvement. *Becoming* thereby trumps being. We remain inherently meaningless in our *being*.

Q. Suppose, as theists generally believe, that there was a single couple, Adam and Eve, who became the father and mother of all humans on the planet earth. How could the human community get its start without the children of this couple engaging in incest?

R. That is a good question and it displays one of the reasons I do not think we have developed sufficient knowledge regarding the *how's* and *when's* of human origins in space and time.

The "one and only first couple" idea (monogenism) would seem to involve necessarily some kind of incest, at least at the beginnings of human *existence*. But the idea of there being "more-than-a-single-couple" (polygenism), taken for granted by evolutionists, would also likely involve incest.

That the human community would start out mired in incestuous relations is a solid testament to the punishment for both originative and original sin. Even if Adam and Eve had not fallen and had begun the activity of procreation in paradise, would not incest be inevitable?

This predicament is *especially symptomatic* of the originative sin at the moment of creation *ex nihilo*. Therein we freely, if partially, engaged in direct intercourse with ourselves—ontological incest—instead of uniting *completely* and *ecstatically* with God.

Q. You seem to be using the term *energy* as applicable only to a *creation out of something*, but not to the *creation out of nothing*. Did God really create energy only in the second kind of creation and not in the first?

R.   Yes. Energy is the capacity to do *work*, and *effecting the activity of redemption* takes "effort."

There was no effort at all for God in creating all person-beings "out of nothing." Nor was any exertion intended for the created ones in their *receiving* of this gift of be-ing.

We could have received, freely and effortlessly, our own be-ing and could have exercised it with perfect freedom in uniting with God. Our gifted *independence-with* God affords no scope for work and energy. Struggle, striving, and any other form of effort come from the passivity that *we* effected through causing the conditions of *independence-from* and *dependence-on*.

Salvation is *work* on our part and, in a sense, on God's. Infinite power respects the activity of our finite freedom even when it is exercised resistantly. Christians, at least, regard redemption and salvation as the *work of God*, quite particularly through the *passion and death* (*work*) of Jesus, the Word Person of the divinity. In addition, many theists recognize the *work* of the six days of creation touted in the first passages of *Genesis*.

In the new theistic perspective, the forming of the earth and all of its creatures is one crucial part of the second or redemptive creation. However long it took, *this* world was created through time. Time is required for the works of effort.

We redeemed person-creatures, however, are not simply "doing time." We are *integrating time*. Moreover, that endeavor is part of our work that is done by means of the expended energy from our fractuality. We need time in order to awaken from the shock of being self-wounded, as well as to begin receiving our being to an appreciable extent.

At the moment of our creation *out of nothing*, rebelling human actuality split itself, resulting in two basic kinds of energy. From this primal fracture, one kind of energy was extrinsic; the other, intrinsic.

Chapter 17   Critical Questions: Challenging the View   261

Sub-personal matter is *extrinsic human* energy. Yet this extrinsic energy or fractuality ("alienated actuality"), in accord with its super-multitudinous forms (animal, plant, mineral, and so forth), provides grounds for the attempted human recovery. While it represents a primal effect of our originative sinning, this extrinsic human energy is likewise gifted (*ex aliquo*) by the divine activity on behalf of our redemption.

Extrinsic cosmic energy forms the matrix for the conception, birth, and development of sinful human persons, including their potential contrition, conversion, and repentance—the quasi-placental life of becoming redeemed.

But more proper to us self-fractualized human persons is intrinsic cosmic energy. Within the vast spatiotemporal matrix, whole human persons—bodily, mentally, emotionally, and spiritually—work by exercising their own personal energy. This energy is *intrinsically* proper only to *humans-in-recovery*. It comprises the *human* body and the functions of humans who are undergoing redemption and potential salvation.

So, we can say that there are two basic kinds or forms of human energy, as the result of the primordial fractuality within human personhood.

The first is *fragmentive energy*: energy of the whole cosmos that is *functionally* other than that of the integrative human persons who are struggling from within it to awaken and to convert. God worked with this *extrinsic human energy* that had been caused by the initial human cataclysm, coming from the "big bang of being." This energy had emanated from the fractualization of personal freedom at its *primal moment of irresponsibility*. It is *reactive* actuality, reacting positively from within our *maybe*. This energy interfaces with earth-bound human persons, who are extrinsically depending upon it for their cosmic sustenance. It is a effluent of our own originative crash.

The second kind of energy is *integrative energy*: the *intrinsic* energy of the individual human person that includes the person's own bodily, mental, emotional, and spiritual condition.

Intrinsic energy is the main part of the *nature* of being human *as God physically constitutes the person in the world*. This auto-energy of the whole individual person has not been explosively fragmented by his or her originative sin. Rather, it has implosively lodged in the practical being (ex-istence) of every fallen person. Such energy is actively, if constrictively, exercised by each person. By means of this intrinsic source of total endeavor, the redeemed person copes with the cosmic *struggle* to awaken self and to receive salvation—all the while interacting fluently with extrinsic human energy (the energy of the cosmos), also caused by originative sin.

Our lives as prebirth children might serve to suggest our energy situation in the *larger womb* of space and time. In the mother's womb, the child's placenta is a kind of necessary functional part of life: serving as a kind of extrinsic energy or self-environment that came from the same unitary source as the intrinsic energy that forms the child's body. The fetal body itself represents a kind of intrinsic energy on the way to maturation. Upon the "death" of being born from the womb, the child loses its placental (extrinsic) energy and goes into extra-uterine life with the same *intrinsic* energy, ever manifest in the growing bodily self.

Paradoxically, these two forms of human energy—extrinsic and intrinsic—can be understood as dramatically interactive at death. The dying person can be seen to be "in touch." Not only in touch with cosmic energies, but with the timeless dimension of his or her *being*, wherein originative failure occurred.

And *at the moment of death*, there is a kind of recapitulation of the activity that caused the need for death. The *maybe*-saying that was responsible for originative fractualization of being is manifest in the mega-*maybe* with respect to our everlasting destiny. No one escapes this major measure of self-immolation.

Death has been rightly called a *substantial* change, quite different from, and transcendent to, all the motions and actions of the person in *this* world. Within the midst of myriad accidental or secondary changes of any given substance, every substantial change in this processing world happens in an instant. At the death of a person, this instant of substantial change makes "contact" with the timeless from which we are normally self-blocked, and yet toward which we move inexorably.

When the human being is seriously ill and dying, there comes a point at which the whole human being ceases to *ex-ist* in space and time. What remains observable to us after the change that we call death is the non-living ("dead") matter: being-based *residue* (the corpse). At the point when a human person no longer exists in this world and when only multiple non-living elements such as carbon, nitrogen, and other cadaverous substances exist as remains, there has been a substantial change.

The multitudes of accidental modifications of the living human as he or she is sliding *toward* death, however, are characteristics of the human substance itself. Yet at the instant the person "loses life" *in tangible space and time,* only a complexus—an extrinsic unity—of non-living substances results. The person no longer exists in this world after that point. And the new substances—particles of the *corpse,* the dead "body"—*start* to exist. They are *not* particles of the living body, but multitudinous *new* elements *caused by* the death itself.

So, *that instant* constitutes a break in time—a timeless moment. Such an instant is *not a part* of time. The *instant* is a *non*-temporal divider: right within time, dividing absolutely all that is past and all that is to come.

In order to appreciate this, we might consider a simple geometrical analogy. Draw the line AB. Place an X somewhere in the middle of the line. That point X on the line AB is a *not a part* of the line. The point X marks the end of the AX part of the line AB, and it also marks the beginning of the XB part of that line.

Similarly, the *instant* of death for the human substance marks its termination in this world. At that instant, there is, in this world, the beginning of wholly new substances. Their array might "look like" the original—a corpse looks like a living body without being one. But every molecule in that corpse is substantially *quite other* and is *not the same molecule* as its living "look-alike" counterpart that was there the moment before death.

In space-time existence, the timeless intrudes at every "point." Every instant is *not a part* of time, but is itself timeless: serving as a division of past from future. We are *both* time-full *and* timeless.

From a more fundamental point of view, however, the whole of space-time happenings can be seen as within the "larger" realm of the spaceless-and-timeless. Space itself is a wounded circumstance within the spaceless. And time itself is a wounded condition within the timeless. Space and time also serve redemptively as windows in our longing for union with a spaceless and timeless destiny.

If fulfilled, that destiny is to *be* a pure act of *love*. Energy will be literally useless in divine union.

The Two Kinds of Beginning and Our Repression

Q. You actually say we have two kinds of beginning, with no *time* between them. How can this be so?

R. Our time-bound, human minds have insulated us from most of the meaning of *being*. So, first, we ought to distinguish *existence* from *being*.

"Existence" is the *manner* of being by which we "*ex-ist*" (*ex-sistere*). Somewhat in accord with the roots of the word, we *stand outside ourselves* consciously and make our choices.

Ex-istence is the result of a self-determination about sheer *be*-ing. This *standing-outside kind of being* applies to everything in this world of time and space, but especially to us fallen persons with our "cast out" spiritual, mental, emotional, and physical selves.

Non-persons also exist, but in a partial or fragmentary way, with no capacity for true *self*-conscious reflection and choice. These sub-personal creatures are, as it were, remnants of energy. They are fashioned by God out of the results of the originative crash of human personal *freedom*. God creates *ex nihilo* only pure freedom.

This formative actuation of all subhuman creation—whether it developed by creationism or by evolution—is a major dimension of our fallen human *origination—of our clearly derivative, second kind of beginning*.

All subhuman realities might be called *excidents*, since they "fall out of" or away from (*ex-cadere*) the human substances that exist. Animals and plants, as well as all organic and inorganic substances, are creations of God *out of the energy* caused by the originative crash.

These subhuman entities are fashioned from the energy formed by the self-fractuation of originatively sinning human persons. They provide paradoxically a remedial base for the redemption of fallen human persons, who eventually come to be conceived and rooted among them.

Chapter 17   Critical Questions: Challenging the View   265

These *excident* entities—from molecules to monkeys—are *partial* beings. They are not whole beings because they do not exist with the powers or potential for self-reception and self-identification. But they are all directly related beingfully (ontologically) to us human persons who have crashed originatively. Originative sin affected not just human wills, but *caused* every molecule in the universe *through the original, defective activation of those human wills.*

In order to surmise the character of sub-personal (partial) beings, one might imagine animals as "partial humans." Animals would be appreciated as something like fingers that have no base in a hand. These "detached" fingers would wiggle and point and react similar to "real" fingers on the hand of an integral human person. These partial beings—from animals to subatomic particles—are fashioned to be as humanlike as their constitution of energy (fallen-off human fractuality) affords.

Excidents are *elements* that are material, incomplete substances and that are extrinsic to human substances. In contrast, there are what the traditional philosophy has called *accidents* (*ad-cadere*, to "fall toward"). The term *accidents*, in this usage, does not refer to a "fender bender on the boulevard," but to everything about a person or a thing that truly belongs to it without *being* the reality *in itself.*

Accidents of a person include *powers* to think and to walk, as well as the individual and collective *acts* of these powers. Examples of *accidents*, would be both the power to talk and acts of talking by a human substance, both the power to bark and acts of barking by a canine substance, and both the ability of a bush to produce or grow roses and the roses themselves. These features of a substance exist *in and through* the substance and *cannot* really exist on their own, as though they were "little substances."

As a wag once put it, "I have seen many faces without smiles, but never a smile without a face." The smile, and even the face, of a human person are accidents: features that *cannot be* without existing *in* and *through* some particular person or thing. No one has ever encountered barking without a barker or thinking without a thinker. Nor even a face without a "facer." Accidents stand as *part* of the substances *in* and *through* which they exist.

In contrast, the *manner of existing* of a substance is *in and through itself*, and not *in and through another*. The substance may be dependent for its existence on many other substances, but as such *the way in which* it exists is in and through itself, not in and through another.

You and I are not accidents any more than a tree is an accident. People, animals, plants, and so forth do not exist in and through any other substance. They indeed *depend* on many other substances for their existence; but the *manner in which they exist* is *in and through themselves*.

Both *excidents* (in the way the new view conceives sub-personal substances) and *accidents* (features or parts of existents) emanate from the fragmental nature of *fallen* human persons. At the moment of immaculate creation, these persons self-defected.

Excidents are "breakaway energy" that is developed or matured through divine power in the recovery process. They comprise all sub-personal substances and their accidents.

Accidents of human substances in this world comprise all of the "extended or distended energy" that helps to form the recuperative powers and the actions of the redemptively recovering *persons*. We might say that *accidents* are developed within us from fragmentive human energy that did not "break away." That energy had imploded upon us and remained *within* us and *of* us. It was not lost *by* us, but was lost *in* us and *for* us.

Strictly speaking, all things resulting from the second beginning, the beginning of be-coming, both *are* and *exist*. They *are*, but in a "cast out" manner of being—that is, they *ex*-ist. They are beings, but they *are* in a way that is "outside themselves within themselves."

God and the positively responding angelic and human persons, however, do not "exist." They simply *are*. Lots of false problems could be wiped away if theists came to realize that God does not *ex*-ist. God simply *is*. God is the *infinite presence*, to whom we have given, and are giving, incredibly little response.

We fallen persons are *full beings* that *exist*. We *are, and* we *exist*. Our egocentric consciousness impedes us and we think existence—the "cast out" *manner* of being—is the *same* as being. God is even "honored" sometimes as the supreme *Existent*, rather than as the supreme *Being*.

Chapter 17 Critical Questions: Challenging the View

Moreover, we surmise unconsciously that *being* is *in* a temporal framework—that it is somehow framed by time. But being is not a mode of time. Rather, time is a mode of being—a defective mode—consequent upon our dive into ex-istence.

Both time *and* being are real, without any "time" between them. One must not be played off against the other, as is the inclination in Platonic, reincarnationist, and even Origenistic thought.

When people think that there must have been a pre-existence—a kind of "time before time" or "being before being"—they are, perhaps among other things, trying to develop room for the idea of our pristine, radical freedom. A "pre-existence" might sound like a good platform for a *totally free* self-determination, because we can hardly conceive of any such thing occurring under the conditions of space and time.

But, in order to postulate perfect human freedom, there is no point to a "pre-existence" as *functional before* the existence we are now living. The unity and the integrity of God's *perfectly created beings* provide "all the room in the world" for those perfectly free persons to respond and either to consummate or to mess up the gift of total union with God.

The term, "pre-existence," however, might apply to the crashed condition resulting from our act of flawed response to the creation *ex nihilo*. It would be actually something absolutely "pre" or prior with respect to our existence at the moment of conception. It would constitute the duration between the timeless act of creation *ex nihilo*—including our timeless, bad response—and our personally being conceived by our parents' gametes: the start of formal time for us as individuals who are actively responding to being redeemed.

At the moment of creation *out of nothing*, we crashed or collapsed into a state of *passive* existence where we "waited" until we could attain *active* existence in space and time on planet earth. We are now ex-isting (*ex-sistere*, to stand outside) actively, having been actually brought into active existence by way of our parents' conception of us.

In those vast ages, before we were conceived at a particular time and place, we were "pre-existing," that is, passively existing or *being* in a crashed manner prior to conception. With conception, we became *formally* existent. Our active existence began formally at conception. Our *be-ing badly*—the immediate result of originative sin—might be called a "pre-existence" that had no active existence; it was really a faltering form of *being*—and of *being* our "plunged" self—strictly before our active ex-istence.

We who "messed up" *caused* the need for *existence*—for time and space to be. We are now trying, here and now in formal time and space, to "wake up" and to decide whether to admit our need for redemption and sanctification. The decision *to admit* is likewise a momentous activity of freedom, in which *we* are now engaged.

Having botched our *creation in be-ing*, we are now charged in this life—this ex-istence—with the opportunity to "come back to" sheer *be-ing*—to receive *fully* the gift we partially rejected. Our space-time life has been caused *both* by our crash *and* by God's infinitely merciful attempt to recover us, despite our profoundly unconscious resistance. God creates our be-*coming*, too.

We are subjects of the two kinds of creation, the two beginnings. Both creations—our *creation in be-ing* (*creation out of nothing*) and our *creation in becoming* (*creation out of something, out of the mess*)—began at the same *timeless* moment.

In being created, we immediately failed to receive fully our be-ing. This *caused* the crashed condition and we were thereby immediately in dire need of be-coming, and of another *creation*.

That other, derivative creation *began* immediately to be effected, but only through the saving love of God. This second beginning—at the same timeless moment as the first—is the redemptive creation that is likewise continuous. This *originative* moment was *both* the absolute beginning of our *being and* the definitive *beginning* of our redemption. It is no wonder that we conflate these creations.

Jews and Christians, for instance, believe firmly in the coming of the Messiah or the Savior. His mission is to crown personally—right in our face, so to speak—the global work of God: redemption itself in space and time. For Christians, the definitive *culmination* of this liberation from sin comes in and through the death and resurrection of Jesus Christ.

In effect, all theists can come to appreciate how it could be that, in one non-durational moment—freely and immediately—God created us *out of nothing*, we responded defectively, and God responded to

Chapter 17   Critical Questions: Challenging the View   269

our response by lovingly and forgivingly beginning the work of our be-*coming* (our "coming back"). This did not mean that we were necessarily going to be *saved*, but that we were necessarily being *redeemed*.

Our redemption is *effectively* the work of God incarnate alone. Our salvation is *effectively* the co-work of God *and* of our repentant hearts.

This series of questions and responses will be continued at the conclusion of the third volume of the trilogy: *God Will Say, We Will Say: The Interpersonal Act of Salvation*.

About the Author

Robert E. Joyce is *professor emeritus* of philosophy at St. John's University in Minnesota. He received a B.A. in philosophy from the University of St. Mary of the Lake, Mundelein, Illinois, 1957; an M.A. in philosophy from De Paul University, 1960; and a Ph.D. in philosophy from International College, 1978. The doctoral courses of study were completed at the University of Notre Dame, 1959-61. At Notre Dame, he served with a Teaching Fellowship, 1959-61, and was appointed instructor of philosophy, 1961-62. He has taught courses at De Paul University, Loyola University, and the College of St. Benedict. His principal teaching has been done at St. John's University, 1962-94. At St. John's, for several years he served as Director of the Tri-College Honors Program and for several years as Chair of the Philosophy Departments at St. John's and the College of St. Benedict.

Dr. Joyce is the author of various books and numerous articles in scholarly and popular publications. He published with Mary Rosera Joyce, his wife, the first pro-life paperback in the United States, *Let Us Be Born: The Inhumanity of Abortion* (Chicago: Franciscan Herald Press, 1970). In the same year, Mary and Robert published their unique introduction to the philosophy of man and woman, *New Dynamics in Sexual Love: A Revolutionary Approach to Marriage and Celibacy* (Collegeville, Minn.: St. John's University Press, 1970). Robert's doctoral dissertation was published in 1980 by the University Press of America. *Human Sexual Ecology: A Philosophy and Ethics of Man and Woman* has been used in University courses and by several leaders in the natural family planning movement.

Works Cited

Bible. The Holy Bible, Douay Version.

Blumenthal, David. *Facing the Abusing God: A Theology of Protest.* Louisville, Ky.: Westminster John Knox, 1993.

Buber, Martin. *I and Thou.* Edinburgh: T. and T. Clark, 1950.

Burrell, David. *Freedom and Creation in the Three Traditions.* Notre Dame, Ind.: University of Notre Dame, 1994.

Fromm, Erich. *Forgotten Language: An Introduction to the Understanding of Dreams, Fairy Tales and Myths.* New York: Rinehart, 1951.

John Paul II. *The Theology of the Body: Human Love in the Divine Plan.* Boston: Pauline Books and Media, 1997.

_____ *Fides et Ratio.* Vatican: Libreria Editrice Vaticana, 1998.

Joyce, Mary Rosera. *The Future of Adam and Eve: Finding the Lost Gift.* St. Cloud: LifeCom, 2009.

Joyce, Robert E. *God Said, We Said: The Interpersonal Act of Creation.* St. Cloud: LifeCom, 2010.

_____ *God Will Say, We Will Say: The Interpersonal Act of Salvation.* St. Cloud: LifeCom, 2010.

Kushner, Harold. *When Bad Things Happen to Good People.* New York: Avon, 1981.

May, Gerhard. *Creatio Ex Nihilo: The Doctrine of "Creation out of Nothing" in Early Christian Thought.* Edinburgh: T. and T. Clark, 1994.

Maritain, Jacques. *Creative Intuition in Art and Poetry.* New York: Meridian Books, 1955.

Muller, Julius. *The Christian Doctrine of Sin.* 2 vols. Edinburgh: T. and T. Clark, 1868.

Quran. The Holy Quran, paraphrased from multiple sources.

Ratzinger, Joseph Cardinal. *Truth and Tolerance.* San Francisco: Ignatius, 2004.

Wiesel, Elie. *Night.* Westminster, Md.: Bantam Dell, 1982.

Meeting the Challenge Posed by the Perennial Conflation of Creations

I am interested in gaining various responses to the new perspective that is briefly introduced in the present trilogy of books, including this one, *God Says, We Say: The Interpersonal Act of Redemption*. The first book of this set is entitled, *God Said, We Said: The Interpersonal Act of Creation*. The third book is *God Will Say, We Will Say: The Interpersonal Act of Salvation*. The series is called *When God Said Be, We Said Maybe: An Inside Story of the Creation, the Crash, and the Recovery of Being*.

God's acts of Creation, Redemption, and Salvation are momentously intertwined. So, each book deals with all three interpersonal acts of God, but emphasizes one of the three themes, respectively.

On behalf of this project, any observations, suggestions, or objections will be afforded careful attention. Also, any suggested relevant material will be welcome.

I also encourage dialog by email.

Robert E. Joyce, Ph.D.
Professor Emeritus
St. John's University
Collegeville, Minnesota

Phone   320-252-9866
email   robertjoyce@charter.net
Website www.Lifemeaning.com

Glossary

Coming to Terms

The new theistic view requires an adventure in revisiting traditional terms. Faith and reason need an increase in depth-perspective on perennial truths.

Painters, for instance, once rendered their images in largely flat, 2-dimensional presentations. They seemed to be incapable of knowing how to represent the third dimension successfully. Similarly, because of a cosmological crunch, traditional philosophy and theology tend to be 2-dimensional in presenting the great truths. If possible, our effort here is to change *not the truths, but the perspective* for the sake of better vision.

The following definitions and delineations of key terms might assist the reader's thinking about prospects for a better theistic view. These words and phrases are analogical, not univocal. They do not have one single, exclusive meaning. For brevity and practicality, however, only one or two main meanings are set down for each term.

Some of the following terms are not used in this particular book, but might serve to fill out the perspective for readers interested in philosophical and theological "details." The Glossary may be read in itself as a review.

Being and Becoming

Being (*ens*) can mean the totality of a given being: who or what it is. But, more specifically, be-ing (*esse*) is the *act*uality of being-at-all. Be-ing is the most important *act* of a whole being. All other acts and actualities, such as thinking, drinking, walking, talking, *et al*. are "branches of the act of be-ing." Somewhat counter to the traditional theism, being is regarded, in this book, as what we *are* and *do*. Be-ing is the gift God gives us to *be* and to *do*. *We* do our being. God does not. Being is an act, not merely a fact.

We do not simply "have" being. We *are* the entire be-ing God gifted us uniquely to *be* and to *do*. No part of our being is *of* God or *of* anyone else. We are fully and forever our own unique being, thanks to the *infinitely* powerful gifting of God.

Only persons are *whole* (complete) beings. Subpersonal beings (from molecules to monkeys) are *part* (incomplete) beings. They cannot receive themselves within themselves and so are not, and *cannot be, fully* what they are. (See *excidents*.)

To *be* is to be *unique* (to be not the same as anything else) *and* to be *uniquely related* (to every other being that is). For person-beings, to *be* is (also) to *be-with*.

Existence is a *way* of being, of standing outside of self and other things. *Ex-sistere* means to "stand out of." But God and all created persons who said fully *yes* to creation *ex nihilo* do not *exist*; they simply *are*. They have no passivity to "overcome" by striving to get out of or go beyond their condition of being.

All material beings, as we know them now, not only *are*, but *ex-ist*. Subpersonal beings exist by having "parts outside of parts," by being extended, material realities. Personal beings who, like us, have fallen—who are defective—*ex-ist* also by reflective consciousness, whereby they "stand outside" themselves by being conscious of themselves, the better to direct themselves and make choices (the existentialist aspect).

Failure to distinguish meaningfully between *being* and *existence* (in any language equivalent) can be seen as a particularly instructive sign of our originative repression of our *first* act of *be*-ing and of the ex-istence that this act caused.

The *pre-conceptive latency of our fallen being* (*ontological latency*) is the coma-like, disordered way of being from which we emerge at conception. It was caused immediately by the crash of saying *maybe* at the moment of creation *ex nihilo*.

This condition of collapsed being before existence (conception) has nothing to do with reincarnation or even incarnation. There was no "taking on" of any kind. The perfect (finite) ontological structure with which we were gifted at creation *ex nihilo* was compromised by our imperfect response. Immediately, we became imperfect created persons by way of *adding* an *imperfect receiving* to our originative perfection or giftedness. We became, as it were, "bloated in our being." Our perfect, God-gifted essence remained, but our nature—the disposition to act according to essence—was self-distorted.

Maybe-sayers thus subsist prior to their ex-istence in space and time at conception. Our pre-conceptive latency results from the condition of our being following the moment of *our imperfect response* given to originative creation right up to the moment of conception. Our self-conflicted be-ing (including powers to know and love) was relatively dysfunctional until that event. We were not fallen angels, but simply fallen humans.

Energy is the natural capacity to work: to struggle, strain, move forward, exercise potencies to do and to be done to. It arises from the fractuation (fractured actuation) done by the *maybe*-saying of originatively sinning persons and it comes in many forms at various levels of redemptive causality. Without any originative sin, there would be no need or occasion for energy. Every reality would be itself a *pure act* or *actuality*—whether infinite or finite. No work to be done. Simply, the play of everlasting life.

Glossary

Essence is *what* someone or something *is*. While one can focus on the essences of qualities and activities of entities, the prime signification relates to the *fundamental what*: *what* is a person, *what* is this thing or that thing as such. Fundamentally, what *kind* of person or thing is this as different from other kinds of reality?

But there are really two different—almost always confused—kinds of essence: *common* (e.g., human) and *individual* (e.g., *this* human). The confusion between, say, the humanness and Jamesness of James makes for much metaphysical mischief in giving an account of being *as being*. What James is as this unique human (his uniqueness of person) is not at all the same as his being a human kind of being.

Nature is the essence of someone or something as this essence is disposed to act. What kinds of activity can be expected from a particular entity? Granted the essence of a peach tree is to produce peaches—not apples, oranges, *et al.*—its nature is the inexorable disposition to do just that. The way the being expresses itself, or can express itself, in action is its nature. *Nature* is, so to say, *how* the *essence* can reveal itself in acting. In saying *maybe* to being and God, the *self acts through* its essence, but *in and by* its nature.

Form (substantial form), traditionally conceived, is that principle in the essence of a person or thing *by which* the entity is *fundamentally what* it is. It is an intrinsic *part* of the essence. All things have substantial forms: one for each kind of thing.

This traditional meaning is considerably modified by the theses of this book. In the new view, substantial form is the principle of the person (not of things) *by which* he or she is able to give self to self and to all others as a principle of essence. In the new view, it is called "givity": the capacity specifically to give in a receiving way. It is the principle that is co-active with matter and is a dimension of the *act* of *be*-ing. To be is to be giftive (and to be receptive).

In the new view, human *souls* are the substantial forms *as they serve* human persons in their recovering from defective exercise of "givity" at the moment of their originative creation. Souls as (reparative) substantial forms serve fallen humans in their struggle to attain the pristine, God-intended condition of gifting selves fully at the moment of creation.

Matter (prime matter), traditionally conceived, is that principle in the essence of a human person or of a thing *out of which* the entity is *fundamentally what* it is. Matter is an intrinsic part of the essence. All things in matter and motion, space and time, involve prime matter, from which every diverse kind of thing is developed. It is the ultimately common feature of substances in the cosmos. None can exist without it.

This traditional meaning has been, however, considerably modified—not negated—by the theses of this book.

Prime matter (reconceived in the super-light of Faith and of ontological reflection), first of all, is the principle of the human *person* (not of any *thing*) *by which* he or she is able to receive self from within self as a characteristic of essence. (Angels have no prime matter. Their kind of essence itself is pure receptivity to their be-ing.) (God's Being is pure *infinite* receptivity, as well as infinite givity.) This pure receptivity-power, co-constitutive of the essence, was gifted at the moment of creation *ex nihilo*.

In the new view, matter is a kind of *receptivity*: the capacity to *receive* one's essence in a giving way—and not at all "to be done to" or "to be determined." The prime matter and substantial form are totally correlative as the roots of all receiving and giving in the human person from the moment of originative creation.

Originative matter was *purely* **active receptivity**—*the active power or potency to receive who and what* we are. It was not—originatively—the *passivity* or passive receptivity delineated by Aristotle.

Pure originative receiving is actually as active and real as giving. *Originatively*, there is no passivity.

With our bad originative response, prime matter as sheer receptivity within our essence had to begin functioning as prime matter that is passive, a capacity to "be done to" right within the essence and to function in common with the extrinsic energy of subpersonal creation. Out of this passive condition, human bodies were formed. Our bodies are prime matter *as it serves* human persons in attempting to attain the pristine condition of receptivity intended by God at the moment of creation.

Angelic persons, however, in their greater simplicity and likeness to God's infinite receptivity, are without this co-principle within their essence. Originatively, angels are simple, sheer receptivities for the act of be-ing.

Soul and Body are terms we use unconsciously, for the most part, to indicate the form and matter principles of human essence in their self-weakened condition. By these principles of becoming, we humans grope for salvation. Soul and body, however, are distinct from the originative **form** and **matter** that are purely active.

In the tradition, the soul is the principle of life in that which has life and comes from Aristotle's philosophy of nature. The body is the "stuff" of matter that the form specifically determines. The body is 'supinely' related to form as to its virtually sole principle of intelligibility. This manner of conceiving represents the unawareness in the tradition of an originative sin that has passivized both form and matter into the conditions of crash and hopeful recovery now recognized as soul and body.

Glossary

The following terms—except purely active potency—apply strictly to existents in the cosmos, not to angelic creatures.

Substance is, above all, quite like what Aristotle said it was in the first instance (primary substance): this whole being...its essence, with all its attributes and weaknesses, concretely and singly. More specifically, in accord with the common tradition, substance (second substance) is also that principle in the being of a person or thing *by which* the entity is or exists *in and through itself* and not in and through any other. Every created substance is its own principle of intrinsic being and activity (but not its own ultimate cause). It remains the source of natural stability in the midst of accident-modifications or changes. In space and time, substance relates to accidents as passive potency (*q.v.*), out of which qualities and acts develop.

Accidents are not the substance, but parts of the substance, through which the substance *manifests itself*. An accident, such as the color of a tree or the thought of a human, does not be or exist in and through itself, but only *in and through another* (a substance). The act of walking and even the power to walk, as instances, are accidents and cannot be or exist "on their own" or in and through themselves. There is no act of walking without a walker, nor act of thinking without a thinker. Yet the acts are real; they express or manifest the substance or the agent; they are never discounted —even if minor.

Excidents, according to the new theistic view, are the super-multiplicity of substances and their accidents in the cosmos that are not *entitatively* human. Excidents are *everything in the whole of space and time*, including every particle of organic and inorganic matter—and excluding human substance (persons) with all their accidents. At the base of all excidents lies the supremely low level of human (non-entitative) fallen freedom that empowers the telic character of all matter and motion. All material things tend, however erratically, to an end or fulfillment of inherent purpose by virtue of their being entities created by God out of fallen human freedom (energy).

At the absolute moment of creation *ex nihilo*, *excidents* resulted from the ontological explosion caused by our immediate response. They are forms of the passive-reactivity (i.e., energy) emanating from the originative sin that was constituted by the first acts of innumerable humans who said *maybe* to their be-ing. These elements of discarded human freedom were separated from malreceptive, freedom-abusive sinning persons themselves. As subpersonal (partial) beings (from molecules to monkeys), they were developed by God's *infinitely* loving activity of compassion on the *maybe*-sayers.

Energy originally emanated from the partial rejection (the fractuality) of perfect personal beings as we were gifted to be. All energy is originatively human energy—frustrated human freedom—and is of two basic kinds: *fragmental* and *non-fragmental*. On the one hand, excidents are *fragmental* energy, "broken off" from the substance of the *maybe*-sayers in and by the ontological "big bang." On the other hand, fallen human substances retained a kind of *non-fragmental* energy that is therapeutic and intrinsic to them. The result is our defective substances ex-isting with their accidents (including bodily life in the cosmos).

Active potency is the ability or capacity to *do* something or to *perform* a certain kind of activity. By creation *ex nihilo* we were gifted to *be* pure active potencies of be-ing—each person fully able both to receive and to give personal be-ing. After originative sin, fallen human being has the active (natural) capacity (whether functional or not) to reason and to love; a dog does not. A dog has the active potency to bark and wag its tail; a human does not. *Pure* active potency, however, is the kind of being we were gifted to be *out of nothing* with the angels. It was not mixed with any passive potency. We created the latter by our less-than-full response.

Passive potency is the ability or capacity to *be done to*, to *be affected by* or determined by someone else or something else. A tree has the capacity (passive potency) to be bent by the wind; a boulder does not. A boulder has the capacity (passive potency) to be rolled down a hill; a (living) tree does not.

Moreover, "prime matter" in the traditional sense is a sheerly passive receptivity—prime passive potency. In the new view, however, prime matter is *originatively* a supreme, purely active, receptivity of essence right within the essence—an *active potency*. God does *not*, and cannot, create *directly* out of nothing any passive potency.

As perfectly self-actuated, angels and saints in heaven are purely active potencies that co-act *with* God and the others, without being acted *upon* or determined in any way. There is no *passive* potency in beatitude.

Creation

Creation *ex nihilo* (out of nothing) is the *originative beginning of all finite being*. God infinitely loved persons into being. In this creation, only persons resulted—out of nothing, and not out of any preceding substance. The creation was immediate, non-durational, and immaculate. Each person was unique and perfect in every way, including the freedom (purely active potency) to say *yes* fully. There was no temptation or ability to *be* tempted. Simply, there was gifted an invitation to *being with* God and all others 'ecstatically' forever.

Glossary

This creation was perfectly *interpersonal* in divine intent and solely an act of God.

Creation *ex aliquo* (out of something) is the *secondary* or *derivative* act of creation: a creation of *be-coming* or of being coming back to itself from a crash and from its own ontological self-conflict. This remedial act of God began at the same moment as creation *ex nihilo* and our response. God "works with and out of" the results of the originative crash of those persons who said *maybe* to the gift of being at the moment of the *ex nihilo* creation. Infinite love and power interacts with finite, free resistance that is both conscious and unconscious.

This redemptive opportunity for saving these "fallen human persons" is what is directly the subject of *Genesis* and other Scriptures. According to Christian teaching, this redemptive creation of *becoming* culminated in the death and resurrectional life of Jesus Christ. At least, it can be said that, for all three theistic traditions, only God can redeem and save us.

Originative *creation* is interpersonal, yet solely the act of God. But the act of *salvation* itself is more. It is an interpersonal action of finite freedom completely cooperating with infinite freedom.

Immaculate creation is another name for the interpersonal, immediate, durationless originative creation *ex nihilo* by which God gifted into being perfect persons with perfect freedom. Being pure and unique acts of personhood, these persons are able to receive their being perfectly. The result of God's act of creating was beings unstained by any passivity at all. All gifted persons (angelic and human) were purely (immaculately) who and what they were by the power of the infinitely loving heart of God and necessarily gave their interpersonal response (*yes*, *no*, or *maybe*). The act of angels was either *yes* or *no*. The act of humans was *yes*, *no*, or *maybe*.

Freedom and Sin

Freedom is the correlative capacity of intellect and will to let the person be present to, and unite with, the Being of God *and* to participate in the fundamental goods of human personhood. Essence-freedom is structured to unite directly with—*not an identity with*—the essence of God, if or when beatitude is attained.

Natural freedom is, then, the *essential disposition* to know and to love, to the fullest extent of one's capacity of be-ing.

Functional freedom is the actual ability to do the knowing and loving. Both natural and functional freedom are gifted in originative creation. But the defective response of the first *act* of our freedom maimed them both, functionally separating them from each other and also from the freedom of essence, the being as originatively gifted.

The alternatives of *yes*, *no*, or *maybe* were not set up "ahead of time." Our originative freedom was "pre-alternative." Before we broke out into the alternative conditions of being-and-becoming, we were—like God—*free* only to say *yes*. But being finite, we were *able* to say *no*. We were not *free* to say *no*; but we were *able* and did, *de facto—severely damaging our freedom*. Only with that defective response did there arise the passively based kind of freedom with its alternatives and choices.

Originative sin is our *first maybe* (less than a full *yes*), said to God and ourselves with perfect, untempted freedom, given at the non-durational, immediate moment of creation *ex nihilo*. The degree of *no* in that *maybe* is not the only cause, but it is the ultimate cause, of all evil *in which we find ourselves involved*.

This primal sin caused *our very exposure* to the evils done by others—including the forces of Satan—as well as evils done by ourselves. Without originative sin we would be completely blissful in be-ing. By this abuse of perfect freedom we are now in the cosmic world of space and time—"all spaced out" and "doing time."

Original sin in Eden is a subject for *reportorial* Revelation. It is known by Faith in Scripture and Tradition. *Originative* sin, however, is a subject for our *personal* admission. It was not at all one of our temporal decisions or events, and thereby it could not be readily "reported." But it can be *admitted* in the light of Revelation. This signature sin is surely received unconsciously by Faith in Scripture and Tradition; and it is discerned, at least somewhat, by the awareness of our being as *be*-ing—by beingfully (ontologically) received Faith.

Original sin is the first recorded historical sin. Adam and Eve committed this disobedience as they were tested through the serpent. God "predicted" it in saying that on the day you "eat of it (the forbidden fruit), you will die the death." This sin manifested to Adam and Eve their own weakness, already present in the Garden of Eden, as the result of their *ontologically* prior and repressed *originative* sin, committed along with all the rest of us. The *original* sin in Eden has initiated the execution of the punishment of *originative* sin for all of us. It has included our generation in the world of space and time, that made it possible for us to wake up to our sinfulness and our need for a Savior.

Knowing

Knowing is, quintessentially, a personal activity by which we are related intentionally to the being and essence of everyone and everything. It is proper to all persons. Every person is *knowing*, even if unconsciously. Despite our present degree of consciousness, therefore, knowing is also

Glossary

vastly unconscious for us in the fallen world. The largely repressed origin of our unconscious knowing is our response in the moment of creation *ex nihilo*.

Starting from our present fixation on an implicit framework of space and time for everything, *we think that* conscious knowing in this world *initiates* the connection between knower and known, that is, between ourselves and the world we are knowing. But the connection or "intactness" is already there—having been buried by our initial ontological repression.

Knowing in the spatiotemporal world, then, is remedial. It is a knowing derivative of the primal knowing, done by our being as be-ing. It is the tip of the iceberg.

We cannot not know—however remotely and confusedly—all that is. To be is to know (finitely, for created persons) all that is—at least to some degree. God is known by everyone, whether consciously or unconsciously or partly both. So, too, is every being in creation, spiritual and temporal (past, present, and future). Unconscious, subconscious, and preconscious knowing are bases, out of which ordinary *conscious* knowing occurs.

Sensory knowing is also real, but peripheral, and not as such personal. By sensation *alone* (i.e. as in animals)—whether internal or external sense knowing—the *essence* of something can never be known. *Human* sense knowing, however, is essentially intellective.

We have been hardened perennially by the idea that there is nothing in the intellect that was not first in some manner in the senses. So, we are inclined to think that substantial knowing is a kind of "gap jumping." By the power of its "intentionality" (other-directedness) and by the light of an "agent intellect," the ordinary (potential) intellect is thought to initiate contact with the essences of people and things (called "objects" of knowledge) by 'jumping the gap' between knowing power and known realities.

Such a knowing, however, is to be found only in redemptive creation (*ex aliquo*). This knowing is itself founded on the gapless and super-dynamic radiation of knowledge coming from the nurturing originative knowing at the moment of creation *ex nihilo*. In that originative creation, we knew, *and still know, all that is*, by our *finite* powers of intellect and will, now so sorely self-damaged. The common practice that identifies our knowing as *solely within* our earthly predicament reinforces our originative repression and keeps us "locked out" of the depths of our be-ing and of the much fuller meaning for *who we are* even at present.

The empirical and quasi-empirical dimensions of intellection here and now must be supported by strictly non-empirical, but archetypally relevant dimensions. Wisdom is a loving kind of knowing and a knowing kind of love.

Conscious is the manner of knowing that we all rightly desire now. As experienced in the spatiotemporal world, conscious knowing is necessarily narrow and focused. It precludes much. Yet, before we know things consciously, we know them unconsciously, perhaps also subconsciously, definitely preconsciously, and above all, protoconsciously. Conscious knowledge and awareness of someone or something can come about in various ways (such as immediate intellection or intuition, instruction from another, recalling or memory, individual or collective probing and investigation, meditation, contemplation, and so forth).

Subconscious is the manner of knowing things that are just below the surface of ordinary consciousness. We are always knowing subconsciously particular things, many of which are semi-conscious, or at least partially conscious. Subconscious things often can be brought into consciousness. How to do ordinary tasks such as eating, washing dishes, playing tennis, playing the piano, and all manner of "automatic" activities constitute one major area of the subconscious.

Unconscious is the repressed manner of knowing persons, things, and meanings that are buried deeply away from conscious life. Much is rarely accessible to consciousness as formed in this world. But the whole of the unconscious plays a large part in influencing thought and behavior. It is meaningful to distinguish the emotional, that is, the psychic unconscious (recognized psychoanalytically) from the ontological unconscious, so prominent in this book.

We might even speak of the physical unconscious. It includes all human physiological and physical actions of which we are not overtly conscious. Together, the physical, the psychic, and the spiritual unconscious—including the "collective and archetypal unconscious"—form a virtually horizonless ocean of potential meaning.

Some have represented the unconscious as featuring levels. Included are the subconscious, along with various kinds of deeply buried meaning.

From the ontological standpoint of this book, we know *protoconsciously* everything that is. Such knowledge was "smashed and packed down" by the sin forming our *unconsciousness*. Therefore, when we consciously know something in this world, especially new meanings, we do not simply come to know it "out of the blue." Rather, we come to *know that we know* it finitely, and yet with much inadequacy.

Preconscious (non-Freudian) is the immediate manner of knowing persons and activities that are *spiritually unconscious*. Persons and activities that are critical to our sheer *being* are particularly known in this way. The preconscious area of reality occurs prior to the development of ordinary consciousness. It is most directly beingful in its bearing upon us. This

Glossary

ontological level of knowing—in this book, the spiritually unconscious—is quite closely associated with the protoconscious, our originative act of freedom in creation *ex nihilo*.

Protoconscious is the pure manner of knowing by which we originatively received our be-ing from God. It is our originative knowing of God, self, and all others at the non-durational, first moment of creation. This is the archetype of what we now know and call our consciousness: ordinary consciousness that is partial, functional, and privileged as redemptive.

Repression is the unconscious denial that we know some event, actuality, emotion, feeling, or value even as we *do know it unconsciously*. This mechanism of human knowing is an attempt to protect the knower from impulses, images, concepts, memories, meanings, and values that would likely cause anxiety and various disturbances. Repression is never good, but often inevitable.

The supreme instance of such "protection" is our immediate denial to ourselves of what we failed to do at the moment of being created out of nothing. This prime repression keeps us from recognizing our originative sin, the ultimate cause of *all* evil in our lives. It virtually requires blaming Adam, Eve, the serpent, and God for originating our predicament.

Psychoanalytic repression—repression of unwanted emotional and mental content—is better known at present and to be taken seriously; but it does not even get near to the root of our spiritual denial of originative sin. The latter is the supreme reason for all repression and suppression.

Suppression is the *conscious* attempt to be unaware of, or not to attend to, the multiplicity of events, actualities, emotions, feelings, or values that flood our everyday lives. Generally, it is a good and necessary endeavor that is ongoing and allows us to concentrate on one thing at a time. Often it is the explicitly deliberate attempt to block, however rapidly, awareness of something undesirable. This activity can be good or bad, depending on the issue at hand.

Suppression is a conscious activity, even if quick and minimally explicit. Repression, however, is always an unconscious activity.

Intellect

In the new view, intellect and will are co-dimensions of the *be-ing* that each created person *is*. They are the "know and love" powers of *be-ing*. To be, for a person, is to *know* and to *will*. A person cannot *be* without also knowing and willing *protoconsciously*—however well or poorly.

Intellect and will are more than simply faculties of reparative and recuperative action in the world of be-coming, as we first come to be aware of them. They *are* the created being as knowing and willing (loving or hating) originatively and forever.

Potential Intellect is the power to know *by which* we are in touch with, and called to become wedded to, the essence and being of everyone and everything good.

In our common earthly life, this power does the conceiving, judging, and reasoning. It operates in being determined ("stimulated") by the objects of knowledge. It is the ability to be-done-to by whatever it conceives. It is ecstatically fulfilled in heaven, and is an instrument of supreme self-torture in hell.

Agent intellect, in traditional thought from Aristotle onward, is a pure act of intelligibility-giving. It is characterized as a supreme light that renders what is potentially knowable by the potential intellect actually knowable. It is a supreme instrument of knowledge, without itself being a knowing power.

In the new view, however, agent intellect is the originative capacity to *know* (fully and directly)(a purely active power to know)—to be united with all persons, infinite and finite, in their being and essence. It is the only way *knowing* transpires in heaven.

Will

Potential Will is the power, in space and time, to love *by which* we affirm, and are called to unite with, the essence and the being of everyone and everything good. The objects of the will determine or "act upon" it in the holistic processes such as loving, desiring, delighting, being repelled, and the like. Thus will functions in the redemptive creation as a critical means of coming to what God has prepared for those who would love forever.

Agent Will is the power to love, to say *fully yes* to God, self, and others immediately and forever—right from the originative beginning. From "moment one" in creation, we did not fully exercise it. This power is now almost totally repressed.

In classical philosophy, the missing elements are curious concerning the agent (active) intellect and the agent (active) will. The agent intellect is portrayed as not knowing anything. And the notion of an agent will is virtually non-existent. But one cannot reasonably conceive of intellect without a corresponding will, and *vice versa*. That idea has been axiomatic in terms of the traditional understanding of potential intellect and potential will. Such can be no less true for active intellect and active will.

It is interesting to realize that the classical tradition recognizes, from the thought of Aristotle, the reality of an agent (purely active) *intellect*. But it

Glossary

fails to acknowledge it as *both* a light *and* a purely receptive knowing power for executing a pure act of knowing.

Nowhere, however, do we find acknowledgement of the truly agent (purely active) *will,* by which we committed our personal originative sin, but could have instead related perfectly with God forever.

At the heart of all knowing and loving, **agent intellect** is our purely active power of emphatically receiving ourselves and others, even as **agent will** is our purely active power of emphatically *gifting* to ourselves and others. In hell, **agent will** represses itself so severely that one can blame all adversity on God. In heaven, **agent will** is our central loving power, uniting us with God in utter bliss forever.

By their originatively defective activity, **agent intellect** and **agent will** are found in this world to have been largely passivized (contaminated). Yet every passive condition of intellection and of volition requires, as its base, a purely active agency, as gifted by God at the core of one's being. Only by **agent will**, for instance, can we love God with our "whole mind and heart." The slightest passivity prevents wholeness of activity.

Loving

Loving is willing the truest and best for self and *all* others, despite the cost. Not wanting or wishing, but *willing.* Our loving comes in degrees of intensity. At any given time, however, we love everyone, including God, with the same intensity. Often confused with liking, loving has nothing *essentially* to do with pleasure and pain. Love of enemies and of friends is the call to all that they may live well the be-ing with which they were originatively gifted.

At any given moment, we love everyone with the same *intensity*, but we know and love some persons with much greater *richness* than with others, based on our mutual experience, affection, and value sharing. If we were to consider whom we *love* least in this world: we can know that *that* is how *intensely* we love God, all others, and ourselves.

Affirmational love (see *loving*) is the central form of at least five kinds of love. Affirmation is the attitude of spontaneously delighting in another person and giving the other to himself or herself in an unqualified manner. The beloved feels loved and gifted as good unconditionally by the lover. Obviously, God is the supreme Gifter of being: of gifting to another (the created person) his or her whole being, without any "strings" attached.

Traditionally, *storge, eros, philia,* and *agape* are often cited. In general, they are forms either of giving others to self (such as *eros*) or of giving self to others (such as *agape*).

None of these, however, expresses the central meaning of love found in the *originative creation*. And when created persons come to realize *existentially* how they have been gifted by God, they are much better able to "pass it on" in attitude and in deed to their companions in being. God's act of creating was an *infinite willing* of each of us to *be*, to be this unique person, and to *be-with* God—literally giving us to ourselves to *be* forever.

Friendship is a relationship that is of genuine love (see above) in which the persons share some sense of equality and esteem, including affection, and an ever-increasing participation in common values. The depth of the friendship can be assessed by the degree to which the friends participate in the most fundamental, spiritual values of human life. We *love* our friends more richly than others, but not more intensely.

In brief, friendship is loving plus liking. It is opposite to "enemyship," that is, loving plus disliking.

Assorted Terms

Experience is the conscious participation in the world of space and time. It is essentially a *felt being-done-to*. It can be pleasant or unpleasant, happy or unhappy, by virtue of how one's consciousness is affected by the interaction with others and the movements of the self.

Experience is a bit like the wrapping or insulation on an electric wire. It can serve as a protection from what is really going on, what is going through the wire. Or it can be stripped away...by death. Experience is the conscious impact upon us of the world of passive potency.

But our activities or acts that the experience surrounds are independent of the "wrapping" or experience. We inveterately fail to identify the difference between acting and being acted upon while acting, even as we fail to identify the difference between being and existence. Ex-perience happens only in ex-istence and in our outsideness kind of agency. Every experience—including the mystical—"hides" an act or acting that is at least a little bit other than the experience itself, even as every existent—being that ex-ists—hides the act that is the be-ing of it all....However positive our experience is, it is basically passive (passive-reactive in the ontological sense).

There is no experience in heaven. No beatific *experience*. Just sheerly ecstatic, egoless participation in the Being of God and of one another—incomparably more joyful than any *experience*. The heart of acting and co-acting is passivity-free, existence-free, and experience-free. All is be-ing and lov-ing in consummate joy.

Glossary

Experience provides opportunity for learning here in creation *ex aliquo*. But experience is not "the best teacher." It is not a teacher at all. The one who experiences teaches self or is taught *through* experience, not *by* it.

Perfection is a term that literally suggests the fulfillment of a process, a making (*per-ficere*, from *per-facere* to do or make through and through). Nevertheless, traditionally, it seems to be purged of any suggestion of process as when it is applied to God and angels. For the most part, it means *flawless, without blemish or defect.*

The scholastic philosophers and theologians made much of a distinction between what they called pure and mixed perfections. Pure perfections are those attributes such as intellect, knowledge, love, truth, *et al.* that do not necessarily suggest any passivity or "limitation." Mixed perfections are those qualities that necessarily are a mix of actuality and passive potency, such as colors, sounds, bodies, *et al.*

In the new view, these perspectives on perfection are included, but a new and critical emphasis is placed on the difference between perfection (flawlessness) that is *finite*, including the immediate *effects* of the divine Creator's action, and perfection that is *infinite* (God).

Created goodness, for instance, is not fulfilled in infinite Goodness, but in its own kind of *finite* gifted *perfection*.

We are fulfilled *by* God—and by our cooperative selves. But God is not (pantheistically) our fullness. This fullness is finitely perfect, not infinitely perfect. Infinite goodness is the only ultimate *cause* of our complete fulfillment, but not the fulfillment of our perfection itself.

Conception (human) is our individual entry into the cosmos. Prior to conception we were redeemable, but we would have been almost entirely dysfunctional. Conception is not the beginning of the person's *being*, but the *beginning* of the *becoming* (positive growth and awareness)—the person's coming back, within God's redeeming action, to a condition of originatively-intended *being*. Conception really *happens to* the person and initiates formal participation in the challenging spatiotemporal dimension of redemptive activity.

Death is the exit of a redeemed person from the opportunities of the awakening, alerting life in the cosmos. It is entry into everlasting destiny, through divine judgment—into heaven, hell, or final purgation for heaven. What is left in space and time are the *remains* of that person's cosmic participation. The corpse is not the body itself, but "exhaust" from the person's dynamic thrust through space and time.

The internal or spiritual body by which the earthly participation was specifically effected goes with the person and is not separated from the soul. What happens to be separated is the person's empirical (placenta-like) connectedness with life in cosmic matter.

The soul and the ontological body are reparative dimensions of the originative form (givity) and matter (receptivity) of the person. They could not really separate from each other, without loss of *essential ontological integrity*. In hell, they are "impossibly united" as essential parts and are inexorably at war with each other forever. In heaven, they are "radiantly harmonious" with each other forever.

Grace is the infinitely affirming Being of God as gifting us with the union of love and of perfect friendship. The grace of creation—being brought to be "out of nothing" in an unlimitedly unconditional way—is the supreme gift that we failed to receive *fully*. The grace involved in redemption and in salvation is the same open union of love offered to us in myriad ways.

Temptable is the condition of human persons who said *maybe* to the gift of being originatively. God's creation *ex nihilo* could only be infinitely perfect, yielding finitely perfect effects. These created persons were not temptable as gifted, but *as received*. "God's best" needs no test. But they immediately rendered themselves imperfect. They were thereby in need of testing or revealing—to themselves and to others—how reliable they could be.

Adam and Eve and their historic children, with two notable exceptions, were to be tested by being tempted throughout their lives, however long or short these might be. Death might bring on some of the most dreadful temptations for many. Temptability itself indicates the need of salvation and provides a necessary sign of anyone who has committed an originative sin.

Reincarnation is impossible. The intrinsic integrity of body and soul as the remedial dimensions of the *originative* matter (receptivity) and form (givity) of human being make such theory absurd. The form and matter of the person are absolutely *essential, correlative parts* of the very *essence* of human personhood.

Reincarnation is an attempt to make intelligible the 'law of karma' that is supposed to need many bodies for mediation over lengthy periods of soul activity, picking up and discarding bodies. Personal identity is egregiously compromised. And body is demeaned, along with the soul.

Likewise, in the Western world, the traditional theory of hylomorphism (matter-and-form) has not succeeded in telling adequately of the integrity of human beings within their essence. If God's absolute act of creating perfect essences *ex nihilo* is adequately recognized, the soul cannot be *separated* from the body, in the way that classical theology has conceived it, any more than the form can be separate from the matter. The activity

Glossary

essential to persons receiving redemption—who are *becoming*, that is, being *created ex aliquo*—requires genuine self-identity at every point in the process, including especially the period between death and ultimate resurrection.

Human Life and Sexuality Series

Along with others, this book by Mary Rosera Joyce:

The Future of Adam and Eve: Finding the Lost Gift

(LifeCom, 2009) 267 pages

Adam's Puritan-Playboy America; True Sexual Freedom; Friendship; Sexual Likeness to God; True Feminism; Sexuality and the Trinity; the Meaning of Personhood; the Origin of Evil; *et al.*

Two Creations Series

God Said, We Said: The Interpersonal Act of Creation

(LifeCom, 2010) 170 pages. **First book in the trilogy.**

The Shock of a Lifetime; The Condition for Temptation; The Missing Link; Freedom's Wider World; The Origins of Humility, Another Way of Knowing, *et al.*

In addition to this book, there are others by R. E. Joyce:

Affirming Our Freedom in God:
The Untold Story of Creation

(LifeCom, 2001) 100 pages.

The Cry of Why, beneath the Holocaust; Are We Hiding Something? God Freely Creates Our Freedom to Create, *et al.*

Facing the Dark Side of Genesis:
A New Understanding of Ourselves

(LifeCom, 2008) 84 pages.

The Genesis Gap; Originative Sin; Theology of the Person's Being; Two Creations: Originative and Redemptive; Consequences for a Life of Faith, *et al.*

A Perfect Creation:
The Light behind the Dark Side of Genesis

(LifeCom, 2008) 170 pages.

From Cosmess to Cosmos; The Missing Infinity of God; God's Intimate Act of Creation; The Meaning of Evil and Its Cause, *et al.*

The following three books including the present one form a trilogy and are part of the comprehensive volume: **When God Said Be, We Said Maybe: An Inside Story of the Creation, the Crash, and the Recovery of Being**

God Said, We Said: *The Interpersonal Act of Creation* (LifeCom 2010)

God Says, We Say: The Interpersonal Act of Redemption (LifeCom 2010)

God Will Say, We Will Say: *The Interpersonal Act of Salvation* (LC 2010)

The following comprehensive volume may be pre-ordered: **When God Said Be, We Said Maybe: An Inside Story of the Creation, the Crash, and the Recovery of Being** LifeCom, 2011) c. 500 pages

LifeCom   Box 1832, St. Cloud, MN 56302
www.Lifemeaning.com

www.ingramcontent.com/pod-product-compliance
Lightning Source LLC
Chambersburg PA
CBHW022105150426
43195CB00008B/282